Storytelling Strategies for Reaching and Teaching Children with Special Needs

Storytelling Strategies for Reaching and Teaching Children with Special Needs

SHERRY NORFOLK AND LYN FORD,
EDITORS

Foreword by Kendall Haven

LIBRARIES
UNLIMITED™
An Imprint of ABC-CLIO, LLC
Santa Barbara, California • Denver, Colorado

Copyright © 2018 by ABC-CLIO, LLC

All rights reserved. No part of this publication may be reproduced, stored in a retrieval system, or transmitted, in any form or by any means, electronic, mechanical, photocopying, recording, or otherwise, except for the inclusion of brief quotations in a review, without prior permission in writing from the publisher.

Library of Congress Cataloging-in-Publication Data

Names: Norfolk, Sherry, 1952- editor. | Ford, Lyn, 1951- editor.
Title: Storytelling strategies for reaching and teaching children with special needs / Sherry Norfolk and Lyn Ford, editors ; foreword by Kendall Haven.
Description: Santa Barbara, California : Libraries Unlimited, [2018] | Includes bibliographical references and index.
Identifiers: LCCN 2017029263 (print) | LCCN 2017050053 (ebook) | ISBN 9781440853647 (hardcopy : alk. paper) | ISBN 9781440853654 (ebook)
Subjects: LCSH: Storytelling in education. | Special education.
Classification: LCC LB1042 .S838 2018 (print) | LCC LB1042 (ebook) | DDC 372.67/7—dc23
LC record available at https://lccn.loc.gov/2017029263

ISBN: 978–1–4408–5364–7
EISBN: 978–1–4408–5365–4

22 21 20 19 18   1 2 3 4 5

This book is also available as an eBook.

Libraries Unlimited
An Imprint of ABC-CLIO, LLC

ABC-CLIO, LLC
130 Cremona Drive, P.O. Box 1911
Santa Barbara, California 93116-1911
www.abc-clio.com

This book is printed on acid-free paper ∞

Manufactured in the United States of America

Dedicated to the students from whom we have learned so much
and to the parents and mentors who have shared their love
and learning with those students and us.

Love ... is the final purpose of the world story.
—Novalis, poet and philosopher, 1772–1801

Contents

Foreword: The Science behind the Startling Power and
Effectiveness of Storytelling xi
Kendall Haven

Acknowledgments xvii

Introduction xix
Sherry Norfolk and Lyn Ford

1. **Storytelling: What? Why? How?** 1

   Introduction 1
   Sherry Norfolk

   What Is Story*telling*? Orature as a Very Special Gift.................. 2
   Lyn Ford

   Why Storytelling?... 4
   Sherry Norfolk

   What Happens When Storytelling Enters the SPED Classroom?
   One School District's Experience with Storytelling in Special
   Education 7
   Dr. Mollie E. Bolton

   Notes for Storytellers: A Little Preparation Goes a Long Way........ 13
   Donna Washington

   A Language of Empathy: Etiquette of Interaction with
   Disabilities... 17
   Lyn Ford and Sherry Norfolk

   Notes for Teachers: Storytelling Tips and Techniques............... 20
   Sherry Norfolk

   A Story Is Coming! Modeling and Nurturing Effective Audience
   Behaviors through Adaptable Storytelling Openings
   (Skill Levels: Pre-K through Grade Two) 24
   Lyn Ford

2. **Storytelling Strategies for Children with
   Emotional/Behavioral Disabilities** 31

   Introduction 31
   Lyn Ford

Yipes! I'm Going to Special School District!........................... 32
Annette Harrison

A Wish Granted 39
Asha Sampath

Getting Real: Public School Residencies 42
Judith Black

Thinking beyond Violence: First Steps toward Peace................. 47
Sherry Norfolk

Incorporating the Five Senses in the Autism Classroom:
    How to Spice Up "The Gingerbread Man"......................... 50
Katie Knutson

Programming for Children with Special Needs...................... 56
Emily Nanney

Sensory Storytime at the Denver Public Library 62
Rachel Hartman

**3. Storytelling Strategies for Children with Intellectual/
    Developmental Disabilities** **69**

Introduction 69
Sherry Norfolk

My Story, My Voice: Storytelling with Nonverbal Students 70
Dr. Amanda M. Lawrence

Making Meaning from Images: Predict and Infer.................... 76
Sherry Norfolk

On-the-Fly Tales: Creating Stories with Young Children............. 80
Jeri Burns (The Storycrafters)

Sing Me a Story: The Language of Music for Students
    with Verbal Challenges 86
Cherri Coleman

Storytelling to Improve Literacy Learning (and Self-Esteem!) 92
Sherry Norfolk

Can Every Student Tell a Story? Making Storytelling
    Accessible for Everyone! 97
Darlene Neumann

The Wide Mouthed Frog: Understanding Setting in Story 103
Sherry Norfolk

Accessible Aesop: Fables for the Best in Us (Skill Levels:
    Grades Two through Five) 110
Lyn Ford

**4. Storytelling Strategies for Children with Physical
    Disabilities**... **115**

Introduction 115
Lyn Ford

Storytelling with Children Who Are Deaf or Hard of Hearing 116
Erika Van Order and Geneva Foster-Shearburn

The March Wind: Interaction and Adaptation for Children
  with Physical Disabilities (Grades K through Four) 120
Lyn Ford

Storytelling with Children Who Have a Visual Impairment 123
Christine Moe

Paths to Literacy: Adapting "The Three Little Pigs" for a
  Learner with Dual Sensory Impairment (Deafblindness) 126
Betty Braun

**5. Storytelling Strategies for Children with Multiple
    Disabilities** **129**

Introduction 129
Sherry Norfolk and Karen Young

Multisensory Storytelling with Children with Complex
  Additional Needs 131
Ailie Finlay

Scaffolding Learning for Children with Multiple Disabilities 138
Sherry Norfolk

The Magic Tree: Creating Engagement through Interactive
  Storytelling 141
Sheila Wee

Touching Stories: Connecting to Students with Cognitive
  Disabilities through Multisensory Storytelling 149
Gwen Bonilla

Stories in Motion: Creating the Path to Inclusion 155
Cassandra Wye

**6. Strategies for Inclusive Classrooms and General
    Audiences** **165**

Introduction 165
Lyn Ford

They Didn't Tell Me Some of These Kids Are "Special":
  What to Do with a Mixed Audience 166
Patty Carleton

Talking about Those Bears: Folktales for Social Considerations
  in the Special or Inclusive Classroom 172
Lyn Ford

Spinning the Words: Deliberate Storytelling for Framing
  Vocabulary in the Minds of Scholars 176
Ken Wolfe

Teach Them to Fly: Creating On-Ramps to Learning in the
  Inclusive Kindergarten Class 182
Sherry Norfolk

To Boo or Not to Boo: Spooky Stories for Middle School
Students as the First Step on a Path to Prereading, Reading,
and Writing 188
Lyn Ford

Inclusive Embodied Storytelling Strategies: Power Words 194
Arianna Ross and Suzanne Richard

Oral Communication and Narrative Formatting: Five Everyday
Ways to Share Storytelling in the Special Needs or Inclusive
Classroom—Show, Tell, Read, Reflect, Share 199
Lyn Ford

Index.. 205

About the Editors and Contributors 211

Foreword

The Science behind the Startling Power and Effectiveness of Storytelling

Kendall Haven

Why Storytelling?

As you see throughout this book, virtually every teacher who has employed storytelling reports tremendous success. But is this just selective anecdotal evidence, or is there hard science research to back up a classroom devotion to story and storytelling?

The short answer is: absolutely, yes! There is overwhelming, compelling, and conclusive solid science evidence to both establish that storytelling is effective and to explain *why* stories and storytelling are so important in the teaching environment. But let's unpack that short answer a bit and lay out exactly what we know and how it applies to your classroom.

Why do humans pay more attention to stories than to the same information being delivered some other way? (And, yes, all experiments on this topic show that we do.) Why do we remember stories better than the same information delivered in other ways? (And, again, yes, we do.) Why do we so readily and naturally transport ourselves into the world of a story? What is it about the human brain that makes us so naturally and universally storytelling animals? These are the kinds of questions that have driven storytelling research.

If you are already convinced that storytelling is the most effective and most powerful teaching tool in your arsenal, then feel free to skip this article. However, take comfort in knowing that the science research (especially neuroscience) is there to fully justify your reliance on storytelling in your own special education (SPED) classroom.

Your Brain

But first, a quick word about this thing we call a brain that is so controlled by story structure and story thinking.

Ancient Egyptians thought so little of the brain that they made a practice of scooping it out through the nose and throwing it away before mummifying the body and placing "important" organs (liver, lungs, stomach, and intestines) in elaborately decorated jars. Aristotle believed that consciousness resided in the heart, not in the head. In 1662, philosopher Henry Moore scoffed that the brain showed "no more capacity for thought than a cake of suet or a bowl of curds."

As late as the mid-1700s, scientists believed that thought, intelligence, and consciousness were lodged almost anywhere in the human body other than in the brain. Some thought it happened in the heart. Others favored the intestines. Some chose the stomach. Others tried to prove that intelligence rested in the lungs. Those beliefs are the origins of phrases such as "Trust your gut." "What's your gut reaction?" or "Listen to your heart." When first used, those phrases meant, "Stop and think about it!"

Through recent neural lab experiments, we have established that *story* is the gatekeeper of the brain, controlling all access to your mind and memory.

Ball your hands into fists and hold them together, knuckles touching with thumbs on top and pinkie fingers on the bottom. That's about how big your brain is. No wires, sparks, batteries, or flashes. Just a wrinkly, soft-to-the-touch lump that is 85 percent water and weighs typically less than three pounds. But that glob of wobbly goo controls everything you do, everything you feel, everything you think, everything you dream and wish. Your brain faithfully performs thousands of functions every second.

The typical brain contains 100 billion brain cells (100,000,000,000)—about the same as the number of stars in the Milky Way. Each cell is linked by synapses to as many as 100,000 others. Your brain has created over 500 trillion (500,000,000,000,000) wiggling string-like fibers called axons and dendrites that connect with other neurons at junctions called synapses.

Neurons link with others to form *networks* of brain cells, inked with thick ribbons of dendrites and synapses. Networked regions and subregions of the brain wire together so that they automatically fire together. Different networks are in constant cutthroat competition to expand and to increase their dominance over brain activity. The network of central concern in this article, your Neural Story Net (NSN), forms before birth and, by the time you were only a few months old, it assumed a dominate role in making sense out of incoming information. In the typical brain, the NSN never loses that powerful and important position.

Neural Story Science

Neural story science is a new field of research. Much of the information in this chapter has been experimentally verified only within the past 10 years. My books (2009, 2014) are the best overall presentations of this emerging field.

Research over the past 20 years has conclusively established it: the human brain has been evolutionarily hardwired to initially make sense of, and to understand, experiences and incoming information in specific story elements and in a specific story structure. It's not that your students *can* think and make sense of the world in story terms. It is that they *must*. It happens automatically at a subconscious level.

Why are stories so powerful, alluring, and engaging? Turns out, it's because that's the way your brain is wired! We are preprogrammed from before birth to seek specific story information when we try to understand and create meaning from the world around us. We think in story form. We make sense in story form. We create meaning in story form. We remember and recall in stories. This drive to focus on story information can be seen in babies as young as two months old.

To see the incredible importance of that concept, let's follow a bit of incoming information from sensory organs (eyes or ears) up to the conscious mind and memory.

Let's say you *see* something. That information travels as an electrical signal down the optic nerve to the lower back part of the brain. There the signal scatters to almost 30 separate tiny subareas that interpret the electrical impulses as squiggly lines, then as letters, words, and then as a visual thing and give it dimension. (Oh, it's a chair, or an apple, or a human.) Other areas try to identify more specific information about it and then send their findings to the *fusiform gyrus*, a small area responsible for basic visual recognition identification (a spider, my wife, a folding chair, my boss).

Now this signal goes in two interlinked directions. First, it travels to the *amygdala* (gateway to limbic system) to add emotional response. (Uh-oh. I hate my boss!) It also lights up the rest of the NSN that tries to make sense out of this image of your boss appearing at this time in this sequence of visual images. We have been able to experimentally show that this fixed and dominant network interprets all incoming information and experience in story terms and elements.

Note that this visual image has not yet traveled to your conscious mind in the *frontal cortex*. It is still rumbling about in the subconscious regions of your brain. The same pattern is true for audio signals. The NSN lies *between* your sensory organs (eyes and ears) and your conscious mind. Information flows through the NSN to be reformed into story structure *before* it flows to your conscious mind!

Couple this positioning with a second huge concept. We have been able to identify what directs the NSN's efforts to transform information into story form.

Developmental psychologists have documented the supreme mental drive to make sense of incoming information. We have started calling it the Make Sense Mandate. My recent research has confirmed that this Make Sense Mandate is an incredibly powerful and dominant force in human mental activity. If you can't make sense out of it, you tend to ignore it. At some evolutionary time in the past, the job of making sense out of incoming narrative and experiential information was assigned to the NSN.

How does the NSN make incoming impressions from your sensory organs "make sense"? It uses the elements of effective story structure. It organizes the information around those essential elements. It identifies those elements that are missing or unclear. It then tries to infer (or create) those missing bits of story information. In short, it converts the incoming information into a specific story form.

Here is the final kicker: if incoming information does not—on its own—make sense to your NSN, those subregions of your mind that make up this network rush in to *make* it make sense.

To do that, your NSN is routinely (and automatically) willing to:

- change (*even reverse*) factual information in your source material;
- make assumptions;
- create new information;

- ignore parts of the provided information;
- infer connections and information;
- infer motive, intent, significance (even when no supporting information is provided); and
- invent new information and detail.

Your friendly NSN will do whatever it needs to do to make the incoming information make sense as a cohesive story!

Put those extraordinary research findings together and what do you get?

1. What reaches your conscious mind is always your own self-created, story-based interpretation of what your sensory organs actually recorded—altered (distorted) from that original source material by your NSN to make it make sense to you.
2. When you provide information to your students in story form, you minimize that automatic distortion in each of their minds. A more vivid, detailed, engaging, compelling, and accurate image reaches the conscious mind and memory. In more straightforward terms, use story and you teach (communicate) more effectively.

We think in story terms because we are hardwired and preprogrammed to do so. We invent (infer)—as needed—story elements to make the world around us make sense because that is the way our brains are wired and programmed to operate.

A Final Thought on the Importance of Story

There is a clear implication to the advances in neural story science over the past few years. This is something storytellers have long claimed. However, we have always meant it metaphorically, symbolically. Our research findings mean that we can state it physically, factually, and biologically.

Story is literally and physically scripted into our DNA.

DNA scripting directs our developing brains to create an NSN and to strengthen it into a dominant part of our thinking and interpretation mental apparatus. DNA scripting preprograms us to make sense, to think, to learn, and to remember all in specific story terms. DNA scripting creates our predilection for stories and storytelling.

We are story. Story is us. It is woven into the most basic fabric of human life: our DNA. We are story animals. The value of the science of story is that it makes clear and specific this inseparable linkage between storytelling and being human. There can be no doubt, therefore, that story and storytelling should be central to any and every form of teaching.

The Value of *Telling* the Story: Storytelling Science Research

So far, I have laid out the value of presenting material to your SPED class in story form. However, there are many ways to share a story with your class. Does oral storytelling hold any substantiated advantages and benefits for you and for your students?

Short answer: absolutely, yes.

I have collected over 1,850 anecdotal reports of the use of storytelling in classroom environments. One hundred percent of them report that storytelling was an effective and engaging addition to their programs that enthused students and efficiently taught essential story content. Storytelling works.

I have also collected over 150 research-based studies (both quantitative and qualitative) that assessed the effectiveness of storytelling. *None* reported that storytelling was ineffective or even that storytelling was less effective than available alternatives included in the studies. Again, 100 percent of the available studies supported the value of storytelling. That result is, in itself, amazing.

I must mention a third reference book here. My books *Story Proof* and *Story Smart* focus primarily on story. More of my collected references on storytelling are included in the book, *Crash Course in Storytelling*, that I cowrote with fellow storyteller, Gay Ducey.

Many of the biggest and most respected names in education and literacy research—from Cliatt and Shaw, to Snow and Burns, to O'Neill, Pierce, and Pick, to Schank, to Dalkir and Wiseman, to Chang, to Mallan, to Bransford, to Boyce, and so many others—conclude that "the relationship of storytelling and successful children's literacy development is well established." Some studies have also correlated classroom storytelling with subsequent student success in math, general problem-solving skill, academic engagement, reading, and—especially—comprehension.

Why is oral storytelling such an effective and efficient means of communication? The answer lies in recent memory research. That research shows that there is a direct correlation between the density of sensory details associated with a memory and the probability that the memory will be (a) recalled at all and (b) *accurately* recalled. The more detailed and vivid an image is when it is filed into memory, the greater the likelihood that it will be successfully and accurately recalled out of memory.

The mind translates the words of a story into sensory detail. However, orally telling the story adds several important additional streams of detail-rich information to that which comes from the story, itself. Gestures, facial expressions, and movements, combined with vocal tone, pitch, pace, volume variations, and pauses, create a flood of detail-rich information to augment, amplify, and clarify the words of the story. Every time it is experimentally tested, the mental images created by a storytelling event surpass those created from other modes of story delivery for their richness, vividness, physical extent of the recalled image, emotional involvement, and the student excitement their recollection generates.

Storytelling maximizes the moment-to-moment flow of sensory detail information (audio, visual, physical). Each student's self-created story-based version will be both richer and more accurate with a multisensory flow of input detail.

There can be no doubt that storytelling is a powerful and effective teaching tool for every classroom. The natural attributes of storytelling I have described previously pay an even greater dividend in an SPED class where the additional flows of detail provided by storytelling serve as a needed interpretive tool to correctively understand and internalize story material.

We are stories. Stories are us. Storytelling provides the key to unlocking the full potential of your teaching. Enjoy!

Resources

Haven, K. (2009). *Story proof: The science behind the startling power of story*. Westport, CT: Libraries Unlimited.

Haven, K. (2014). *Story smart: Using the science of story to persuade, inspire, influence, and teach*. Santa Barbara, CA: Libraries Unlimited.

Haven, K., & Ducey, M. G. (2013). *Crash course in storytelling*. Santa Barbara, CA: Libraries Unlimited.

Acknowledgments

A very special thanks to the organizations and individuals who have encouraged and supported my work with children with special needs and to those whose patience and expertise have enabled that work:

The Department of VSA and Accessibility at the John F. Kennedy Center for the Performing Arts. Through the Intersections Conference, I learned more about the intersection of arts and education for children with special needs; through the VSA Arts Connect All—Professional Development Program and the Mississippi Arts Commission, I was privileged to offer training and guidance to teams of teaching artists and classroom teachers providing services to children with special needs; and through the VSA Arts Connect All—Workshop / Residency Program, Springboard to Learning, St. Louis, my work has expanded and grown.

Special School District (SSD) teachers, paraprofessionals, and students—especially Dr. Mollie Bolton! The very special students and faculty at SSD continue to teach me, inspire me, and leave me awestruck.

Milbre Burch, storyteller and friend extraordinaire. Milbre not only listens but also responds with insights, ideas, and materials when my creativity runs dry.

Annette Harrison and Karen Young, storytellers and partners in delivering storytelling residencies in the SSD classrooms. We encourage each other, inspire each other, console each other, and celebrate our victories together.

Bobby Norfolk, partner in all that I do. He commiserates with the frustrations and cheers for the victories, and through it all, he listens and listens and listens.

—Sherry Norfolk

Thanks to all those who have encouraged my work and added to my knowledge base about developing special programs:

Amy Fihe, elective / art instructor and senior capstone at Encore Academy, Reynoldsburg, Ohio. Amy was the art teacher at Herbert Mills Elementary School, with whom I worked for about

12 years to connect storytelling, visual arts projects, and curricular studies for all grade levels and types of learners at the school.

Judy Beck, retired from her position as a collaborative teacher at Herbert Mills Elementary School in Reynoldsburg, Ohio. Judy invited me to her special needs classrooms every year for 14 years, and many of her students were included in those art-room storytelling sessions. I learned as much as I shared with her mentors and students.

The Franklin County (Ohio) Board of Developmental Disabilities Early Childhood Education Partnership, in which I have spent time playing with story with all types of learners and their mentors as they approached their potential in a learning environment where everyone participates in our storytelling, in his or her own way.

My friends, with all their unique challenges, gifts and voices, age differences, and abilities, have never limited our love.

—Lyn Ford

Introduction

Sherry Norfolk and Lyn Ford

Why do we believe that storytelling belongs in inclusive and self-contained classrooms? Why did we develop this book? Because storytelling *works*!

Storytelling provides natural, organic pathways to learning language and communication, socialization and collaboration. It makes math, social studies, and science concepts relevant and meaningful.

Storytelling is important—impactful and effective—and *joyful* for both the students *and* the teacher/storyteller!

Why is this so? Here are just a few of our favorite answers:

Storytelling Allows Instant Response

In a world of instant gratification, with students whose attention spans are limited and whose needs are incredibly diverse, the face-to-face, live performance art of storytelling allows the storyteller to observe his or her listeners and respond to them immediately, changing the tone of voice, the gesture, and the vocabulary in reaction to paralinguistic feedback. A questioning look is met with a restatement or definition of language or concept; a giggle is rewarded with repetition of the gesture or sound that occasioned it; boredom is instantly detected and replaced by engagement. A bond is created.

Our Human Brains Are Hardwired for Story

Not only do we learn language by hearing language, but we also learn, evaluate, store, and retrieve information through story (for more on this, read Kendall Haven's Foreword).

Storytelling Engages Learners

Storytelling provides a new point of entry for learning, helping to level the playing field for children with disabilities by engaging all learning styles and multiple ways of knowing. It has the power to transform the special needs classroom, reaching children who have not responded to other strategies, and provides students with the means to achieve and demonstrate understanding.

And, perhaps most importantly. . .

Storytelling Breaks Down Barriers

Watching bewildered, frustrated, angry, lost kids relax into wide-eyed innocence in the trance of story; oh, that's the *best*!

How do we know? We are storytellers! And we are teaching artists. We have had the privilege of bringing storytelling into hundreds of inclusive and self-contained classrooms across the country, and we have had the pure, unadulterated joy of seeing it transform learning over and over again. We want to share the joy!

If You Build Stairs, Some People Can Use Them. If You Build a Ramp, Everyone Can Use It

This metaphor is used by Universal Design for Learning (UDL), a framework to improve teaching and learning for students with special needs. Based on new insights from the learning sciences, it helps educators improve and optimize learning experiences for all individuals, providing an "on-ramp for learning". The precepts were originally designed to support the use of technology but apply equally to the arts:

> Provide Multiple Means of Engagement in order to create *purposeful, motivated learners.*

> Provide Multiple Means of Representation in order to create *resourceful, knowledgeable learners.*

> Provide Multiple Means of Action & Expression in order to create *strategic, goal-directed learners.*

Storytelling provides multiple opportunities for *engagement, representation,* and *expression.* Language is layered on top of *sensory experience* and *physical activity,* allowing learners to *store, access,* and *exhibit understanding* of information in *multiple modalities.* Students connect with stories as active listeners, writers, performers, and collaborators, exploring a wide variety of options for learning, retelling, creating, and presenting narratives.

Storytelling creates an "on-ramp for learning" for children with special needs.

So what does a "special needs classroom" look like? What is special education? Let's take a brief look at what the term "special education" encompasses.

Special education is a broad term used by the law to describe specially designed instruction that meets the unique needs of a child who has a disability. There are 13 categories of special education as defined by the Individuals with Disabilities Education Act (IDEA). In order to qualify for special education, the Individualized Educational Plan (IEP) team must determine that a child has one of the following:

- Autism
- Blindness
- Deafness
- Emotional disturbance
- Hearing impairment
- Intellectual disability
- Multiple disabilities
- Orthopedic impairment
- Other health impairment
- Specific learning disability
- Speech or language impairment
- Traumatic brain injury
- Visual impairment

More than 57 percent of more than six million American children with disabilities are in inclusive (i.e., general) classrooms; "self-contained" classrooms serve children whose disabilities are either more severe or disruptive. As much as 20 percent of the children in an inclusive classroom are identified as "disabled" (the highest percentage of these have learning disabilities).

For our purposes, we are combining the above categories into four overarching groups:

- Emotional/Behavioral disabilities
- Intellectual/Development disabilities
- Physical disabilities
- Multiple disabilities

Each of these groups will be addressed in a separate chapter, providing examples of storytelling strategies and modifications that are specific to these needs. In addition, a chapter on inclusive classrooms and general audiences provides strategies for leveling the playing field for *all* learners.

In developing this book, we have solicited the help of other storytelling teaching artists, librarians, and teachers who use storytelling with students with special needs. Since we are well aware that there is no one-size-fits-all approach to teaching, we offer a wide variety of experiences and approaches for your unique and special classroom.

Why do we believe that storytelling belongs in inclusive and self-contained classrooms? Why did we develop this book? Because storytelling *works*! We know it can work for you!

—Lyn Ford and Sherry Norfolk, Storytellers

1

Storytelling: What? Why? How?

Introduction

Sherry Norfolk

It has been said that next to hunger and thirst, our most basic human need is for storytelling.

—Khalil Gibran

Before we begin exploring storytelling strategies for learning, let's take a moment to agree on *what* storytelling is and *why* it's so powerful that wise men call it a "basic human need." Let's consider *how* storytellers, teachers, and librarians use story to reach and teach.

Come then, and let us pass a leisure hour in storytelling, and our story shall be the education of our heroes.

—Plato

What Is Story*telling*?
Orature as a Very Special Gift

Lyn Ford

*Orature is more than the fusion of all art forms. It is the conception
and reality of a total view of life. It is the capsule of feeling, thinking, imagination, taste and hearing. It is the flow of a creative
spirit.*

—Pitika Ntuli, South African sculptor, poet, and storyteller.
Orature: A Self-Portrait. In *Storms of the Heart,*
edited by Pitika Ntuli and Kwesi Owusu, 215.
London: Camden Press, 1988.

In the 21st century, storytelling is recognized as an educational tool, a
communication characteristic, a masterful marketing device, a promotional
technique, a digital technology, super screenwriting, and superb journalism,
and everything seems to be carrying the label "storytelling." But what happened to recognition of storytelling as spoken narrative, *talking* story?

In Hawaii, storytelling is called "talk story." It is an informal way of getting to know one another. Mo'olelo is presentation and preservation of tradition; it is mythology, genealogy, legend, history. Ancient storytelling is still
an honored cultural tradition in these islands, where it may be offered among
other story presentations shared as dance (hula), chants and songs, and
verses, often surrounded by the representative legends of sculptural imagery
and the visual legends and mythology of natural imagery such as mountains,
waterways, and rock formations. But when people come together as family or
want to get acquainted, they *talk story*. No television, no technological applications, just narrative conversation, *talk*.

In most of the countries of Africa, what tourists might refer to as "art" is
a part of the everyday life story of a specific culture; bowls and chairs and
tools were, and are, decorated with meaningful or playful symbols and
designs, and wearing jewelry and other physical adornment may have deeper
meaning as familial or cultural tradition. Nowadays, Western clothing fads
have had their impact on the styles worn just about anywhere in the world,
but one can still see story in the patterns of kente cloth and proverb symbols
printed on adinkra cloth in Ghana. The drums speak story; the dances show
story; the art in traditions maintained from the coast of West Africa to the
continent's eastern countries visualizes the story. The poets speak story,
even in their adoption and adaptation of the contemporary stylings of rap
music. The old storytelling traditions still live alongside the new. And among
the elders of the continent and their descendants on many continents, storytelling thrives in its diversity.

This diversity can be called "orature." Storyteller Tim Sheppard says,
"... in many old traditions storytelling is synonymous with song, chant,
music, or epic poetry, especially in the bardic traditions." These old traditions
still exist, as living narrative art.

Orature is orally transmitted creative expression, including any types of
stories told: epics; bedtime tales; folklore; narrative poetry and songs; stories
spoken and accompanied by drumming and dance; interactive tales with call
and response or choral response and so forth, *anything that is not read* by its
performers or to its participants. Although Ngũgĩ Wa Thiong'o is often given
credit for this word, Thiong'o states, "The term orature has been used

variously since the Ugandan linguist Pio Zirimu coined it in the early seventies of the last century to counter the tendency to see the arts communicated orally and received aurally as an inferior or a lower rung in the linear development of literature" ("Notes towards a Performance Theory of Orature," published in *Performance Research* 12, no. 3 (September 2007): 4–7).

Zirimu, a victim of the genocide perpetrated by Idi Amin Dada in Uganda in the 1970s, was a scholar and linguist who introduced the term to remind the world that seemed to define "literate populations" as those who can read and write that centuries-old cultures had preserved and perpetuated knowledge through a living, spoken literature long before the printing press was invented.

The *Encyclopaedia of African Literature* (edited by Simon Gikandi. Routledge, 2003) defines "orature" as "something passed on through the spoken word, and because it is based on the spoken language it comes to life only in a living community."

In other words, storytelling as orature is now, this moment, shared in communal communication, face-to-face and heart-to-heart. In this form, it is adaptive, interactive, and empathetically transmitted. It is what we want to offer as a special gift for *all* types of "listeners" and learners:

> *While literacy extends human possibilities in both thought and action, all literate technologies ultimately depend on the ability of humans to learn oral languages and then translate sound into symbolic imagery.*
>
> —Orality, from Wikipedia,
> https://en.wikipedia.org/wiki/Orality

When we are being told a story, not only are the language-processing parts in our brain activated, but any other area in our brain that we would use when experiencing the events of the story is activated, too.*

What does all this mean for the book you are reading? Our goal as editors is to give educators, storytellers, and other mentors skills and resources for sharing a story in ways that take it from any limitations for usefulness and comprehension in printed format and make it a functional learning tool and teachable moment that will communicate, inform, educate, and, yes, entertain *everyone*.

---

*See Leo Widrich's article at http://lifehacker.com/5965703/the-science-of-storytelling-why-telling-a-story-is-the-most-powerful-way-to-activate-our-brains.

Why Storytelling?

Sherry Norfolk

Experts tell us that children need to hear a thousand stories read aloud before they can learn to read for themselves.
—Mem Fox (*Reading Magic*, 2001)

Storytelling is integral to English Language Arts language learning, building an organic understanding of narrative story structure (e.g., beginning, middle, and end) and story elements (e.g., character, setting, problem, solution) along with vocabulary and world knowledge.

Let's look at vocabulary acquisition. It's generally accepted that the more that children understand language, and the more of that language they know, the easier it is to read it. Children will never read well if they don't understand the meaning of words. But children who are not talked to, read to, and surrounded by words—children whose families perhaps do not believe that they can *understand* language—are at a severe disadvantage.

In the 1960s, Betty Hart and Todd Risley were studying language development in preschool children. Their research led them to a startling discovery. They found out that a child's exposure to language at a very early age had a profound effect on whether or not they became lifelong learners. Children who came from homes where the parents did not use complex language and expected simple answers to their questions heard, on average, 30 million fewer uses of language than their peers by the age of three. They called this discrepancy the Thirty Million Word Gap. By the time these children entered kindergarten, their deficit was even more extreme, and they were never able to catch up with their peers. The Gap profoundly affected their abilities in every subject in school.

Storytelling, however, allows children to encounter rich, descriptive language in meaningful ways. Not only are new words placed in context, but they are also interpreted paralinguistically through the storyteller's facial expression, body language, and tone of voice. All of these circumstances help the listener comprehend the meaning of the new words—and repetition through student retellings and dramatization reinforces understanding. In addition, the storyteller is able to watch the faces of the audience and respond to cues. A look of bewilderment can easily and quickly be responded to with a restatement and defining of vocabulary within the story (Brand & Donato, 2001).

Comprehension also depends on being able to predict and infer and recognize cause-and-effect. According to researchers, the basics of inferring and understanding cause-and-effect are learned through *oral* comprehension: through hearing and actively participating in stories (Hirsch, 2006).

In *7 Keys to Reading Comprehension: How to Help Your Kids Read It and Get It!* the authors explain that visualization—"The Motion Picture of the Mind"—is the number one key to making meaning out of the words on the page. Children are losing the ability to visualize through constant exposure to television, video games, and computer screens that supply all of the images for them. But *visualization is strengthened by storytelling*. As a story is being told, listeners have the opportunity to create sensory images of the characters and events, unhampered by the need to decode words on a page. By practicing and strengthening their visualization skills, learners are better able to apply the same techniques to the written word.

Storytelling provides natural, organic pathways to learning language and communication, socialization, and collaboration. It is essential to oral language development. Research indicates a close correspondence between language development and cognitive processes and the need for integration if children are to achieve their cognitive potential (Feuerstein, Falik, & Bohacs, 2012). Storytelling—clearly narrating and acting out a story—serves this same purpose and helps to achieve the same goals.

Storytelling provides opportunities for differentiated instruction. In inclusive and self-contained classrooms, teachers must provide students with different paths to their learning. Each student will have a unique path to success. Forcing all students to learn the same way means some will always struggle, a few will be very successful, and the majority will just get by. Being prepared with various teaching styles for the same material gives each student the opportunity to learn with the class. Even on separate paths, students can reach their learning goals (Concordia University, 2013).

Storytelling/Theater strategies provide students with multiple opportunities for engagement, representation, and expression. Storytellers engage learners with expressive character voices, facial expression, sound effects, meaningful gestures, and body language. Language is layered on top of sensory experience and physical activity, allowing learners to store, access, and exhibit understanding of information in multiple modalities. Students connect with stories as active listeners, writers, performers, and collaborators, increasing academic achievement and intellectual development.

Storytelling can also be effective for children with profound and multiple learning disabilities, combined with sensory and physical impairments. Sensory stories—stories that offer a variety of stimuli—provide experiences that help these children learn to understand and interact with the world.

In addition, storytelling is holistic—it addresses the integration of the left and the right side of the brain, the corpus callosum (Siegel, n.d.). When listening to a story, the left side of the brain is processing sequence, vocabulary, and cause-and-effect, while the right side is creating images. Both sides of the brain have to work together to *make meaning*. The combination of words, images, and spatial orientation really empowers young brains!

Storytelling belongs in inclusive and self-contained classrooms. It is impactful—effective—and *joyful* for both the students *and* the teacher/storyteller!

Resources

Brand, S. T., & Donato, J. M. (2001). *Storytelling in emergent literacy: Fostering multiple intelligences.* New York, NY: Thomas Learning, pp. 10–11.

Concordia University. Advice on the best practices for teaching special education. Posted February 11, 2013, in Special Education, http://education.cu-portland.edu/blog/special-ed/advice-on-the-best-practices-for-teaching-special-education/

Feuerstein, R., Falik, L. H., & Bohacs, K. (2012). *A think-aloud and talk-aloud approach to building language: Overcoming disability, delay, and deficiency.* New York, NY: Teachers College Press.

Fox, M. (2001). *Reading magic: Why reading aloud to our children will change their lives forever.* San Diego, CA: Harcourt, p. 17.

Hart, B., & Risley, T. R. (2000). *Meaningful differences in the everyday experiences of young children.* Baltimore, MD: Paul H. Brookes Publishing Co. Inc.

Hirsch, E. D. (2006). *The knowledge deficit.* Boston, MA: Houghton Mifflin, p. 49.

Siegel, D. (n.d.). How storytelling connects both sides of the brain. Kidsinthehouse: The Ultimate Parenting Resource. Retrieved from http://www.kidsinthehouse.com/teenager/parenting-teens/talking-with-your-teen/how-storytelling-connects-both-sides-of-the-brain

Zimmerman, S., & Hutchins, C. (2003). *7 keys to reading comprehension: How to help your kids read it and get it!* New York, NY: Three Rivers Press.

Storytelling Enters
om? One School
with Storytelling
ducation

. Bolton

" was the first question I was asked
s coming into our schools. We are a
rict. I oversee the separate special
truction, which serves students with
lly, mentally, and physically. I was
t had received a contract to provide
self-contained special education pro-
the agency, I was extremely excited;
past to bring programs that focused
edback from students and staff had
s very nervous. Our students can be
and behaviorally. I was told that one
e with special education, but I was

the early fall at one of our centrally
the details of the grant and discussed
schools. He also asked if I would come
the program and help plan the activ-
gram director and the three storytell-
program. I was very nervous about
he same time, I wanted to be honest
s of working with our students.
long table. The storytellers chatted
ject. I presented the strengths and
would be working with. Two of them
students before, so they were a little
had worked with special education
we walked through what that might
nts. I explained that there was a wide
tion and participation all the way up
would need to be flexible enough to
e also have the challenge of some sig-
what they were used to experiencing,
ect as well. I reassured them that we
nd paraprofessionals who would be
e very used to doing on-the-spot mod-
a particular student.

The storytellers had previous experiences in the past where teachers left the room and they were on their own with the students. I assured them that would not be the case in our situation. The teachers would learn from them to continue the students' learning after they had completed the session as our students require much repetition to master skills.

It was decided that the storytellers would come visit the schools and observe some of the students and classrooms that they would be partnering with. We arranged a date and time. We discussed the best way to measure the results of our project, both quantitatively and qualitatively.

Table 1.1   Student Engagement Rubric

Teacher Name:				
Student Name:				
Category	**3**	**2**	**1**	**0**
Alertness	Student is fully alert and paying close attention.	Student is alert most of the time and is paying attention.	Student is somewhat alert and sometimes paying attention.	Student is not alert, not paying attention, and needs to be reminded to focus on the lesson.
Participation	Student is asking or answering question or making choices pertaining to the lesson.	Student is trying to answer questions and asking question or making choices.	Student only participates if prompted by teacher or staff.	Student is not interested in participating.

We decided to use a rubric for the storytelling that the students would participate either individually or as a group depending on the needs of the students. We also utilized an engagement rubric to determine how engaged students were in the activities (Tables 1.1 and 1.2). Teachers would also fill out an anonymous survey about their experience.

Now my next task was to convince teachers that this would be a worthwhile experience for themselves and their students. I met with the teachers monthly and brought it up at our meeting. "Do they understand our students?" was the question that was repeatedly asked. I assured them that the storytellers were aware of the needs of our students and were coming to visit. This would be a partnership in which all would work together to give our students a wonderful experience. It was voluntary for the teachers to participate, and I was able to get all the classes that wanted to participate scheduled into the time slots we had. Teachers anxiously awaited the visits from the storytellers.

The day of the initial observations went smoothly. The storytellers were so enthusiastic and soaked in all that was happening in the classrooms. Teachers and staff greeted them warmly and demonstrated students' communication and participation levels. Everyone was so excited!

The students who would be served were located at three schools. The first two shared a campus and were located in the north part of our district. The northern part of our district is categorized by having pockets of extreme poverty and racial divide. A large portion of these students live in a children's home or are in foster care. The elementary and middle schools are together in one building, and the high school is in another brand-new building. The third school is centrally located and services students from a variety of socioeconomic classifications. The elementary schools service students ages 5 to 13, and the high school services ages 14 to 21. All students have diagnoses of Multiple Handicapped, Intellectual Disabilities, Autism, or Emotional Disorders, and these schools are considered the least restrictive environment for them to receive their education. The storytellers left the visit with a good idea of the strengths and needs of our students and were going to reach out to the teachers to finalize their plans.

Table 1.2 Storytelling Rubric

Teacher Name: _____

Student Name: _____

Category	4	3	2	1
Focus on Content	There is one clear, well-focused topic. Main idea stands out and is supported by detailed information.	Main idea is clear, but the supporting information is general.	Main idea is somewhat clear, but there is a need for more supporting information.	The main idea is not clear. There is seemingly random collection of information.
Sequence	Details are placed in a logical order, and the way they are presented effectively keeps the interest of the listener.	Details are placed in a logical order, but the way in which they are presented sometimes makes the story less interesting.	Some details are not in a logical or expected order, and this distracts from the story.	Many details are not in a logical or expected order. There is little sense that the story is organized.
Characters	The main characters are named and clearly described (through words or actions). The audience knows and can describe what the characters look like and how they typically behave.	The main characters are named and described (through words/actions). The audience has a fairly good idea of what the characters look like.	The main characters are named. The audience knows very little about the main characters.	It is hard to tell who the main characters are.
Story Elements (setting, characters, problem, solution/resolution)	All story elements are present.	Three-fourths story elements are present.	Two-fourths story elements are present.	One or no story elements are present.
Voice	Always speaks loudly, slowly, and clearly; is easily understood by all audience members all of the time	Usually speaks loudly, slowly, and clearly; is easily understood by all audience members almost all the time	Usually speaks loudly and clearly; speaks so fast sometimes that audience has trouble understanding	Speaks too softly or mumbles. The audience often has trouble understanding
Collaboration	Listens and accepts others' ideas Contributes thoughts and ideas Completes given task Allows each person to share information/opinions	Completes three-fourths components	Completes two-fourths components	Completes one or no components

Table 1.3 Student Engagement Averages on a Three-Point Scale

Alertness	Participation
2.4	2.2

$N = 111$

Each storyteller spent five one-hour sessions in each classroom. The activities that they focused on were differentiated to meet the needs of the students in that particular classroom. Sometimes puppets or props were used, and sometimes it was music or the intonation and actions of the storytelling that kept students engaged. Storytellers shared and modeled storytelling and then supported the students with the opportunity to participate individually or as a class to create a storytelling experience that they then performed.

Teachers then completed the storytelling and engagement rubrics and a teacher survey. Those were returned to me for compilation. We had 27 classrooms participating with a total of 111 students. The quantitative data are shown in Tables 1.3 and 1.4. For the storytelling rubric, students averaged 3.5 out of 4 points on the categories measured. These categories included focus on content, sequence, characters, story elements, voice, and collaboration. These elements are also covered in the state standards and alternate standards for English Language Arts strands. The engagement rubric showed a total average of 2.3 on a 3-point scale that measured alertness and participation. These areas are often goal areas for our students with the most significant impairments. We had more students who were rated on the engagement rubric than the storytelling rubric, again depending on the level of students in the classroom. Teachers were given the choice of rating the storytelling rubric if they felt it was a true measure of their students' abilities during the storytelling experience. Some teachers felt the engagement rubric was more suited to their students' performance and needs.

Teachers were also given sentence stems to respond to about their storytelling experience. The stems were "The best part about storytelling was . . ."; "My students thought storytelling was . . ."; "I learned the following from participating in the storytelling experience . . ." "I would/would not be interested in participating again because . . ."; and "Opportunities for improvement would be . . ."

Teachers overwhelmingly responded that their students were so much more engaged and excited about reading and writing. We saw many students who were not actively participating in daily activities becoming more involved and asking for more. Teachers appreciated that the storytellers were so flexible to meet the needs of their students, and students often asked when the storyteller was coming again. Some teachers stated that they saw their students respond in ways that they, as teachers, had never or rarely

Table 1.4 Storytelling Rubric Averages on a Four-Point Scale

Focus on Content	Sequence	Characters	Story Elements	Voice	Collaboration
3.6	3.6	3.5	3.6	3.5	3.5

$N = 78$

seen before. All teachers were so grateful for the experience, and all stated they would do it again.

There were also many lessons learned. Several teachers proclaimed that they now had new strategies to incorporate into their lessons such as music, props and puppets, and emotion. These strategies brought excitement to the classroom and levels of discussion of the characters and characters' feelings that teachers had not seen before. One hundred percent of teachers agreed or strongly agreed that the storyteller introduced educational concepts and resources related to the four Cs in 21st-century education (critical thinking, communication, collaboration, and creativity) that they would continue to use in the classroom.

Our journey with storytelling was amazing! Our teachers and students benefited tremendously from this experience. We saw performance from some our students that we would never imagine. The following e-mails I received from a teacher and a storyteller after the very first day say it all.

Teacher

Just wanted to let you know that it (storytelling) was awesome! Students were engaged and the storyteller was very comfortable with my students. A para had made picture cues with sound animations which the storyteller used on the smart board. The storyteller was so animated and I felt she had a good experience. She is super excited to bring her other puppets and stories tomorrow. Just wanted to let you know it was a wonderful experience for everyone.

Thanks for bringing the opportunity to our school!

Storyteller

Ladies:

I had a good first day with the kids today! Out of three classes, only 3 kids had an ability to verbalize. Several did not have much eye contact with me and a few would turn their wheelchairs around because they wanted a time out. Yet all 3 teachers said the kids were "very engaged."

The picture table and sound effects (displayed on the smart board) a para made for my Wide Mouth Frog story were quite successful. She has made one for The Mitten, which we will start tomorrow, and The Mermaid's Magic Seashell which will be next week.

I brought my speaker with me and it was great playing some music in between stories today. I bought a kid nursery rhymes album and a song from The Little Mermaid movie which I will use with the kids. Story, music, story, music seemed to work pretty well. A few of the kids could make hand movements to go with the songs.

My puppets were a hit and I am confident the menagerie I will be bringing will delight them. I am borrowing another storyteller's idea and transporting them in a suitcase.

There were many smiles today—from the kids, the teachers and me. I quickly adjusted to the fact that my storytelling would not elicit the kind of response I have been used to. It is not easy to see if my efforts are having an impact. With this audience, one girl who finally looked at me at the end of our time together was as meaningful as a standing ovation.

These e-mails demonstrate what a great team effort this project was and how rewarding it was for the students, staff, and storytellers. This nonprofit organization has received another contract in order to continue the project this year with our schools. Our teachers are so excited, and now I have a waiting list for teachers to participate. The storytellers were amazing advocates for us to continue this project, and we are so grateful to them.

"Do they understand our students?" I think you can see from our journey: yes, they do! This was a great example of how we all learn: teachers, paras, storytellers, and, most importantly, students. In our challenging world today, it is so great to see folks working together for the common good to give students like ours opportunities that they may not have received otherwise.

Notes for Storytellers: A Little Preparation Goes a Long Way

Donna Washington

It is not uncommon for schools to ask if they can include students with "special needs" in the audience during storytelling sets. I have never said "no." I have, however, learned that the term "special needs" alone means absolutely nothing. If you tell me some of the audience members have special needs, but you aren't specific, then I can do nothing whatsoever with that information. There are many things that would classify someone as having "special needs" that would have no impact at all on a performance and other things that would be really useful for me to know before I begin.

Audience members with special needs run the gamut from hearing or sight impaired to those who have combustible behaviors. There are some simple rules of thumb I follow when working with audiences who need extra considerations. They only work, of course, if you know what sort of challenges you are likely to face.

Performance Tips

Hearing Impaired

If there is an interpreter, speak to him or her before you begin. The interpreter is a partner in the telling. Give him or her the outline of the story before you begin so he or she can follow you. If you are going to make some odd noises or animal sounds, tell him or her ahead of time. Get his or her name, introduce him or her to the entire audience, and tell the audience that this person is an interpreter. If there is no interpreter, then slowing down the telling and articulating well will help those who are lip reading.

Sight Impaired

Your language must be very visual. Consider making sure you are speaking and not "showing" things. Figure out how your presentation needs to be adapted *before* you ever arrive.

Sensory Issues

Some audience members cannot handle loud or sudden sounds, bright lights, or sudden movements. If you have audience members who are bothered by these types of stimulation, then adjust your tales so that you do not lose the story's efficacy while keeping the rest of the audience engaged.

Tips for the Classroom

As a performer, I have all sorts of ways of keeping audiences focused, but when I am working as a residency artist, it is a bit trickier. I believe it is necessary to ensure that everyone can participate in safety and comfort. This requires a different approach than simply adjusting the material. Here is the process I follow.

Clear Instructions

Make sure you tell your participants what you expect. Let them ask questions. I also repeat instructions three or four times and ask the students to repeat what I just said. The more certain the participants are about what they have to do, the better the outcome.

Monitor

Make sure the participants are on track, but don't hover. Your presence changes the outcome of the work.

Adjust

If you find that you have lost your group or parts of the group or that everyone is making the same type of miscalculation, then you need to adjust something. Be flexible!

Repeat these three steps until you and your participants arrive at the same place.

Recently I was working with the fourth grade doing something I call "mini-residencies." In these two-day exposures, I model a very specific technique for a classroom teacher while having the students go through exercises. The techniques and processes are applicable to multiple areas of study and can be adapted for social studies, language arts, and mathematics.

I realized early on that every single person in my class is going to have myriad abilities. When it comes to storytelling, everybody is on a different rung, and some folks aren't even on the same ladder. Meet them where they are and see if they are willing or able to take a step forward. If they are, help them take it. If not, then let them practice standing where they are until they are so comfortable that they feel like they might just want to see what is on the next step. I believe in helping people feel safe in workshops and residencies because it is always easier to strike out from a place of safety.

Fear of speaking in public is called glossophobia. Apparently, 75 percent of the population suffers from this disorder. In fact, there is the amusing anecdote that people are more afraid of speaking in public than dying. This means if you were at a funeral, you would rather be the guest of honor than giving the eulogy. Either way, creating a safe space is the only way you'll get some people to tell a story!

The first day of my "mini-residency" is a story swap. Students create short stories in small groups, and then they tell in pairs, swapping stories after each partner. We start with 5 or 6 stories; we always end up with 10 or 12. Afterward, we share some of the stories. The second day we either use the tableau technique to create short stories, or we play story games.

This school asked for story games for their second day. They informed me that they wanted to bring some of their students from a self-contained class in for the entire residency. These students were not physically or emotionally challenged but had been identified as having very low IQs. It was decided, who knows how long ago, that they would be unable to keep pace with kids in the regular classrooms. Some of them could not read or write, while others had trouble with basic language. There was some concern that they would be unable to handle the material I was offering. My attitude was to let them see: you can always leave an educational experience, but you don't know how you feel about it unless you have it.

Knowing I would have students who struggled with the mechanics of language, I didn't even bother adding that to the residency. I encouraged the teachers to take the stories and write them out after I was gone if they wished. The educators were enthusiastic about this idea.

The "special needs" kids blended well, with the exception of one who was so overwhelmed by people that he couldn't speak. His aid walked with him the whole first day and helped him get through it. He enjoyed it but elected not to try day two. In fact, there were two students who did not return for day two. The second day was all about games that required lots of verbal interaction, and one of the students from the self-contained classroom did not do well if he didn't win every single time. Despite his interest in attending day two, the staff decided game day would not have been a good fit with his personality.

One of the fascinating things about having the "special needs" students try the activities was that they thought about language, concepts, and images very differently from their peers. Their ideas added a dimension to the stories and games that impressed everyone. My favorite interaction came on the second day when we were playing a game called "Rock, Paper, Scissors, Everything!" The rules are simple.

1. Every group has three people. Two people are "shooting," and the third person is always on deck. The third person also acts as a judge if there is a dispute.
2. If you lose the round, the judge takes your place, and you become the judge.
3. You cannot choose anything immortal.
4. Don't use any religious icons from anywhere.
5. We limited our game to real and imaginary things found on earth, but that was just a choice. You could use this game for a space unit by using things in space. To make it challenging, you could activate the rule that you aren't ever allowed to use the same object twice.
6. The "shooters" say, "Rock, Paper, Scissors, EVERYTHING!" They are required to make a sound and physicalize whatever it is they have chosen to be. For example, one could be a rabbit and the other a hurricane. Who would win that? Well, a hurricane could wash a rabbit out to sea unless the rabbit was down a hole and safe from the storm. When the storm was done, the rabbit could come up and be just fine. So, who won that round?
7. The two "shooters" must agree on who won. If they can't, the third person becomes the judge. Each person advocates for himself or herself—*not against* the other person—for one minute. Afterward, the judge makes the choice. (Be fair, because you might need either of these people to help you in the next round.)
8. If the judge decides it is a tie, then the round goes again until a winner emerges.

One of the "special needs" kids was in a group of three playing this fun, ridiculous language game. One of the participants won time after time playing an especially strong character. We had not activated the rule that you couldn't use the same idea twice. At first I heard frustration from the other two players as they tried to come up with things to beat the thing they knew was coming, but even if they came up with something good, the kid with the powerful character was very good at arguing for his choice. Then, I heard an eruption of "Man! That was a good one!" I went over to check it out, and it turned out that our "special needs" participant had played "germ" on the overly strong person, and everyone in the group agreed that "germs" would beat a person no matter what. The teachers were surprised at how well the extra students did, and they were all talking about ways to use storytelling to get these groups together again.

This demonstrated to both teachers and kids that these students had strengths in areas nobody bothered to consider. We also saw success with some students who had issues that did not qualify them as "special needs," but by any standards they certainly had special needs.

In one of my classes, there was a girl who came to school in clothes that were too small. She kept to herself, and according to the teacher, she never spoke to anyone. I was told there were "issues" at home. She jumped into the games and exercises with a gusto that surprised the teacher. Over the course of two days, the teacher watched this kid in disbelief. The girl actively participated and really enjoyed the interaction. I don't know if she felt a bit more comfortable with her peers after that, but she certainly spoke to me (something the teacher didn't think she would do). Not every special needs kid is in a self-contained class. Sometimes they isolate for reasons of their own. I have had great success using stories to draw these children into their classroom community.

- When we use the words "special needs," we are talking about people whom we do not expect to process the world the same way "most people" do.
- When you have audience members who need specific things, adjust so that you can accommodate everyone.
- If you are teaching, don't make any assumptions before you begin. As you move through the exercises, adjust as you encounter new information.
- There is no hard and fast rule about *what* to adjust. You are going to have to rely on your participants to tell you when you have taken a wrong turn.
- Last but not least, remember that every single audience has special needs. As teaching artists, performers, librarians, and educators, it is important to allow students to crash up against the arbitrary boundaries we have erected. You never know what could happen.

At the end of the "mini-residencies," one of the fourth-grade teachers offered this thought: "When you first started I noticed that you didn't tell them exactly what to do. That worried me, but they all managed to produce something. They were all different, and they were interesting. I never thought they could do things unless you told them exactly what to do every step. I'm going to have to watch that. I guess I need to trust them more."

That sentiment goes for all teaching and performing whether you are working with identified "special needs" populations or not.

A Language of Empathy: Etiquette of Interaction with Disabilities

Lyn Ford and Sherry Norfolk

The difference between the right word and the almost right word is the difference between lightning and the lightning bug.
—Mark Twain

Regardless of our intellectual capacities and our knowledge bases, many of us fear what we don't know or understand. That's evident in the difficulties with and misunderstandings within some cross-cultural communication. We forget that, beneath the skin and beyond what our eyes think we see, we are all pretty much the same. We all want to be recognized as people, with rights and feelings, and names.

When I was in the fourth grade, I had a friend, Linda, whom I didn't get to see very often. Linda lived in a housing development in the community bordering ours, and she went to a different school. We played together on Saturdays or Sundays as our mothers chatted and planned Girl Scout outings and drank coffee. One afternoon, I ran into her home to use the bathroom and ran back outside to find Linda standing, fists on hips, facing a taller girl I didn't know and frowning as she yelled directly into the girl's face, "My name is not *retarded!* My name is *Linda!*"

I ran to Linda's side, not sure what was happening but certain that my friend needed me. The taller girl just looked at both of us, shrugged, and walked away. Under her breath, she muttered about my race and Linda's intellectual abilities as a person who had Down's syndrome.

We stood there, both of us at attention with our fists on our hips as we watched that taller girl leave the common yard. I can remember my heart racing as I tried to think of what we should do next and what I should say if Linda was upset and started to cry. I figured a big hug would help. But Linda didn't cry. She hugged *me* and smiled a wide grin. "Come on, my friend," she said, "we've got some big playing to do!"

Linda and I were friends. The language we spoke with and about one another and the experiences we shared were those of friendship and unconditional love, a language of empathy.

Students with disabilities are individuals, with names, not problems. They each have their own personalities, abilities, and needs. They are a part of our families, our neighborhoods, our communities, our societies, and our world. They are the largest minority populations in the United States (about 19% of the population, or 56.7 million people, according to the 2010 report of the U.S. Census Bureau. "Nearly 1 in 5 People Have a Disability in the U.S., Census Bureau Reports," an article released July 25, 2012, https://www.census.gov/newsroom/releases/archives/miscellaneous/cb12-134.html).

People with disabilities constitute our nation's largest minority group, which is simultaneously the most inclusive and the most diverse. Everyone is represented: of all genders, all ages, all religions, all socioeconomic levels and all ethnic backgrounds. The disability community is the only minority group that anyone can join at any time.
—https://www.thearc.org/who-we-are/media-center/
people-first-language

As in any cross-cultural communication or discussion, we should honor the person, not the characteristic. Speak to, with, for, and about the *person*. Avoid words that label as if they are names. Increase your own vocabulary to include the following:

- "Person who has ..." or "a person with a disability" (recognizing that the term "disability" is a very broad and nonspecific one) rather than "the handicapped," "disabled," "learning disabled," "afflicted with ...," "a victim of," or "suffering with"
- "Person without disabilities" rather than "normal" or "healthy"
- "Person who uses ..." (a wheelchair, or a walker, or a communication device, or any assistive device) rather than "wheelchair bound" or "confined to a wheelchair" or "mute" or "blind"
- "Person who receives ..." (assistance or special education services) rather than "special education student"
- "Person diagnosed with ..." (a mental health condition, a developmental or cognitive or intellectual disability) rather than "mentally ill," "emotionally ill," "disturbed," "slow," "retarded," "handicapped," and so on

This list could go on and on. The main point can be made more simply by breaking it down:

- If you don't know what to say or how to say it, ask. And, yes, you can ask the person.
- When you meet the person, learn his or her name first. Use it. Often.
- Use common sense. Learn to look at the person and to use nouns of empathy: participant, class member, friend, and so on.

It's important for you to be comfortable and at ease in the special needs classroom if you want the students and teachers to be able to relax and enjoy your visit. Following these basic principles of disability etiquette, suggested by the National Easter Seal Society, will reduce anxiety on all sides:

- If you would like to help someone with a disability, ask if he or she needs it, and listen to any instructions the person may want to give.
- Be considerate of the extra time it might take a person with a disability to get things done or said. Let the person set the pace in walking and talking.
- Relax. Don't be embarrassed if you happen to use common expressions that seem to relate to the person's disability such as "See you later" or "I've got to run."
- Don't lean or hang on someone's wheelchair. Remember that wheelchairs are an extension of personal space. Ask permission before touching someone's wheelchair.
- Don't place strains on both your and the students' necks by standing over them for too long. Place yourself at the wheelchair user's eye level to spare both of you a stiff neck if you are talking for more than a few minutes.

- Don't grab a person with a vision impairment's arm in order to guide him or her; rather, allow a person with a vision impairment to take your arm. This will help you to guide, rather than propel or lead, the person.

- When you are with people with a hearing impairment, don't shout. Instead, tap the person on the shoulder or wave your hand. Look directly at the person and speak clearly, slowly, and expressively to establish if the person can read your lips. Not everyone with hearing impairments can lip-read. Those who do will rely on facial expressions and other body language to help understand. Show consideration by facing a light source and keeping your hands and food away from your mouth when speaking. Keep mustaches well-trimmed. Written notes may also help.

- It's okay to ask people who have speech problems to repeat what they said if you didn't understand the first time.

- If an interpreter is helping you speak with a deaf person, make sure you talk to the deaf person, not the interpreter.

- Don't speak loudly when talking to blind people. They hear as well as you do.

- Ask permission before touching a child with multiple disabilities and wait for a response.

- Don't offer scents or tastes to students without checking with the teacher first. Respiratory issues, medical fragility, and sensory sensitivities must be respected.

- Ask about sensory sensitivities—sound, light, touch, and so on—and adjust accordingly.

Again, common sense is the key. People deserve an empathetic point of view from those who care enough to teach them. Our actions and attitudes affect others, and our effective, caring choices make a difference.

> *I've learned that people will forget what you said, people will forget what you did, but people will never forget how you made them feel.*
>
> —Maya Angelou

Notes for Teachers: Storytelling
Tips and Techniques

Sherry Norfolk

Storytelling is communication, and long ago, you developed your own communication style. You might be the one who uses lots of gestures—or you might typically stick your hands in your pockets. Perhaps you mimic people's voices, or you talk in a quiet, soothing voice. To tell stories effectively, you are simply going to use your own communication style—but more so!

Tip One: Don't Memorize the Story!

No, storytelling is not about memorizing and reciting words on a page. Instead, you need to *know* the story—know who the characters are, where the story takes place, what the problem is, and what the sequence of events is. Know how the characters attempt to solve the problem, how it is finally solved, and how the story ends.

Knowing the story gives you the leeway to manipulate it in response to the needs of your listeners, rather than march steadily through a litany of memorized phrases. Consider this: You know the story of Goldilocks and the Three Bears, right? You know the characters, what they do and what they say. If you were asked to tell that story, you wouldn't need to rely on a memorized text—you would simply begin at the beginning and go on to the end, using your own words and imagination to fill in the details.

If a child looked puzzled when you mentioned "porridge," you would immediately notice and respond, explaining that Goldilocks called oatmeal "porridge." If, however, you were depending on a memorized text, stopping to add something into the story might very well cause you to lose your place and forget what came next.

"Learning the Story in One Hour" in Margaret Read MacDonald's *The Storyteller's Start-Up Book: Finding, Learning, Performing and Using Folktales* (August House, 1993) provides suggestions for quick and painless story learning.

Tip Two: Bring the Story to Life!

One of the many reasons that storytelling is such a successful teaching strategy is that it is *multisensory*—facial expression and body language provide visual stimuli; character voices, sound effects, and expressive interpretation provide auditory stimuli; and, kinesthetic participatory techniques allow children to embody the story. It's also easy to augment these sensory stimuli with scents, textures, and three-dimensional props to help learners fully comprehend.

Use Your Voice

All kids delight in silly voices and sounds (yes, even children who are noise sensitive delight in *quiet* silliness). We have found that children with multiple disabilities are especially responsive to goofy voices and sounds—they'll sit up straighter, focus longer, and smile or laugh!

If attention is wandering, a creaky *squeeeeeak* or deep MOO is guaranteed to bring the focus back to the story. In addition, making distinct character voices helps listeners identify and visualize individual characters; they don't have to ask, "Who said that?" They know!

Don't know how to create character voices? In *Reading Magic: Why Reading Aloud to Our Children Will Change Their Lives Forever* (Harcourt, 2001), Mem Fox explains that there are only seven things that you need to do with your voice to expressively read or tell aloud:

Speak HIGH
Speak LOW (DEEP)
Speak LOUDLY
Speak SOFTLY
Speak QUICKLY
Speak SLOWLY
Set the PAUSES

Used individually or in combination, these variations can create a wide variety of voices. And yes, you *can* do this!

Practice and you'll find that those seven simple ways to use your voice can result in a multitude of options. And here's a trick for maintaining the character voices throughout the story: *visualize*! If you envision the Big Bad Wolf as you say, "Hey, where are you going, little girl?" you are less likely to mistakenly speak with Red Riding Hood's voice.

Expressive Reading and Telling

There is simply nothing more boring than listening to someone read or tell a story in a monotone. You wouldn't do that, right? Expressive voices *interpret the text*; they give it meaning, and they help it come alive! Mem Fox's seven ways to use your voice apply to sharing expressive narration as well as to creating character voices. When the suspense is building, the pace slows. Pauses increase tension; the voice becomes softer and, perhaps, softer to pull your listeners to the edges of their seats.

Using your voice effectively is a key skill when sharing stories with kids. Consider when to use soft, whispery voices (they can be really sinister!), conversational tones, loud voices, or angry voices—and your storytelling will bring the tale to life.

Sound Effects

Most stories that you will want to share will include *lots* of opportunities for sound effects! Doors can creeeeeeak; mice can squeeeeeeeak; coyotes can howl and moan and yowl! OOOOOOooooooooOOOOooo!

Sound effects engage listeners! Try making those sounds—the kids will love 'em! Tell the kids to make those sounds *with* you—the kids will be totally hooked! Put your effort into *not* making those sounds, perhaps because you feel silly, or, maybe, you are concerned that your attempts will fail, and the story will fall flat. *Splat!* Get over your grown-up inhibitions, and let yourself play!

If you have trouble making the sounds, don't worry. First of all, no one will come to assess your endeavors and judge whether the sounds are precisely accurate. It's the effort that counts. And, in the second place, you can always ask the kids, "What sound would that make?" They'll be happy to do the work for you!

Tip Three: There Is a Time and a Place

Try to create a quiet, cozy atmosphere—distractions are inevitable, but the fewer the better! Make sure the kids can see you and that you can see their faces and meet their eyes. This may require you to move from child to child if they have trouble holding their heads up. And make sure that there is enough time to leisurely share and the opportunity to talk a bit after the tales are told. It's really frustrating to only hear half of the story!

Tip Four: Repeat, Repeat, Repeat

When sharing stories like "The Three Pigs" or "Goldilocks," some adults are tempted to skip the repetition: "And then they did it again." Please don't! Repetition is essential—it builds comprehension and increases retention. As the repetitive episodes and phrases appear and reappear, you'll notice your listeners beginning to repeat the phrases with you—actually beginning to tell the story! That could not happen if you skipped the repetitions!

And that is not all. The repeated episodes and phrases allow the listeners to practice recognizing the patterns within the story—and research tells us that the key to our intelligence is the recognition of patterns and relationships in all that we experience (Schiller, 1999).

Tip Five: Participation

Provide lots of options for participation—movements, sound effects, chants, rhythms, and songs. Note the use of the word "options"—these are not required, and certainly you should *never force kids* to participate! Offer the chance to participate, but allow the kids to determine what's right for them.

By modeling the desired participation and inviting kids to join in, you can allow them to choose exactly the way and level they wish to participate. Some will sing but not move; others will do the actions but not sing; others will sing and do all of the movements; and, still others will simply watch and listen and imagine. It's all good!

Tip Six: Build Vocabulary

Your expressive voice and body language will also aid in comprehension: you are helping your listeners *make meaning* (and that is the key to literacy—being able to make meaning of the text, whether it is presented orally, in print, or through visual arts). Vocabulary acquisition is also increased when students encounter new words in context, accompanied by *eloquent gestures, facial expression*, and *tone of voice.*

Tip Seven: Pay Attention to Your Audience

Watch the audience! Children's facial expressions and body language will tell you if they are understanding the story, if they are bored, if they are engaged, or if they are distracted. Pay attention, and adjust accordingly.

Tip Eight: If It's Just Not Working

Assess the problem—a sound effect or a big gesture might be all that's needed. Or you may be using too many words, or the story may be dragging on too long, so cut to the chase! If you try some adjustments and they fail, simply stop that story and move on to another one. Try it again after you have had a chance to identify the issue and find a solution.

Tip Nine: Don't Try to Be Perfect!

Kids truly don't care if you are a fabulous storyteller—they just care about the story! The more you practice, the better you'll get; so what are you waiting for? Go tell a story!

Resources

Fox, M. (2001). *Reading magic: Why reading aloud to our children will change their lives forever.* San Diego, CA: Harcourt.

MacDonald, M. R. (1993). *The storyteller's start-up book: Finding, learning, performing and using folktales.* Little Rock, AR: August House.

Schiller, P. (1999). *Start smart: Building brain power in the early years.* Beltsville, MD: Gryphon House. "Patterns in the brain," 85-93.

A Story Is Coming! Modeling and Nurturing Effective Audience Behaviors through Adaptable Storytelling Openings (Skill Levels: Pre-K through Grade Two)

Lyn Ford

"Be an effective listener." "Know when to speak and when to listen." "Respectfully respond to what is said, without yelling or making unnecessary comments." "Be still when it's time to be still." "Keep their hands off their neighbors and their comments to themselves." "Be attentive." "Look at me!"

Those were just a few of the responses I received when I asked in a workshop for educators and mentors of grades K through 2: What would you like for your students to do when it's time to listen and prepare for the learning experience you offer? To me, the answers I received and listed earlier spoke to a need for four skills:

1. Cooperation
2. Communication
3. Comprehension and retention of effective social skills
4. Continued application of those effective social skills

In order to prepare and keep students attentive to what is taught, to facilitate their learning experience, and to communicate ideas and reinforce concepts, an educator must be *heard*, with his or her spoken messages *received* and *understood*. When the educator is working with little ones under the age and skill levels of an eight-year-old listener (a student at the second-grade language-arts speaking and listening competencies level) or with those who have had little success in classroom or audience settings, just getting the process of sharing an informative moment *started* can be a challenge. Educators also face the challenges of getting and retaining the attention of many children with attention deficit disorders and of other students who may lack basic skills of body awareness and self-control.

Across the United States and in many places around the world, this "time to be attentive" mode is initiated with some form of active motivation to participate: rhythmic hand-clapping, short songs or rhymes, classroom cheers, countdowns to silence, and so on.

I prefer to call all of that what it really is: call and response (or choral response).

Why? Because I'm a storyteller, and call and response is traditional to many of the cultures from which my stories were inherited. I'm a fourth-generation storyteller of multicultural Appalachian (Affrilachian) heritage. Call and response is a part of who I am, how I know, and what I do. But the traditional and cultural aspects of call and response don't mean it can't be a part of any educator's classroom-behavior toolbox.

What is call and response? In storytelling format, a statement is made. The statement is immediately followed by an answering statement. That is "call and response." Simple, right? It can be used to open and close a story or story program; it can also be used to enhance the story and maintain attentive and active listening as it is being told. This article concentrates on call and response as an opener and closer to the story experience. The format that I use can also be called "choral response"—everybody gets in on the act.

Call and response is a way of letting the storyteller's participants know that he or she is ready to begin the story or program; their response lets the storyteller know that they are in agreement to participate as a community experiencing the story together. This is the essence of the basic give-and-take of *communication*—someone talks, and in turn, someone listens. It is also a form of *cooperation*. When the call and response format is routinely used in a story-sharing experience, the response is better understood and repeated by the storyteller's participants (*comprehension* and *retention of effective social skills*). And when the storyteller uses it in the next story or program, he or she can usually expect to see the same responses repeated (*continued application of effective social skills*).

My preference is call and response with some form of rhythm or rhyme, song, gesture, or movement incorporated into it. Interactive call and response that incorporates rhythm, rhyme, repetition, and some physical activity effectively approaches teaching for all styles of learning.

Call and Response and the Storytelling Connections to the Seven Learning Styles

Visual (spatial): Story participants need to see a teacher's body language and facial expression in order to fully understand content. Call and response and storytelling can include both.

Aural (auditory-musical): Story participants prefer using sound and music. Tone of voice, pitch, speed, rhythm, rhyme, and other nuances have more meaning than written expression. Call and response (and, most definitely, storytelling!) addresses this.

Verbal (linguistic): Story participants prefer using words in both spoken and written format. Call and response and storytelling provide that opportunity.

Physical (kinesthetic): Story participants prefer using body, hands, and sense of touch. Call and response can be enhanced with hand movements and clapping or snapping, body language, drumming or patting on knees, and so on.

Logical (mathematical): Story participants prefer using logic, reasoning, and systems. Call and response is a pattern of language usage and can incorporate distinctive rhythms and rhymes (more patterns); call and response also lets participants know that something is about to happen and leads to the rationale that a story, or action within a story, is about to begin.

Social (interpersonal): Story participants prefer to learn in groups or with other people. Call and response is a communal experience in the give-and-take of oral communication, an important social and career-oriented skill.

Solitary (intrapersonal): Story participants prefer to work alone and use self-study. In a storytelling event, most participants feel that the story and all its experiences are a form of one-to-one communication. (Thus, many younger students who are still learning the skills of oral communication tend to speak to the teller or verbally respond to the actions and events during some story moments, as if the teller is speaking only with and for them.)

Call and response is a modeling and mirroring moment, wherein the story participants begin to await cues that let them know it's their turn to speak, gesture, or react to what has been said. The effective teller can encourage participants to attentively sit, patiently wait for cues, speak in tones that are acceptable for communication, take control of their own voices and movements, and respond in socially acceptable manners. (See the Call and Response activities that follow this article.)

Call and response is also easily adaptable: a participant who can see but cannot hear can distinguish the gestures; a participant who can hear but can't see can follow the directions given for the response and recognize the call; a participant with difficulty with motor skills may recognize the call and be able to speak the response; a participant who cannot speak, for whatever reason, may be able to hum the voice pattern of a rhyme; and the participant who has difficulty sitting still, for whatever reason, has an outlet in the gestures and movements of the call and response.

Because call and response uses simple syllabic sounds, they can be repeated to help reinforce the placement of teeth and tongue and the creation of sounds for students who are working on clearly and effectively speaking. The sounds can be exaggerated in a mirror (always a silly exercise!), and, because of the joy of making them, they are more easily remembered; of course, we know that memorization is an important skill to have in a student's toolbox for learning. And we more easily remember and replicate those things that we enjoyed hearing, saying, or doing.

Obviously, call and response is also fun. Now, you can't beat that one for a workable classroom tool, can you?

I am not saying that call and response openings and closings should replace whatever is already working to gather students, gain their attention, and reinforce their working together in a teachable moment. I'm offering it as another tool for both the student *and* the educator/mentor toolbox. In this day and age, educators, mentors, and parents appreciate owning as many tools as they can discover!

> *Children are going to class with bodies that are less prepared to learn than ever before. With sensory systems not quite working right, they are asked to sit and pay attention. Children naturally start fidgeting in order to get the movement their body so desperately needs and is not getting enough of to "turn their brain on." What happens when the children start fidgeting? We ask them to sit still and pay attention; therefore, their brain goes back to "sleep."*
>
> *Fidgeting is a real problem. It is a strong indicator that children are not getting enough movement throughout the day. We need to fix the underlying issue. Recess times need to be extended and kids should be playing outside as soon as they get home from school. Twenty minutes of movement a day is not enough! They need hours of play outdoors in order to establish a healthy sensory system and to support higher-level attention and learning in the classroom.*
>
> *In order for children to learn, they need to be able to pay attention. In order to pay attention, we need to let them move.*
>
> —Valerie Strauss, "Why So Many Kids Can't Sit Still in School Today," *Washington Post*, July 8, 2014

And, of course, physical and social learners learn more comfortably when they are physically active *together* during their learning process. From my own experience as a former preschool teacher and a teller who used to tell for several special needs programs, I can state that many early-learning classes include a large number of these types of learners.

"Preschoolers can't understand complex rules and often lack the attention span, skills, and coordination needed to play sports. Instead of learning to play a sport, they should work on fundamental skills."—kidshealth.org/parent/nutrition_center/staying_fit/active_kids.html#

Some call and response experiences can open a door to multicultural studies. Learn the call and response. Connect it to an appropriate story. Research the culture from which both came. Enjoy the learning experience!

A Few Culturally Connected Openings

Because many of the stories that I share can be traced to storytelling traditions from West Africa and the African diaspora (the historic dispersion of African peoples from their original cultures and homelands), I offer these call and response openings gained from my research and program preparations.

Please note: Before we begin to share any call and response as a communal effort, I have shown the gestures as I said the words, or described the gestures as I model them, or added any tune I might want to use in a rough-draft form of participation. And I always say, "If that's not easy, do ___," and I model other possibilities, including simply smiling as a form of participation.

Nigeria (Language Group Unknown)

CALL: Tohio! ([tō-hee-ō] "A story is coming!")
RESPONSE: Hia, Hia, Hia Hia, Kpoo! ([hee-a, hee-a, hee-a, hee-a, kpoo] "Tell it quickly, we are listening!")
The enhancements I have incorporated with this call and response include the following:

- Teller holds hands at the sides of his or her mouth, as if shouting, and gives the call. Story participants clap with each "Hia" and then put their hands beside their mouths as they shout "Kpoo!"

- Participants shake their hands excitedly as they call out "Hia" and then hold their hands above their heads as they shout "Kpoo!"

- Participants who had difficulty with the vocal sounds simply clapped four times and shouted the "Ooooh!" sound of Kpoo.

Stories/books that have a cultural connection to this call and response include the following:

Gerson, M.-J. (1995). *Why the sky is far away: A Nigerian folktale.* New York, NY: Little, Brown Books for Young Readers.

Walker, B. K. (1990). *The dancing palm tree and other Nigerian folktales.* Lubbock, TX: Texas Tech University Press.

Akan Language Group, Ghana and Other Parts of West Africa

CALL: Ago? ([ah-go?] "Are you listening?") or Ago! ([ah-goooooo]), with extended long o sound
RESPONSE: Ame! ([ah-may!] "I'm listening!") or Ame! ([ah-maaaaaay])

The enhancements I have incorporated with this call and response include the following:

- Rhythmic clapping
- Sign-language applause (hands held at shoulder height and waving) when we say "Ame!"
- Jazz hands as we hold the last syllable of "Ame!"
- Participants who had difficulty with vocal sounds focused their vocalization on the long a sound of Ame.

Stories/books that have a cultural connection to this call and response include the following:

Agandin, J. B. A. (2015). *The adventures of Asuom: Folktales from Northern Ghana*. Accra, Ghana: Afram Publications.

Any story of Anansi the Spider, trickster hero of many Ghanaian stories.

Haitian Creole

CALL: Cric?
RESPONSE: Crac!
The enhancements I have incorporated with this call and response include the following:

- My head bent to the left or right as I speak; the participants lean their heads in that direction as they speak.
- One clap as I speak; one clap from the participants as they respond.
- First calling loudly, with an equally loud response, then calling in a softer voice, until we are all whispering our responses, followed by applause and the beginning words of the story.
- Adding the word "yeh" before cric and cric: "Yeh, Cric?" "Yeh, Crac!" I have heard this called out at a few story programs led by tellers from Haiti and Jamaica.

Stories/books that have a cultural connection to this call and response include the following:

Lauture, M. B. (2009). *Bobo, Chen Odasye A / Bobo, the sneaky dog: Mancy's Haitian folktale collection*. Kindle Edition, AuthorHouse.

Wolkstein, D. (1981). *The Banza: A Haitian story*. New York, NY: Dial Books for Young Readers.

A Few Traditional Folktale Openings Waiting for Your Own Enhancements

A fable! A fable! Bring it! Bring it! (Kanuri)
A story, a story, let it come, let it go. (Traditional West African [Ghanaian] opening)
Now here's a story! Tell it to me, yeah!

What we say here . . . teaches the mind. What we say now . . . touches the heart.

Oh, let's go! Let's get into a story! Oh, let's go! Let's get into a story! Oh, let's go . . .

Resources for Contemporary Call and Response Variants

"50 fun call-and-response ideas to get students' attention," *The Cornerstone for Teachers.com*. http://thecornerstoneforteachers.com/2014/01/50-fun-call-and-response-ideas-to-get-students-attention.html

"Listen up, students! Attention signals that work," *Scholastic.com*. Retrieved from http://www.scholastic.com/teachers/top-teaching/2013/11/listen-students-attention-signals-work

"27 attention-getters for quieting a noisy classroom," *Buzzfeed.com*. Retrieved from http://www.buzzfeed.com/weareteachers/27-attention-getters-for-quieting-a-noisy-classroo-h0xt

2

Storytelling Strategies for Children with Emotional/ Behavioral Disabilities

Introduction

Lyn Ford

As storytelling educators, we also nurture and model intrapersonal and interpersonal relationship skills and effective emotional and behavioral responses. As such, we become cheerleaders whose words and actions can make all the difference in the world.

In an old Chinese folktale attributed to one Hsien-Sheng Liang, a group of young frogs were making their way through the woods, when two of the small creatures fell into a deep and muddy hole in the ground. Unable to leap or crawl out, and flailing in the soft and slippery mud, the two unfortunate frogs croaked for help. And the other frogs croaked to the two unfortunate ones in the hole, "Give up! You can't get out! You're gonna die!"

Desperate for assistance, the two frogs thrashed and jumped about even more. But the other frogs kept telling them to stop trying, to give up, to die.

And one of them did.

The other frog waved and smiled to his companions standing safely above him. He continued to jump as hard and as high as he could. And as the other frogs yelled and gestured for him to stop trying, that frog jumped high, high, high, up and out of the hole in the ground.

As the now-fortunate frog laughed with glee, the other frogs gathered around him and asked, "Why didn't you stop trying? Didn't you hear us?" The frog said, "What?" The other frogs yelled, *"Didn't you hear us telling you that you were going to die?"* The frog said, "Ah, I couldn't hear you. I saw you waving your arms, so I waved mine even harder until I got myself loose from the mud. I saw you yelling. I thought you were cheering for me, so I tried harder.

"If I'd known that you thought I couldn't change my plight, that I couldn't make my way up by myself, if I'd known that you had all given up on me, I might have given up on myself."

We learn by seeing and doing and by not giving up. This chapter shares stories and efforts to cheer for effective emotional/behavioral development.

Yipes! I'm Going to Special School District!

Annette Harrison

A week before Springboard in St. Louis, Missouri, sent me into Special School District (a public school district that ensures that all local students receive equal access to quality special education) for two residencies, I found out that I was working with middle school students. I had planned for and worried many hours about working with *young* children. The stories I prepared were too juvenile for middle schoolers. Needless to say, I was terrified. I knew all the paper plate masks that I so lovingly made with my 10-year-old granddaughter, Addy, were not going to work. They were losing their plastic googly eyes at an alarming rate anyway!

What to do? I called the teacher, Wendy Ralston, in a panic and asked the comprehension level of the students. She said that they were mostly on their age level or below, with an average of fourth and fifth grade. I asked her to tell me about them. She said that in the first class there was one student who couldn't speak, one with significant emotional problems, and others with speech problems, autism, depression, and possibly bipolar disorder. A few had mobility problems as well. The other two classes were older boys, ages 13 to 15, with severe emotional problems, who had good and bad days and "you never know how they will feel when they come to school."

When I came early the first day of the residency, I was very anxious. I waited in the classroom down the hall. It was actually two very large rooms and the teacher and her students could not see me, but I could hear them. It was obviously a bad day for one of the boys; he was shouting obscenities at the teacher. Within minutes, two big male teachers came running in to take him away. I saw them grab him and drag him physically into the hall as he continued to shout.

"Oh boy . . . I'm in trouble!" I thought.

I clutched the one-hour-each session plan I prepared for the first day. I had no idea if it would work.

Here is the plan:

- Tell the story "Bird in the Hand."
  - Discuss the meaning of the story.
  - Retell the story with musical instruments.
  - Role-play with the students becoming the characters.
- Tell "The Boy Who Flew Too Close to the Sun," the Greek myth.
  - Retell with music.
  - Role-play with students becoming the characters of the story.
- End the session with a mystery from the book *Stories to Solve* by George Shannon.

This seemed very ambitious, but the teacher, Wendy Ralston, assured me that the students would love it. I think she had her fingers crossed! All the sessions were in her classroom.

The first class arrived, seven students ages 11 to 13. A week before, when I visited the school to observe this class, one of the students was talking about a bad dream she couldn't get out of her head and how she couldn't do her work. Another student had a rubber crab on his head, which kept slipping off. I listened intently to the teacher and watched the students respond to her and talk to each other and to the two aides in the room. None of the students gave me eye contact or seemed to even notice that I was there.

Now, on the first day, in the first class, I was not prepared for the response to my storytelling. I told "The Bird in Hand," and they were entranced.

The Wise Old Hermit

Annette Harrison's Version of "Bird in Hand"

It was a hot summer day. There was a group of teenage boys standing together in the center of the tiny rural village, and they were hot and bored! They had already gone to the watering hole to swim, had their lunch, and now they were standing around trying to figure out what there was to do in this boring town.

"We can go to my house and play with my dog."

"Naw, she is too old and it is too hot!"

"We can go to the library," suggested the only boy who enjoyed books. The library was an old house in the center of town that had musty book shelves.

"Naw . . . not that smelly old place, we need some excitement!"

"Yeah, excitement!"

"I have an idea", said the leader of the boys. "I think we should go and see the Wise Old Hermit."

"Yeah. Why?"

The Hermit was an old retired teacher who was beloved by his students when he taught in the High School many, many years ago. When he got too old to teach, he built himself a simple house in the forest, away from the people of the village, to live out his last years reading and studying in peace. He would come into town once a month for his provisions, and the boys would taunt him.

"What just crawled out of the forest? It sure is smelly!"

"Here comes the smelly old man. Do you ever take a bath?"

"Get a haircut!"

The parents remembered the Hermit as a dedicated teacher and forbade their children to bother him. "He is a wise old man who wants to be left alone. Respect that and stay away!"

"Let's go see how wise he really is!"

Yeah . . . can we go now?"

"We need a plan," said the leader. "Here is what we will do. First, we catch a bird in the forest and then go and test the old man. I will hold it behind my back and let him guess what I have. He will not know, but if he guesses a bird, I will say, 'Is this bird dead or alive?' If he says dead, I will let it fly away, but if he says alive, I will crush it with my hands."

"Yeah. Then we will see how smart he is!"

So they went into the forest looking for a bird. It was not easy to capture one, and by the time they did, they were sweaty and hot. They followed the narrow path deep into the forest to trick the Wise Old Hermit. It was cool and quiet. They were very excited about this new adventure!

They came upon his small, vine-covered, hut-like house and tried to look into the dirty window but could not see anything.

They knocked loudly on the door. Nothing. They knocked again and again. Nothing. They knocked on the window and finally heard a muffled sound and then some footsteps.

"He's there! Let's see how smart you are, old man."

He came to the door, which creaked open, and there was the bearded old Hermit squinting in the bright light, with his reading glasses on his wrinkled nose and an old book in his hand.

"Yes, why are you here?" He looked from one boy to the other.

"We heard you were very smart. If you are so smart, then tell us what I have behind my back."

Now, the Hermit had been living in the forest with the wild birds and animals for a long time and he was very observant. He could hear the wings of the little bird struggling to be free and saw a feather fall to the ground.

"It's a bird," he said.

The boys looked at each other.

"Yeah, it is a bird. Tell us, is it dead or alive?" asked their leader.

Once again the old man slowly looked into the eyes of each boy and sighed.

"We got him now," they thought. "Who is smarter now?"

Finally, the Hermit spoke. "The fate of that bird is in your hands. Whether that bird lives or dies is up to you. If I say he is dead, you will set him free, but if I say alive, you will crush the bird. I hope you make a good choice."

The boys were dumbfounded! How did he know that? They looked at each other and slowly turned away and walked silently out of the forest. The little bird flew happily away!

As far as I know, they never bothered the Wise Old Hermit ever again.

When it ended, students shouted, "You are the best storyteller ever! Tell us another!" The girl with the bad dream and the boy with the crab on his head (no crab today) were smiling.

I let them choose musical instruments from my set of six flat round drums that nestle together with individual wands, a bongo drum, bells, and other various found and garage sale instruments. They chose easily and we began our retelling of the story with musical accompaniment. I gave them a signal for starting and stopping. They followed directions well.

Here is an example:

"A long time ago and on the edge of the forest . . . let's make some forest sounds. This is our *setting*. What sounds do we find in the forest?" Students suggested sounds such as birds, squirrels, trees rustling, and wind blowing. We created a forest with the musical instruments and voice sounds. "A group of teenage boys were hot and bored." Let's make some boring music. And so, the retelling of the story began.

After we put the instruments away, I suggested that we role-play, acting out the story as the *characters*. The students became the teenage boys and the hermit. "What did the hermit look like? How did he walk and what was his voice like?" I asked many questions and they responded appropriately. We played in the story a few times so everyone could try out the part that they wanted. They all volunteered: amazing!

Then I told the second story, "The Boy Who Flew Too Close to the Sun," the Greek myth about Icarus and Daedalus.

The Boy Who Flew Too Close to the Sun

Retold by Annette Harrison

Long, long ago in Greece on the Island of Crete, there lived a fierce, powerful King named King Minos. He hired Daedalus, a famous architect, to build the city of his dreams. Daedalus was a dreamer, but he was also a doer. He designed most of Crete's fabulous gardens, created sculptures that seemed to breathe with life, and built many magnificent palaces. He was known far and wide for his amazing talent.

His final project for the King was to build a Labyrinth, an elaborate maze, to house the King's Minotaur, a horrible man-eating monster who was part man and part beast. Daedalus did as he was told and created a splendid structure that would keep the beast from escaping. There was nothing like it anywhere in the world!

King Minos was very pleased with the Labyrinth but wanted to keep its secret safe, so he imprisoned Daedalus and his son, Icarus, in a high stone tower.

"He will *never* leave Crete—he is my prisoner forever!" said the King.

Daedalus and Icarus were miserable in the tower, kept away from the rest of the world. So Daedalus figured out a way to escape. But once out of the tower, they were still imprisoned on the Island of Crete. The King had made sure that they could not escape by land or by sea.

"How will we get off this island, Father?" asked Icarus.

"He may control the land and the sea but not the air! We will fly off the island, my son!" said Daedalus with a wide grin.

"You joke, Father—that is why you are smiling!" laughed Icarus. "But I am young . . . will I have to spend the rest of my life here?"

"While you've been running and swimming and playing, I have been studying the birds."

"I've seen you, Father, resting in the sand and looking up at the gulls. I was wondering what you were doing," replied his son.

"Your not-so-lazy father was watching them fly, trying to figure out how they sustain flight, how their wings work. I think I have it figured out. Icarus, begin to collect feathers. I will trap a seagull and examine its wings. Together we will make wings and fly off this island!"

As Icarus began to collect feathers of all sizes and shapes, he thought to himself, "How lucky I am to have such a clever father . . . soon we will be free!"

Meanwhile, Daedalus carefully examined many gulls. It took a long time, and Icarus grew impatient.

"Are you ready to make the wings, Father?"

"It takes time, my impatient son. Soon enough, you will be flying!"

Weeks later, Daedalus began his work. He copied the shape of the birds' wings and the way the bones lined up. He carefully studied the way the feathers were placed. Then he began to build two sets of magnificent wings. He used thin, flexible pieces of wood to make the frame and added the feathers with wax and twine. He used leather straps to attach them to their arms.

"It is taking forever!" Icarus shouted after waiting for weeks.

When they were finally complete, Daedalus fastened the larger set of wings to his shoulders spread his arms wide, and took flight.

"You did it!" shouted Icarus. "You're flying like a bird! I want to fly, too!"

"We will practice together," said his father as he put the wings on his son. "We must take this slowly, and we must plan well. It will be very dangerous if you are too eager. You will have to concentrate and listen to my teachings."

"Of course, Father," said his excited son.

They practiced for weeks. Daedalus studied the weather, continued to watch the birds, and made many adjustments. Finally, they were ready for their escape!

It was early in the morning. The sun was bright and the day was clear: a perfect day for flight.

"Today is the day," said Daedalus, "so listen carefully. Remember what we discussed. Do not go too close to the sea or the water will dampen your feathers. And don't fly too high, too close to the sun, because the heat of the sun will melt the wax."

"I know, Father, you have told me many times. I will remember all of your warnings," said Icarus excitedly. "Let's go!"

Father and son reached out their arms, ran along the beach, and caught the wind. They ascended into the sky, looking like two giant birds.

"Stay close, Son!"
"I will, Father!"
Icarus began to sing:

Look at me, I can fly,
Like the birds in the sky.
Look at me, look at me,
I can fly!

For a while, they flew in unison, staying close together. Everywhere they went, people pointed up to the sky in astonishment. They were certain that they were watching gods fly across the heavens. What a sight!
Icarus flew higher and higher. His father could hardly keep up.

Look at me, I can fly,
Like the birds in the sky.
Look at me, look at me,
I can fly!

"Don't go too close to the sun!" shouted Daedalus anxiously.
But Icarus could not hear him. He was feeling the power and the joy of flying. All of his father's warnings were forgotten as he soared with the birds. Then he felt the warmth of the sun on his back! He realized too late that the wax was melting and the feathers were slowly falling from the wings.
Daedalus looked into the sun and saw Icarus tumble down, down into the sea. There was a loud splash, and then it was quiet—only a few feathers floated to the surface of the water.
When he reached land, a broken-hearted Daedalus took off his wings and hung them up on the wall of Apollo's Temple. He grieved for his son and never flew again.
The body of water that Icarus fell into was renamed by the people of Greece. They call it the Icarus Sea. If you visit Greece and you gaze into the Icarus Sea, you will remember the story of the Boy Who Flew Too Close to the Sun.

When I finished, they clapped loudly, and then they were silent.
"Does he really die in the sea?" asked one of the boys quietly.
"Yes," I said.
"Can we change the ending?" another asked.
The teacher got very excited. "How would you change it?"
Some responses:
"I think the people on the beach looking up at the sky caught him," suggested one of the girls.

Yeah, they made a net with their hands and he fell into it and he
was saved.
I think he fell onto a porpoise and was safe.
No he got swallowed by a big fish.
I think he fell into the water and swam to the shore.

Then the teacher said, "Let's make that our next writing project. We will change the ending of the story."
Then I told them a short mystery from *Stories to Solve.* They could not guess the solutions, but they had really good ideas and enjoyed guessing. I promised them at the end of each class we would have a mystery to solve.

All the sessions with this class were positive. They never lost interest in listening and retelling stories. Discussing the meaning or reaction to the characters and plot was much harder for them.

I saw them for five sessions, and at the end of the fourth session, I introduced a photograph from a packet of photos that Sherry Norfolk had generously shared with me. I showed them a photo of a cat looking into a bowl of swimming goldfish. One paw was up, ready to pounce. By answering a series of questions, we created a story together. After I asked, "What is happening in this photo?" I continued with questions about the setting, such as "Where does this take place?" After we established the setting, we began to flesh out the characters with questions, such as "What is the name of the cat? Should we name the fish? Who owns the cat and does he take care of her? What is his/her name?" I followed with questions to help them form a plot, such as "How did the cat get to the fish?" and so on.

The Cat in the Fish Bowl

Ms. Ralston's Class

Luke Lincoln and his sister Polly rushed off to school. The alarm did not go off. They forgot to feed the fish and the cat. They did not put the cat in his cage.

Grandpa Old Man Jenkins woke up just in time. He saw the cat looking at the fish. He fed the cat and the fish. Then he put the cat in his cage and went out and got a traffic ticket.

When the brother and sister came home from school and got to the front door, they remembered that they did not feed the cat and goldfish and did not put the cat in his cage. They expected to see the cat but not the fish because they were sure the cat had eaten them. They were surprised to see Grandpa Old Man Jenkins sitting on the couch with the cat and the fish swimming in the bowl. Grandpa told them about his traffic ticket.

They learned that you need to feed the fish and cat before you go to school.

On the last day, each student picked a photograph and wrote a story. They did it gleefully, but I have to admit that their stories were very short and to the point. Some were very interesting. They wanted to act out their stories and pick students to play the parts. They loved seeing their story ideas come alive; the stories got extended as they got involved. They were sad when our fifth session ended. "There is no justice in the world!" one of the boys said.

On that first day, after the first class, I took a deep breath and thought that maybe this plan would actually work! But then I thought of the young man who was dragged down the hall shouting obscenities. He was in the second class. There were five boys; evidently, all five were having a bad day. Ms. Ralston said that maybe I would not have anyone in my second class. But, one by one, they were allowed to enter and take a seat. They looked at me wearily. When I began the story, they perked up and listened. I caught the teacher's eye; she looked pleasantly surprised. Even the role-playing went very well. They actually got into it, and all of them wanted to participate. The instruments were the big hit, and they followed my lead perfectly. "This is great! I am surprised!" said the teacher.

The third class was composed of three emotionally disturbed older boys who were seated around a table. One of them had trouble being quiet, and he constantly verbally interrupted the story, but an aide sat next to him and kept him relatively quiet. They seemed to enjoy the story and appeared to be processing the meaning. They had a lot of questions, such as "Is that true? How old is that story? What is a myth?" Good questions.

They enjoyed using the instruments and wanted to continue with them. I later found out that the music teacher was ill and that students had not been to music class for months. They especially enjoyed the drums and fought over the largest and loudest one. They really got into role-playing, especially with a crown I brought in to wear after a story about a king. I asked them questions while they were in character about how they felt and why they did what they did; they answered as if they were that character.

There were times when students were unable to come to class because of behavior, but when they did, most of the time, they seemed totally involved.

All the classes were held in Wendy Ralston's Language Arts room. She loved the sessions and wanted to know if I could come every day until the end of school. She was very impressed with the way the students responded to stories. That made me realize how important stories were to these special students, especially the middle schoolers. I truly believe that they would benefit greatly by having a resident storyteller in each school.

Now that I know what to expect (the unexpected!), I can work on making the next time a richer, deeper experience. I learned that I need to devote more time to working on their individual stories. I think we can rewrite these stories after the experience of role-playing in them.

I also learned that five days is not enough!

A Wish Granted

Asha Sampath

Storytelling for children with special needs—why not?

That was the question that popped into my mind early in my storytelling career. So I made the rounds to a well-known school in my area, but after listening to me, the principal said, "I really don't know how it would help our children."

I didn't have much more than my enthusiasm to give her because I am not trained in special education; I only possess a teaching degree for the "normal" stream. I almost gave up my wish.

Then the opportunity came all by itself in the form of a phone call from a very annoyed friend! She volunteered at another branch of the same school for special children and had earlier told me that the principal there was looking for storytellers and she had recommended my name. She had asked me to get in touch with the principal. I didn't, given my previous experience (hence the annoyance of my friend). She asked me, "Are you going to make that call and set up a meeting or shall I drag you there?"

I hastily made that appointment. This principal was deeply interested to offer experiences for her students that the mainstream children had. I explained to her that I had no clue about how to tell stories for special children, but, with the help of her staff, I was willing to learn. So began my experience of telling stories to these children. And what a wonderful two-year stint it was!

The children had a wide range of concerns, from autism to behavioral problems. Many refused eye contact; some never spoke a word; others kept talking to themselves; and there were some who were attentive. They were grouped age-wise into Primary (30 students, ages 4 to 8), Intermediate (two groups: first group—25 students, ages 9 to 11; second group—30 students, ages 12 to 14), and Seniors (25 students, ages 15 to 20). I was told to share with one class per week for each group, which meant a class got to hear the story only once a month; this was eventually changed to twice a month per class.

As storytellers, we know that stories connect everybody on a plane of their own. We are also aware that it is our duty to bring a story as effectively as possible to our audience. That's what I tried to do. The teachers had told me that the children liked action, songs, and colorful graphics/props. With this in mind, I planned each story to use these strategies to the maximum.

The first session, I was nervous. Perhaps the principal and her chief coordinator anticipated this. They gave me the Seniors, who were more attentive and had less behavioral difficulties. The story I chose to tell them was an adapted version of "The Barbers Secret." (My maternal grandmother had told me this story, but a version of this is available at http://greece.mrdonn.org/greekgods/kingmidas2.html.)

Synopsis: Apollo, the god of song, gives King Midas donkey's ears when the king criticizes the god's music. King Midas wants to tell someone; he digs a hole in a shallow pool and speaks into it, "King Midas has donkey's ears!" Then he covers his ears, thinking no one will know. The reeds near the water hear and whisper the secret for the entire world to hear.

"The king has donkey's ears!" was the refrain I used while telling the story with exaggerated movements, props, and much action.

I encouraged students to repeat simple words along with actions: for example, I would walk up to a student as I narrated, "There was once a barber . . ." At "barber" I would stop and do the action of holding the child's hair in my hands and snipping it with an imaginary pair of scissors—"snip, snip." I wasn't sure if they were getting the hang of the story until I had repeated it thrice. The fourth time, the students began to tell the story with me! Oh! What joy! The teachers would sit at the back and watch me involving the class. And for the school's Annual Day (a cultural show featuring performances by students), the Seniors performed this story as a drama! How thrilled I was as I sat watching them perform—I can still feel the tears pricking at the corners of my eyes.

The teachers had gone to great lengths to make this a fabulous performance. Students practiced for almost two months! For the big day, they hired costumes, had volunteers do the makeup for the children, and made big props of trees for the garden. Each student had a role, even if that meant introducing new characters or elements. One girl wore a peacock costume and danced around the trees, and another girl with a beautiful voice sang a song; nonverbal students stood holding the tree props or acted as guards or attendants to the king. The teachers had painstakingly recorded the dialogue of each student (with correct enunciation) and played it for the audience so the dialogue would continue even if the student forgot or just didn't want to say it at that time. They were on stage the whole time prompting and encouraging the students.

I selected very simple stories for each class. But were the children enjoying the stories? That answer came to me in surprising ways! I knew the stories and their telling had made an impact when teachers told me each week I walked in that "Ma'am, the children are singing your 'Welcome Story' song with actions!"

Nonverbal children would sidle up to me and touch my arm, give me a smile, or pull my saree—that was their acknowledgment of me as a storyteller. A verbal child would scream from his class, "Storyteller teacher," as I walked past the window. The teachers told me that children repeated stories in class and at home. The parents were happy about it; the teachers were happy about it; and I was happy about it!

With every class storytelling, my confidence built and along with it, the urge to make a story even better. I constantly spoke with the teachers, the coordinator, and the principal on what else we could do to improve the telling. More songs, more visuals, more physical action!

Then I decided to use multimedia to express the stories even better. I began the second year using GIF images or other colorful images I had patiently collected from the Internet to enhance the stories I chose to tell each class. The children were excited every time I walked in with my laptop and an image appeared on the big screen in the storytelling room.

I used words and showed animated images and then more words and more images. This kept them even more attentive and receptive. For instance, when I told the story of "The Crows and the Serpent," from the Panchatantra (the story can be read here: http://www.culturalindia.net/indian-folktales/panchatantra-tales/crow-and-snake.html), I showed them a GIF image of a crow flying, a moving snake, and a dancing fox that advises the crows how to get rid of the wicked snake that ate up the crow's eggs every time they were laid in the nest.

The children "flew" with the crow, wriggled like the snake, and danced with the fox. Stories had entered the realm of these children too! How great a feeling!

I also believed that using the senses of touch, smell, and taste wherever such stories permit would make that story even more impactful for these children. To illustrate the point, let us consider the story of "The Apple Tree," about a tree that is spared because it holds a beehive filled with honey (http://www.pitara.com/fiction-for-kids/folktales/the-apple-tree/). The children could be given a piece of bark to touch and feel its rough texture; at this point, the word "rough" could be stressed and become part of their vocabulary. A taste of honey could emphasize the word "sweet," and for smell, apples could be used.

As for feedback from the school staff, the coordinator said, "Sixty percent of the students are able to relate to the stories told with exaggerated expression, body movement and voice modulation along with auditory and visual inputs. They have begun to mime some actions; their vocabulary has improved and the verbal students have started answering questions posed by you, the storyteller." The teachers remarked, "Children are responding well. They have become aware of the sequence of events in the story. They have learnt to associate/imitate actions with words, relate to the songs sung —this makes the storytelling interactive. For most students the visuals are appealing and keep them engrossed."

My wish was granted. And I know this: stories can be told to special children, and they receive them as well as anyone who loves a story!

Resources

These stories can be adapted to the needs of the audience.

Aesop. "The Ant and the Grasshopper." (Various versions).

Aesop. "The Fox and the Crane." (Various versions).

Bansal, S. P. (1994). *Mittu and the yellow mango.* New Delhi, India: Frank Educational Aids.

Cultural India. "The Rabbits and the Elephants." Retrieved from http://www.culturalindia.net/indian-folktales/hitopadesha-tales/rabbits-and-elephants.html

Viswanath, T. (2011). *Catch that cat.* Southborough, MA: Tulika Books.

Getting Real: Public School Residencies

Judith Black

Last fall I helped develop a grant proposal for work at a school in Lawrence, Massachusetts. Following is some of the beautifully flowered prose I assembled for that application:

Whereas:

A majority of the student population (80%) represent learners whose primary/home language is not English

The teacher population is not familiar with the culture of origins of most of the student population

This particular student population reads English significantly below standard levels

This particular student population has been slow to acquire social and communication skills necessary for school success

We propose a storytelling residency which will focus on language acquisition and communication via tales from the indigenous cultures of the student population.

Blah, blah, blah, blah, blah . . . .

Completed by the principal and myself, this was all well intentioned and accurate. Then I arrived at the Donovan School. The old brick schoolhouse resembled the tale "Always Room for One More," as children seemed to be oozing out of and pouring into every nook and cranny of the ancient structure. The office was a tiny room jammed with the secretary's and principal's desks and three children at various levels of distress.

"Oh sure, we're expecting you, Honey," called the secretary. "If you can find your way in here, you can hang your coat on the rack next to the desk and I'll try and find Sherry (the principal)." A few minutes later, with a child who was biting and punching at her secured under her arm, the principal called out from down the hall.

"Judy, I'm glad to see you. You made it!" As she closed in, she explained above the din of the angry seven-year-old: "This is my buddy Diego. He's having a bad morning." She put her hand gently on his head and lowered him to a standing position, his arms and legs still beating at anything nearby. She talked to him soothingly in Spanish, but he was not to be dissuaded. I stuck my tongue out at him and began making weird faces and strange sounds. He jumped track to hone in. We started playing a finger game.

"Thanks," Sherry said without his hearing. "Part of it is neurological and he needs to have complete dissonance in order to change response. The other part is that he's just plain angry. He thought he was going to see his father this week, but it turns out that instead of being released from the Massachusetts prison he's been serving time in, they're going to send him straight up to New Hampshire to complete a term there. No home visit." During this explanation, a few other students passed. Not one of them got by without Sherry riffling their hair or touching a shoulder gently and offering an introduction.

"This is Maria. She is a very good reader. This is Pablo; wait till you see him running on the playground. He has feet like wings. Jose, come meet the storyteller. Jose is a math genius." No sooner did she complete her explanation of Diego's issues than the sound of flying furniture was heard from a nearby first-grade classroom.

"*Un momento,*" she said, and was off to douse another fire. At the entrance, a social worker was speaking Spanish rapidly with one of the mothers, and three children were sitting in a front stairwell, the only space available for "time out."

Now, what made me think that our little plan, which outlined exactly what would be accomplished in each classroom session and how, might require some flexibility?

Let me say here and now that this is a good school in the most important way a school can be good. The faculty and staff want to be there. They laugh, joke, and share anecdotes about the kids in the tiny lunch room. The crossing guard and maintenance man are as integral as the language specialist. There is a sense of service to the kids and neighborhood, a warm cooperation among the people working there, and a belief in education. It's good they have these things, because schools, being based on property taxes, leave the kids of urban Lawrence at an enormous disadvantage. They have a building so overutilized that you would need a shoehorn to get another human in there. They have a minimal budget for supplies. Field trips mean that teachers and specialists pool their cars and caravan. Parents, most of whom speak English haltingly, want their children to succeed, but insomuch as they are disempowered politically, socially, and economically, they will often defer to the system rather than take the middle-class route and advocate for their children.

Did I mention that I was here to organize troupes of story actors in grade two, who would share their tales with "underclassmen," parents, and the community? My plan was to introduce the students to movement and story games, tell them stories from their parents' lands of origin, have them choose a tale to act out, and finally facilitate and orchestrate each class's story play and share it at a grand finale to be held at the library.

As part of the residency, I would not only work intensively with the second graders but would also share stories in the other classrooms. Out of the gate, it was clear that these kids needed gripping tales that would speak to their lives and the strengths that would see them through to adulthood. "Sally has a good time on her summer vacation at Disney World" would not cut it.

Two of the first graders were crushed into one end of a small classroom, and in the rear, hiding behind the chair where a teacher sat, was a child of age 6 with the hardened angular face of a 19-year-old gang member. With challenging dark eyes and little features held so tightly that they appeared like a bow string ready to snap, he darted out from behind the chair and retreated again. He would not join the group, and one of teachers, before I began, asked if I wanted him removed.

"Nah, just let him do what he needs to. This is supposed to be fun." The warm-up story was short and funny; during it, he darted from one spot to the other, one step ahead of the enemy. Then I blew into "Hansel and Gretel," only the names were changed to engage the innocent. It became "Juan and Maria," and with a few cultural twists (they were served rice and beans at their last meal), it was the traditional story of betrayal, abandonment, survival, and celebration.

As the story progressed, little Mr. Rebel-with-a-Cause crept closer and closer to the action until he was seated on the edge of the group. By the time the brother and sister had been dumped in the forest for a second time, the rigidity in his body had evaporated, and as Maria pushed the witch into the oven, his face—soft and shining—looked like that of a six-year-old again. For a brief few moments, he allowed himself to enter another world worthy of his own.

Eventually I found and learned appropriate stories for the students to choose among for their reenactments. One story, "The Chili Plant," was a prototypical hardcore folktale. It involved a stepmother abusing her adopted daughter because the child looked like her birth mother. One day the girl is left to guard the stepmother's greatest treasure, a fig tree. When an old man comes, begging water, the girl immediately goes into the house to fetch some for him, and in her absence, he sees no harm in eating one of the figs. He blesses the girl for her kindness and leaves. When the stepmother returns and discovers the missing fig, rage overwhelms her and she kills the girl, burying her in the backyard in a hole with a chili seed. She is deeply missed by her father and brother, who are led to believe that the girl is just visiting relatives, and they watch as the season passes and a remarkable chili plant grows in the backyard. When the father asks for one of the chilies, the son goes to pick it, and the plant sings its anguish to the boy, then the father, and then the stepmother, who falls into a dead faint at the sound of the girl she had buried. The girl is dug up. Safe and sound, protected by the old man's blessing, the family, sans evil stepmother, lives happily ever after.

The other stories were sweet sequence tales and fool's tales. The bilingual class chose a sequence tale, "The Big Bed," but this one was made for another class. When this particular second-grade class heard "The Chili Plant," a shiduck (Yiddish for match) was made on the spot. As a group and individually, their visceral response to this tale was very powerful. It became clear that it was theirs to work with. When the session was over, the teacher took me aside and registered serious concern:

"I don't know if this is such a good choice for my class. A lot of the children are coping with domestic violence issues in their homes."

"Why do you think they chose this story? This story accepts that very fact, and then offers a model of how they can survive that violence by acting with a good heart. Please, let them do this."

With some reticence she agreed, and I sure hoped that Bruno Bettelheim knew what he was talking about!*

Meanwhile, I was preaching the perks of storytelling so often that I forgot that it's real. One day on my way to lunch, I saw Diego (he spent a lot of time outside the classroom) at a little desk in the hall; he was pretending to read a book about Michael Jordan.

"Hey, man, what ya reading?"

His face was a tighter network of rage than any seven-year-old deserves to experience. I looked at the book.

"Hey, he's the man, isn't he? Find out anything interesting? Hey, what's that?" There was a sketch book on the table.

"May I take a look?" He acceded with a nod.

"Wooo, these are great drawings. You do them?" Another nod.

"Cool! What's happening here?" And he started to tell me about a kid climbing up a building to escape and how the guards are trying to shoot him

---

*Bruno Bettelheim, author of *The Uses of Enchantment: The Meaning and Importance of Fairy Tales* (originally published by New York: Alfred A. Knopf, Inc., 1976), speaks to the cathartic value of the ancient tales to accept, play out, and offer models for surviving growing's most traumatic stages.

and "that's what the zig-zag lines are. But there's a really bad man in there and the kid's got to get away."

"Hey, want to hear a story about a really bad man?"

You bet he did, and without knowing exactly why, I launched into "Bluebeard." Sitting in the basement hall with kids, adults, lunch aides traipsing back and forth, his attention was riveted in that little circle of energy that the story created between us. I had barely finished when the principal (by all reckonings a woman soon to be sainted) appeared with Diego's mother. I wanted to tell her what an important part he had in the story we were acting out (he was in the "The Chili Plant" class), but my Spanish was much too halting and she was feeling diffident because he had disrupted his classroom once again. He was taken away. The next day, though—once again sitting in the hall—Diego called me over.

"Hello, my man. What's up?"

"I want to tell you a story." And pulling up a chair, I hunkered into the intimacy of our created circle. He took out his sketchbook, opened it to the same picture we were looking at yesterday, and began:

"This here is a castle and a really bad man lives in there. He has a black beard, so I call him Blackbeard. See this kid climbing the wall? He is super kid and he is climbin' in to save a girl from Blackbeard . . . ."

He went on until school life imperatives forced us to break the circle. The circumstances of Diego's life will only be deeply affected by a new trend in social, political, and economic justice. I'm not holding my breath. His ability to see himself as a hero rather than a victim in his world can be affected by storytelling. I pray that this slight switch in vantage points will give him one more strength to work with in his world.

Some days I would walk out of the classroom and just cry, having absolutely no idea if we had gotten any closer to our goal of internalizing the story, creating scenes, choosing characters, and acting out the scenes. The chaos, constant talking, and little spats of rage, anger, disappointment, and fatigue were as prominent as spots on a leopard's skin. In the bilingual classroom, when their teacher walked out of the classroom, chaos always broke out. The aide tried to rein them in, but eventually my only workable ploy would be to walk out of the classroom after instructing them to pull out their math books. Upon reentry, we could work for a whole five to seven minutes until the tactic would be needed again. (I have a sneaky suspicion that this sequence is not authorized by state curriculum standards or mandated regulations.) In the class where we were working on "The Chili Plant," the scenes where the stepmother hit the stepdaughter were reenacted with such brutality that it made me wince, but I just kept chanting to myself, "They need this story." The classroom that was acting out a Juan Bobo story would often disintegrate into such chaos ("I don't want to be a dog anymore!" "I want to be the princess. She stole my part." "I'm not doing nothing!") that I wondered if we would ever have anything to share.

Well, knock me over with a feather, when it was actually time to put all the scenes together and have the entire tale reenacted by each classroom, they did it. They did it with panache and power and commitment. The flakiest of students remembered their parts. Diego, who was portraying the buried girl's brother in the last scene of "The Chili Plant," had missed the last two rehearsals.

"Diego, do you think you can do this in front of an audience?" All he did was nod "yes," but on that day, with 50 people and local TV cameras running, he stepped to the center of the stage and proclaimed loudly that his sister had been wronged and was alive. He brought his "father" out to the plant and demanded justice. He acted as a member of a team for the first time that anyone could remember, and his mother was there to see it. The bilingual class filed into the four rows of actors representing each scene, and at one point their teacher, who I had feared thought the whole process foolhardy anarchy, prompted one of her students with his line and smiled radiantly throughout his performance. Sherry, the sainted principal, was still emerging with last-minute props and enough pride in her students to launch a thousand careers out of the dust.

After sharing the stories with the rest of the school and larger community, I was down in the teachers' room.

"Judith, 'The Chili Plant,' that story, my mother used to tell it to me all the time when I was growing up in the Dominican Republic."

"Me too," said a woman from across the table. "In Puerto Rico, my grand mama told it to me all the time. I cried like a baby when the kids acted it out."

Then they both spontaneously began singing the song that the chili plant sings to the brother and father. They were singing the traditional tune that I did not know.

"Would you sing that again so I can learn it?" I begged.

Through all the chaos, things were happening. I just needed to develop the eyes and ears to see and hear them. I needed to let who I was and what I could do soak in this world and re-emerge as a hybrid that would both unite and stretch all parties involved. I used every bit of knowledge and trick I knew, but not one of them looked like the things I had done before with young people. This was a new place with its own needs. It wasn't perfect, but the bilingual class understood and told a tale out of their culture in English. They, their teacher, and their parents beamed with pride. A class fraught with the victims of domestic violence experienced a way to digest the realities of their lives and imagine new futures. The chaos of dogs chasing cats, that chased birds, that chased bees, that chased Juan Bobo, who made the sad princess laugh, fell into place and made everyone laugh. Not to mention that we also fulfilled our outlined objectives.

Before lunch ended I noted, "You guys don't need me here. You know all the stories. You just need to start telling them."

Thinking beyond Violence: First Steps toward Peace

Sherry Norfolk

Kids with an Emotional Behavioral Disorder (EBD) diagnosis have low impulse control, are quick to react with anger and violence, and can transform quiet classrooms into war zones with no warning. Working with these kids is very rewarding, always unpredictable—and also somewhat terrifying. Moving them toward peaceful choices is an ongoing goal.

Learning that I would be leading a five-session residency in three self-contained classrooms of middle school boys with EBD, I gave a lot of thought to the stories I would tell and to the kinds of activities that might engage these learners. One of the teachers warned me that these students were never interested in anything, no matter how much fun she tried to make the learning activities. Engagement would be the first, biggest, and persistent challenge.

Once engaged, however, I was also interested in helping them explore nonviolent problem solving. Feeling that a stealthy approach might be best (an announced agenda was likely to alienate them before we even began!), I simply started with storytelling.

Day One

"Wiley and the Hairy Man"—told with lots of character voices, sound effects, facial expression, and gestures—was my opening salvo. Total engagement! After the story, we quickly analyzed the pattern:

Main character (a kid) _____
Is warned about Danger _____
By an Adult character _____
But ends up in danger anyway because _____
He gets away *without violence* by _____

They were ready for another story. I chose "Billy Brown and the Belly Button Monster" because it fit the same pattern but was totally goofy. These guys deserved some laughs.

After noting how the story matched the pattern, we used that pattern to generate a group story. *Collaboration is one of the skills that these students are working on—taking turns and respecting one another's contributions is problematic. We managed to agree by combining some answers and accepting others.*

The problem-solving bit was the hardest, of course—responses included machine guns, bombs, knives, and poison. I pointed out (over and over again) that the characters in my stories had used their brains rather than violence to solve their problems. Heaving huge sighs, the boys finally arrived at an acceptable solution.

After one of the students modeled telling the resulting story, each student used the pattern to generate his own story. No one had to be coerced to write—they dove right in! There were several attempts to "solve" the problems in the stories with violence, but with only a few reminders, the stories became nonviolent.

Day Two

All the students shared their new stories with the class, and classmates seemed engaged in each other's stories. They even complimented the story solutions—"That's pretty good, Man. How'd you think of that?"

I discussed my proposal for the next lesson with the teachers and received enthusiastic support.

Day Three

I began by telling the class a Cree legend about a Skeleton Woman who first eats her own flesh and then wants to eat other humans. Oh yes, complete engagement!

Then, I showed them a collection of very ambiguous photos (superzoom photos of bits of plants, ice formations, etc.). Up close, the photo subjects were unidentifiable and somewhat creepy. I demonstrated how to use one of these photos to create an original creepy story.

I asked one of the students to make a blind choice of one of the photos. This would become the creepy dangerous character in our story. We named the character, decided where it could be found, determined what it would do to a human who came in contact with it, created a voice, sounds, and movement for it, and determined how a human could defeat the creature *without violence*. Then I told them their story, using their ideas plus my own addition of a protagonist who encounters the creature but gets away safely.

"Can we do it?" "I can do that—let me try!" "Let me see the rest of those pictures!" Hah! Gotcha!

After spreading the 50 pictures out and allowing them choose, I distributed forms with questions to help them create their character:

> The creature's name is _____
> Where does it live? _____
> What makes it dangerous? What will it do if it comes in contact with a human being? _____
> What kind of voice does it have? _____
> How does it move? _____
> What sounds might it make? _____
> How can it be defeated without violence? _____
> _____

Every student immediately began shuffling through the photos and discussing ideas for stories and then grabbed a pencil and got to work! By the end of that session or the beginning of the next, everyone had created and told their own creepy stories.

All but one of the stories had nonviolent endings; however, one story simply came to a stop—no resolution at all. The listeners demanded, "So what happened to the guy? How does it end?" When the author confessed that he hadn't been able to come up with a nonviolent ending, everyone spontaneously began to brainstorm solutions. He accepted one of them and finished the story.

This gave me an opportunity to deliver a very short sermon on working together to solve problems, brainstorming to discover multiple alternatives, and evaluating the options. And *that* resulted in the boys offering new and improved endings for the stories that had already been shared!

Day Four

I introduced Jack Tales and told two examples—"Jack and the King's New Ground" and "Jack and the Haunted House"—pointing out the general pattern: Jack needs a job, somehow finds one, encounters an obstacle (typically a giant or witch or other magical creature), defeats the obstacle *without violence*, and gets rewarded.

We used the pattern to generate a new story and I told it to the class—whereupon they began making up their own stories without any prompting! Even better, there were *no* attempts this time to use violence in the stories. Students took more time thinking through the options and developed some very creative nonviolent solutions.

Day Five

Students shared their Jack Tales with the class after promising to provide positive peer feedback. They kept their promise!

Learning that there are options to violence is an important step toward peaceful problem solving. Through our story listening and story making, these kids with EBD took a baby step in the right direction, beginning to discover their own ability to generate, evaluate, and implement nonviolent solutions.

Resources

Bang, M. (2003). *Wiley and the hairy man.* Pine Plains, NY: Live Oak Media.

Chase, R. (1971). "Jack and the king's newground." *The Jack tales.* Boston, MA: Houghton Mifflin.

Ellis, E. (1994). "Jack and the haunted house." In D. Holt & B. Mooney (Eds.), *Ready-to-tell tales.* Little Rock, AR: August House.

Norfolk, B., & Norfolk, S. (2006). *Billy Brown and the Belly Button Beastie.* Little Rock, AR: August House.

"Skeleton Woman" is a Cree legend from the oral tradition.

Incorporating the Five Senses in the Autism Classroom: How to Spice Up "The Gingerbread Man"

Katie Knutson

Thanks to a grant from the Minnesota State Arts Board, I was able to be the storyteller-in-residence for one elementary school for the entire year. As a part of that residency, I saw each of the three center-based (stand-alone) autism classrooms five times. I had worked in neurodiverse mainstream classrooms, but this was the first time I would be able to spend that much time working in small autism classrooms. I had been studying how to create multisensory and sensory-friendly theater and art experiences and couldn't wait to put these new techniques into action.

Before the residencies, I met with each teacher to talk about the special needs of their students. Although there were three different classrooms with vastly different students and ability levels, each teacher agreed upon the same stories and class structure, with slight variations for age, grades K–5.

The basic outline of each session was as follows:

- Gather at the front of the classroom.
- Warm-up and focus activities.
- Set up the story.
- Tell the story.
- Answer questions about the story.
- Do something with the story.
- Say good-bye.

Each part of the day had a specific purpose, and by the end of the residency, we had done activities that supported each learning style. Here, I will focus on "The Gingerbread Man" and specific ways to adapt it for students with Autism Spectrum Disorder (ASD). I hope you will not only be able to use this story but also use this as a framework for adapting other stories. Keep in mind that every student with ASD is unique, so cookie-cutter lesson plans are often inappropriate. I have, therefore, offered several options in hopes that you can find some that will work for your students. Please use them as a guideline and be creative.

Note: if you are not the regular teacher of an ASD classroom, I suggest you observe a class before teaching. This gives you a chance to not only watch the students but also learn what success looks like in this type of classroom, understand the basic structure of the classroom, plan out where in the room different activities can happen, and observe behavior expectations and the specific language or structures used to express and enforce them. If possible, find a time to introduce yourself and then disappear into the background.

Outline of the Class

Gather

Determine the best place in the room for students to gather. In many cases, they will already have a routine of coming together in a certain area. Follow the routines of the classroom as much as possible to allow easy transitions for the students. (You are already a new person coming into their space, who might be doing something very different than what they normally do in school. The more familiar you can make the experience, the better.) It is helpful to have some kind of marker for each student (a carpet square, chair, or letter on a rug) to have as his or her own space.

Warm-Up and Focus Activity: Everybody Go

I use Everybody Go as my catchall warm-up game. It helps me see how big I can get with each group of students and how well they can self-regulate to come back to neutral. Start by explaining the rules: "I will say 'Everybody Go'; then I will move my body and make a sound. *[Do these things as you say them.]* When I go back to neutral (calm, tall body), you do exactly what I just did and then go back to neutral. Let's try it." Start with basic whole-body movements and sounds. Offer simple, specific praises as you go. As the game goes, make the movements, sounds, and phrases longer. Kids love when you incorporate phrases they know, such as "Thank you very much!" and those they don't, like "Would you like a spot of tea?" with big actions. As they become more comfortable with the game (over many days), you can increase the risk level by letting students come up with their own actions/sounds. I give them three rules:

- It has to be appropriate for school (no violence or bad words).
- You have to stay in your spot (to prevent students from running all over the room).
- You need a sound and an action (this may not be possible for all students—adjust as needed).

Sometimes I need to add additional rules, like "Both feet have to stay on the floor," but I usually only add these if they become a specific issue. In general, this game helps students to take small risks, move their bodies, practice oral language and emotions, and prepare for the story. I always end the game with several phrases or actions from the story, especially any phrases I will want them to repeat during the story. For "The Gingerbread Man," I end with phrases like:

> *Run! Run! As fast as you can!*
> *You can't catch me; I'm the Gingerbread Man!*
> *You smell delicious!*
> *Come a little closer . . .*
> *Moooooo!*
> *Buck, buck, buck, buck, buck, ba-GOCK!*
> *. . . I can help you . . .*
> *Flip!*
> *Crunch!*
> *Mmmmmm . . . delicious!*

Set Up the Story

This is the time to show pictures, play sounds, share props, or ask questions about the story. Let students touch everything, and try to make it as interactive and simple as possible to help the students focus on one thing and not get overloaded with sensory details. Incorporate as many senses as you can (see ideas in the General Tips section later in this article), but avoid things that flash or light up.

Suggestions for "The Gingerbread Man" (pick one or two) are as follows:

Discussion: *"Who has ever helped bake cookies? Tell me about it. What did you do? Do you remember any of the ingredients? What kind of cookies did you make? Could you smell the cookies before they were done?" Whenever possible, have students demonstrate what they did (stirring the ingredients together, etc.) and invite everyone to try that motion.*

Setting: *"This story takes place in the country and on a farm. What does it mean to live 'in the country?' What can you tell me about a farm? Who lives on a farm?" You can bring in pictures for this, or have students act out each person / animal on a farm.*

Taste test: *Allow students to taste different types of cookies and vote for their favorite, or taste different ingredients for gingerbread cookies. (Check with teachers before doing this step. See note at the end of this section under "Taste.")*

Sniff test: *Place different scents related to the story into jars (with holes in the lids) for students to smell. Possibilities for this story include the following:*

Food: *sliced ginger root, cinnamon stick, whole nutmeg, whole cloves (scrape or grate a little of these spices before putting them into the jars if the smell is not very strong), shortening, brown sugar, vanilla extract on a cotton ball, molasses, freshly baked cookie, frosting, raisins, any dried fruit you plan to mention in the story*

Things found on a farm: *hay / grass, dirt, feathers, leather, any fresh seasonal produce with a distinct smell*

Pass and touch: *Choose any of the items above that would not make a mess. Pass them around so that everyone can experience them fully. Encourage smelling and feeling as well as looking.*

Tell the Story

The Gingerbread Man

Once upon a time, in a small house in the country, lived a little old woman and a little old man. One day the little old man got a smile on his face and looked at the little old woman. "I'm in the mood for a cookie!" He got up, went into the kitchen, and began to mix the ingredients into a bowl: *(mime grabbing, measuring, and mixing in each ingredient)* flour, baking powder, ginger, nutmeg, cinnamon, cloves, shortening, molasses, brown sugar, egg, water, and vanilla. He started the oven warming while he shaped and decorated one giant gingerbread cookie.

"Raisins for the eyes ... hmmm, what else?" *(Get suggestions from the students on what the other parts of the face/body should be made out of.)* Then he opened the oven door, slid the pan in with the gingerbread man, and closed it. He set the timer for 10 minutes. *(Optional: invite the students to count along with you.)* One—The cookie started to get warm. Two—The cookie got hot. Three—A sweet smell started to come from the oven. Four—The delicious smell filled the kitchen. Five—The delicious smell filled the whole house. Six—The little old man's mouth started to water. Seven—The little old man went to the oven door and peeked at the cookie. Is it done yet? Did we get to 10 yet? Eight—The little old man couldn't wait any more. He opened the oven door wide.

When he did, that gingerbread man moved one arm, then the other, then one leg, then the other, and finally jumped right up off of that pan and out of that oven!

"Wait!" cried the little old man. "You're not done cooking yet, and we want to eat you!"

The gingerbread man looked at the little old man and the little old lady and laughed, "Run! Run! As fast as you can ... You can't catch me; I'm the gingerbread man!" *(Do the same actions and vocal patterns every time you say this. Invite the children to join in with you every time the gingerbread man says this and lists all the people.)*

With that, the gingerbread man jumped up onto the windowsill and hopped right out the window. The little old lady cried, "Wait! We want to eat you!" as she pulled on her boots, jacket, hat, mittens and gloves. The little old man did the same, and they went running after that gingerbread man.

Meanwhile, the gingerbread man skipped along the snowdrifts all the way to a nearby farm, where a farmer who was out shoveling his driveway exclaimed, "Mmmm. You look delicious! Come on over here so I can eat—I mean *meet*—you."

That gingerbread man was too smart to fall for the farmer's trick. He laughed, "Run! Run! As fast as you can ... You can't catch me; I'm the gingerbread man! I ran away from a little old lady and a little old man, and I can run away from you too. I can, I can!"

That gingerbread man disappeared faster than you can say molasses. As he ran toward the barn, he heard the farmer bellow, "Kids! Catch that cookie!"

"What? Cookies?" asked the farmer's son and daughter, who were building a snow fort. They saw that gingerbread man running toward them and shouted, "Wait! We want to eat—I mean, *meet* you."

That gingerbread man was too smart to fall for the children's trick. He laughed, "Run! Run! As fast as you can ... You can't catch me; I'm the gingerbread man! I ran away from a little old lady and a little old man, and a farmer, and I can run away from you too. I can, I can!"

That gingerbread man sprinted away faster than you can say vanilla extract. He squeezed into the barn door and hopped on the back of the cow, but that cow turned her head and uttered, "Mooo! You look delicious! Come a little closer so I can eat—I mean, *meet* you."

That gingerbread man was too smart to fall for the cow's trick. He laughed, "Run! Run! As fast as you can ... You can't catch me; I'm the gingerbread man! I ran away from a little old lady and a little old man, a farmer, his two kids, and I can run away from you too. I can, I can!"

That gingerbread man dashed out of that barn faster than you can say baking powder. He popped into the chicken coop, where a hen clucked, "You look delicious! Come a little closer so I can eat—I mean, *meet* you."

That gingerbread man was too smart to fall for the hen's trick. He laughed, "Run! Run! As fast as you can ... You can't catch me; I'm the gingerbread man! I ran away from a little old lady and a little old man, a farmer, his two kids, the cow, and I can run away from you too. I can, I can!"

That gingerbread man dashed out of the chicken coop faster than you can say cinnamon and raced toward the stream. But the stream hadn't frozen over yet. He looked behind him and saw everyone chasing him. Who was there? *(Kids answer. Help them get all the characters.)* The gingerbread man paced back and forth along the icy edge of the stream.

Out of the brush came a small, gray fox. "It looks like you're in trouble," she said.

That gingerbread man giggled, "Run! Run! As fast as you can ... You can't catch me; I'm the gingerbread man! I ran away from a little old lady and a little old man, a farmer, his two kids, a cow, and a chicken, and I can run away from you too. I can, I can!"

"I bet you can. You look very fast. But if you get across that stream, you can stop running. I can help you get across that stream if you just climb on my back."

The gingerbread man heard the sound of everyone behind him calling, "Get that cookie!" He scurried up the fox's tail faster than you can say ginger, and the fox plunged into the icy water.

"The water is very deep. You should come up onto my head, to stay dry," assured the fox. The water started lapping at the gingerbread man's feet, so he shimmied onto the fox's head. "The water is very deep. You should come up onto my nose to stay dry." The gingerbread man inched onto the fox's nose. Just then, the fox flipped her head backward, sending the gingerbread man flying straight up into the air. When he came down, she caught him with a loud "Crunch!" And that was the end of the gingerbread man. (He was delicious!)

So, the next time you make cookies, especially gingerbread people, remember not to peek too soon, or your cookie might just pop up out of your oven and say, "Run! Run! As fast as you can … You can't catch me; I'm the gingerbread man!"

Notes on Telling

Whenever possible, mime what a character is doing as the character does it in the story. Hold your body differently and use a different voice for each character to help the students (and you!) keep the characters straight and follow the story. Feel free to change the setting, including the season, to match the home climate of the students or a place they are currently studying.

Answer Questions about the Story

Students will often have questions immediately after the telling; answer simply and honestly, encouraging critical thinking when possible.

Do Something with the Story

Here are some suggestions for multisensory activities. Choose one or two:

Give directions as clearly and simply as possible. Practice your instructions before class to see what you can trim. Be prepared to repeat directions.

Regulate your volume as much as possible during the story. Try not to make sudden, unexpected loud noises. Walk the fine line between incorporating movement but not being so big and wild that you will overload the children.

If you will be in the classroom more than once, establish and stick to a routine. It will help students to have a visual indication of which part of the class you are on (e.g., a picture of students standing in a circle for warm-ups, followed by a picture of someone telling a story). Move down the poster as you go through class. Pair images with words to communicate across reading abilities.

Have a clear plan with practiced transitions and backup plans, and be willing to throw it all away. Some days, the warm-ups need to be quick because they just need to sit and listen. Other days, the opposite is true, and you will need to spend twice as much time on warm-ups because it is a kinesthetic day. Pay attention to the children—they will let you know what they need. Special education teachers are very good at reading their students, so trust their judgment too.

Be prepared to be surprised. The arts can bring out the creativity, imagination, and intelligence in all of us. The results of this work often even surprise the teachers.

Incorporate as many of the senses as possible. With each lesson, consider:

Touch: What can they touch/hold? Are there things in the story that I could bring in for the students to experience? For "The Giant Turnip," I might bring in a fresh turnip with greens; for a story where a woman wears a suit coat, I could bring in a sport jacket and let each student try it on and take on the attitude of the woman.

Sight: Are there pictures or other visual elements I can bring in to make the story more real? If I am telling a story set on a farm to city kids, I will bring in a jump drive to plug into the teacher's smart board with pictures of farmers from around the world, local vegetables and fruits, and farm animals. What else might the students need to see to understand the story?

Smell: What smells can I add? Smell is often overlooked yet is the most powerful sense in terms of memory. The "Sniff Test," mentioned earlier, can be done as a guessing game in opaque containers for familiar scents or in transparent containers for new or unfamiliar smells. Essential oil dripped onto a cotton ball is a great way to incorporate stronger smells. Check with teachers about scents, as some students will be so allergic to items that they can't even be brought into a school. There was a student in one of my classes who had such a heightened gag reflex that he couldn't smell anything even slightly unpleasant without throwing up.

Hearing: Are there any sounds or sound effects I should bring? If the students will be acting like animals during the story, maybe I can bring in sound clips of those animals making noises on my jump drive, mp3 player, or CD. This can also be a fun guessing game. (What animal on a farm makes this sound?)

Taste: Taste is wonderfully fun, but you have to be very careful with this one. Many children with autism also have food allergies or sensitivities. Some can be severe, so this is not to be taken lightly. Additionally, some schools have rules that food must be commercially prepared. Check with teachers before bringing anything in.

Finally, relax and have fun! Working with kids on the autism spectrum can be very challenging but is also very rewarding. I will never forget the students I worked with that year. They are some of the most honest, enthusiastic, straightforward, inquisitive, and creative children I have met. Don't miss the chance to work in an ASD classroom!

Programming for Children with Special Needs

Emily Nanney

Charlotte Mecklenburg Library serves over one million customers in Mecklenburg County, North Carolina. "Charlotte Mecklenburg Library's brand promise: Accessible and welcoming to all, our public library celebrates the joy of reading, fosters learning and growth, connects people to each other and the world, and inspires individuals with what they can achieve" (from the "One-page Overview of the Strategic Plan," https://www.cmlibrary.org/about/strategic-plan). By offering programming and services for individuals with special needs, we help serve all our community.

In 2008 and 2009, Charlotte Mecklenburg Library decided to officially begin offering programming for children and their families with special needs and called these Sensory Storytimes. The description of this program is a storytime filled with stories, songs, and activities specifically designed for children with autism spectrum disorders, sensory integration issues, or other developmental disabilities. This initiative arose from parents frequently requesting this program. Staff got feedback from parents both informally and through a focus group.

Focus group questions included the following:

- What would an effective program look like to you?
- What services would you like the public library to offer for parents/families of children with special needs?
- What challenges do you face when you visit the library?
- What tips can you give us for interacting with you and your child?
- Is there anything you would like to share with library staff about the challenges of having a child with special needs in your family?
- What resources would you recommend that the library have that we currently don't?
- Who would you recommend as potential partners for the public library to have?
- What would make the public library the first destination for your family to go to spend free time?
- How often would you like to see special needs programs offered?
- Is there any additional information that you would like to share?

After hearing positive feedback and the need from parents for this type of programming, children's staff, even though most had no official training in this area, wanted to include a program for children and their families with special needs. All families had always been welcomed to any storytime, but families wanted something specifically geared to their children. We used lots of visuals and props, calmer music, and dimmer lighting. We also took away any standing fans or objects that would be distracting.

The storytime was marketed for children and their families with special needs. The parents and children loved it, and we received great feedback. We also provided an opportunity for families to socialize after the program. We learned from parents about picture cards for a schedule board and incorporated those into the program, and we developed a few programming kits for staff to use with families in storytimes. Programming kits centered on themes such as farm, animals, food, colors, and transportation with lots of books, visuals, instruments, bubbles, and picture cards.

We have learned a lot over the years. We worked with Smart Start of Mecklenburg County and the North Carolina Autism Society of Mecklenburg County Chapter to develop a collection of books focused on autism and housed at ImaginOn: The Joe and Joan Martin Center. The Autism Spectrum Disorder Reference Collection is available in Spangler Library at ImaginOn and is a great resource for parents and teachers with children who have been recently diagnosed as being on the autism spectrum. This collection continues to grow and can also be accessed through our online catalog at https://cmlibrary.bibliocommons.com/ search?t=smart&search_category=keyword&q=autism%20reference% 20collection&commit=Search.

By working with Smart Start and the Autism Society of Mecklenburg County, we developed stronger relationships. Representative from both groups have spoken at our Children's Services meetings and provided guidance as we further developed programs and program titles and so on.

Tricia Twarogowski, former children's library manager in Charlotte Mecklenburg Library, can be found sharing tips in videos at https:// www.cmlibrary.org/services/special-needs as well as in her blog, http:// www.alsc.ala.org/blog/2009/06/programming-for-children-with-special- needs-part-one/.

Since the inception of these services in 2008, an Exceptional Experiences Team has been created, which developed fidget kits as one of their goals. Fidget kits contain manipulatives of different colors, sizes, and textures to help calm and focus customers who are sensory seeking. Fidgets can be used to help a child feel relaxed in programs or when they are using re- sources in the library. Fidget kits include items such as koosh balls, puppets, search and find alphabet bags, water sensory objects to hold in the hand, and so on and can be used anywhere is the library.

Programming continues at many locations and has expanded to include school-age children, teens, and adults with special needs. Staff have gone out to share their knowledge with other library systems. Several Children's Service Staff in Charlotte Mecklenburg Library have also trained internal staff on this type of programming.

Over the years, we have developed outcomes for programs that include:

- time to build the program;
- staff learning that it is okay not to have large attendance numbers for programs that involve individuals with special needs; and
- making families feel comfortable in the library and letting parents know they are in a safe place where their child will not be judged.

Over the years, we have learned:

- to have fidgets for children, stuffed animals, puppets, pillows, and so on as needed in programs;
- to have low key music;

- not to provide food since many children have allergies;
- to consider setting out a rug or carpet squares;
- and above all to remain flexible—of utmost importance when programming;
- Saturday mornings seem to be the best time so the whole family can attend programming; and storytime guidelines must be open and flexible so children can enter and exit the program as needed.

Currently, Charlotte Mecklenburg Library offers programming for children, teens, and adults with special needs. Several staff who are leaders in this area (both in the system and the state) now offer trainings for others interested in Sensory Programming. Some of these staff offer their insights later in this chapter.

Tips from Three Library Leaders Regarding Sensory Programming

Viviette White, Children's Librarian in Charlotte Mecklenburg Library

Here are some points I have learned over the years while working with the special needs population and offering Sensory Storytimes.

- I always let the participants do what they can do instead of trying to make them do what I can do because some are limited in speech and mobility. Some participants may be nonverbal and will not be able to sing the songs or do call and response. Many times, I had to engage the caregivers and parents in the room to respond. I let them create the literacy extension the way they saw it and not how I made mine. Sometimes I would just give them the materials to make, for instance, a frog on a lily pad or a fish with scales, and let them design it the way they envisioned it.

- I use trendy and fun songs I like to sing and dance to, not baby songs. The participants enjoy dancing to all types of music including jazz, R&B, rock, pop, and Top 40. Music from the '80s and '90s is always a hit. Even the ones who do not like to dance would sit and rock in their seats or tap their knees to the beat. Songs with directional lyrics are very useful if you want to encourage following directions. You can make up your own choreography for the participants to follow as well.

- Incorporating fidgets into storytime is therapeutic and calming for participants who like to hold on to something. I noticed it made them feel relaxed, safe, and focused. The fidgets helped stimulate thought process by giving them something to look at and manipulate. Textures and colors stimulated several participants because sometimes they would react to a certain texture on their skin or chose a color they liked. I also noticed that fidgets helped them stay focused on the storytime for a longer period by giving them something to concentrate on while other activities were going on in the room.

- Lighting in the room was something that I had to change once in a while depending on who was in the room. Some participants like to look out of the windows, and others liked dimmer lights from the ceiling. Lighting is something you have to gauge based on your audience. If you see someone squinting or covering his or her eyes, it is more than likely your room is too bright.

- Making a timeline or picture schedule of your storytime is very helpful for you as well as your audience because it gives you a lesson plan to follow to stay on course, and it gives the participants a visual program to follow as some may feel anxiety if they do not know what is happening next. You will find it beneficial to use picture schedules with people who are on the autism spectrum or may have other mental processing issues.

Larisa Martin, Children's Specialist in Charlotte Mecklenburg Library

One of Atticus Finch's bits of wisdom in *To Kill a Mockingbird* involved putting yourself in another's shoes. I learned the hard way what visual overload looks and feels like, and while I would definitely not recommend the experience, having a little perspective or insight into what sensory integration issues are like goes a really long way.

To accommodate sensory overload, I always made sure that

- the prints and textures I wore and used were simple;
- I had as little fragrance as possible;
- any fluorescent lights in my room were eliminated; and
- my planning could be modified depending on whether I had sensory seekers or avoiders.

A little extra prep in that area went a long way, and when registration began, I always included a line on the registration sheet reminding the staff member doing the sign-up to ask if any special accommodations would be needed, and if so, what.

I also posted a sign on the door asking that caregivers notify a staff member if extra accommodations might be needed or helpful. This came about because I had one regular participant who needed to see what we would be doing and familiarize himself with the space, props, books, music, and so on. I had another who needed everything hidden, so I balanced both of them by allowing Patrick preview time prior to opening the program to the public.

Using picture cards helped me accommodate the variety of ages and ability levels I have had in programs. Many of my participants were able to become excellent helpers—taking the picture off as we finished, reminding me that we needed to update the schedule and pointing out where we were in the schedule, and placing the cards into the finished envelope, which was often a very fun activity.

I worked pretty extensively to pull together the suggestion list for the fidget kits. I based the list on personal experience (beanie babies, beanbag/fuzzy, heavy animals, and sensory balls were always very popular in my storytimes), input from a professional, and insight from occupational therapy blogs.

When choosing fidgets, be aware of

- latex content;
- age/cognitive level of the intended user (just because something says ages three and up doesn't necessarily mean safe for all users above age three!); and
- potential for breakability.

Anticipate the unanticipated! For instance, Blobby Robby came highly recommended on several occupational therapy sites, but we only had him for a few weeks at Morrison Library before someone squeezed him too hard and Blobby Robby became Empty, Messy Robby. With that in mind, and since our fidget kit was for an extra-program audience (we kept a basket in our office that we lent to users on request/anticipated need), I separated our fidgets into tools that were appropriate for use with all ages/minimal supervision versus fidgets more appropriate for higher cognitive level/greater supervision level. This meant the foam/squeezy animals, the beanbag animals, and many of the balls (sensory, koosh, squeezy/stress/foam) got separated from some of the more technical tools (the expanding bead ball, the letter beanbags—these make a huge mess if they get holes, another lesson learned the hard way!— the squeezy balls a.k.a. Blobby Robby, the water tube).

Keeping a few all-ages fidgets in a handy basket or bucket easily allows for them to be shared from the desk or within the public service realm.

My favorite story of impact involves the fidget kits at Morrison Library. We had a family who came in to use the children's computers on a regular basis. There were five children in the family, and two of the children—the second-oldest and the youngest—were on the spectrum and had considerable challenges. Library visits were sometimes frustrating for the entire family— if the second-oldest and the youngest got overstimulated, no one's homework/library business got finished, and the two were frequently very loud library users (both when they were content and overstimulated).

When we rolled out the fidget kits, I prepared buckets of fidgets for each of them. When the family next visited, the second-oldest and youngest were very excited to be at the library and were letting everyone know that loudly. I explained the fidget kits to their mother, gave each of them their buckets, and then resumed what I was doing in another part of the building. When I returned several minutes later, I was surprised to see the family still in the library. The children's area was nearly silent, and the entire family was occupied. The second-oldest and youngest were very focused on their fidgets, which allowed the rest of the family to complete their library business peacefully. Every visit after that began with the second-oldest and youngest child eagerly exploring the fidgets.

Amrita Patel, Outreach Specialist in Charlotte Mecklenburg Library

Know Your Audience

If time allows, gather feedback/insights (from parents and caregivers) on how to make the room more comfortable for children. I provided Sensory Storytime at the Mint Hill Library, and a little boy came on a weekly basis with his mother. After two weeks, I noticed his mood changed when he walked in the room and asked his mother if he was okay. She said that fluorescent lights bothered him and caused headaches, so I immediately shut off the lights and opened the window blinds. In retrospect, I realize that she wasn't planning on telling me (because she didn't want to cause any issue or single out her son) but the fact that I asked helped her to open up.

It Is Important to Be Patient, Flexible, and Adaptable

It is okay if the children roam around the room, and it is okay if they touch the book or puppets or storytime materials. It is okay if they shout or express themselves in a loud manner. Children express themselves in a variety of ways—in a Sensory Storytime, it is necessary to loosen up the rules of traditional storytime.

Be Inclusive

All children are welcome to programs—whether they have sensory processing issues or not. It is okay for a child without neurodiverse needs to come to the Sensory Storytime and vice versa. Inclusion helps kids with various learning styles and abilities be together in a safe place—and learn to respect differences.

Sensory Storytime Requires Additional Activities

Incorporate music, movement, and manipulatives to engage children with all their senses. I like to include a simple literacy-based activity at the end of each Sensory Storytime, whether it is a coloring sheet and crayons or creating something more hands on. It also provides a social activity and setting at the end of the program.

Make Sure Each Participant Feels Safe and Comfortable in the Room (with Ample Arm and Leg Room to Move Around)

This can be achieved by limiting the number of participants if you have a small room. If you have a large space, place chairs/tables accordingly to allow participants the chance to find their own space.

I encourage you to begin offering sensory or adaptive programs at your library location. Parents and families will greatly appreciate your efforts to include their children in a place that is welcoming and thoughtful about programming and services for all.

Sensory Storytime at the Denver Public Library

Rachel Hartman

Exposure to a literacy-rich environment at a young age builds a foundation that helps all children, including those with disabilities, learn to read (The Access Center, 2007). Libraries can help caregivers provide that exposure, and public libraries in the United States are committed to providing information access to all, including people with disabilities. The American Library Association's (ALA) Intellectual Freedom Manual states:

> *The American Library Association recognizes that persons with disabilities are a large and often neglected part of society. In addition to many personal challenges, some persons with disabilities face economic inequity, illiteracy, cultural isolation, and discrimination in education, employment, and the broad range of societal activities. The library plays a catalytic role in their lives by facilitating their full participation in society.* (ALA Council, 2009)

Offering a storytime for children with special needs is one way public libraries can develop literacy skills in children with disabilities and support their caregivers and families.

The Denver Public Library provides high-quality storytimes that are typically very inclusive. However, when I started working at the Central Children's Library in 2011, the library did not offer any storytimes specially geared toward children with special needs, so with the enthusiastic support of my supervisor, I developed a Sensory Storytime program. Previously, I taught preschool children with a variety of special needs, so I felt comfortable working with children with disabilities. I also researched similar library programs to develop a plan for my storytime. Though my intended target audience was children with any special needs, the actual audience has mostly been children on the autism spectrum and those with sensory processing disorder, perhaps because of the name "Sensory Storytime."

Once I had a pilot plan, I started publicizing Sensory Storytime. I wrote blog posts on the library website and distributed flyers throughout the library system and around the community at schools, therapy centers, and organizations for children with special needs. I also staffed an outdoor booth at an autism resource fair. I was seven months pregnant and the day was scorching hot, but it was worth the discomfort. Many people were surprised and excited to see a library representative at the fair. Parents told me they usually avoided libraries because they worried the library was a "quiet space" and that their child would be disruptive and unwelcome, but, after talking with me, they might try the library again.

After publicizing the event, I held the first Sensory Storytime at the Central Children's Library in August 2012. We provided Sensory Storytime to the public for two years and received wonderful feedback both verbally and through written evaluations. Despite my publicizing efforts and the positive feedback, we struggled with small attendance numbers. Ultimately the low attendance didn't justify all the time and money we spent on the program. Reluctantly we stopped offering Sensory Storytime to the public in August 2014.

Fortunately, my attempts at marketing reached schools and we had interest from educators. Now we offer storytimes upon request for school groups at the library. Currently a few groups come regularly, and we have taken storytime as outreach to many classrooms. Having a guaranteed audience from a school is a much more successful model for our urban library than a regularly scheduled public storytime.

Both the public and the school storytimes follow the same basic structure. The first step is preparing attendees for a positive experience, which starts before they arrive at the library. I let caregivers know what we'll be reading, to give them the opportunity to read the book together in advance.

I also share a pdf of a social story with caregivers via e-mail. A social story is a short, personalized book with photos. Social stories help children with autism (and possibly typically developing children) understand what behavior is expected in a particular social situation (Benish & Bramlett, 2011). Social stories often support children with routines like getting dressed, eating a meal, or going to school or the store. The story I share with storytime attendees has simple, first person text, such as, "I go to the library" and "I find a spot to sit in the storytime room." Photos of the library, the program room, and the librarian leading the storytime accompany the text. I encourage caregivers to print the social story and staple it into a book format and then share the book with their child.

This is the text of the social story I use. Each sentence is accompanied by one or more images:

I go to the Library.
I walk to the Children's Library.
I find a spot to sit in the storytime room.
My mom or dad or other grownup stays with me during storytime.
I listen when the librarian reads stories.
During storytime we dance and sing. I can dance and sing along or listen and watch.
I can play when storytime ends and I can leave when I am ready.
I have fun at the library.

In addition to preparing children and caregivers, I e-mailed library security staff and my coworkers in the Children's Library to explain what behaviors they might see. That way staff would not be surprised or overwhelmed when the program was still nascent and they were getting to know the attendees. One librarian ended up with a few broken mugs despite my precaution.

Creating a comfortable and welcoming environment is imperative on the day of the program; many families have had negative experiences at libraries and are nervous about returning. As children arrive, I greet them and show them to the program room, where they pick up a copy of the book we'll be reading and, if desired, a fidget toy and noise-reducing headphones. Offering children a book to carry into the room provides a transition cue and helps them know what to anticipate, thus easing anxiety they may be feeling (Hume, 2008). Bins holding the books, toys, and headphones are labeled with pictures and words, as an opportunity to build a literacy-rich environment (The Access Center, 2007).

When everyone is settled, I introduce myself again, and we sing our hello song. Singing the same hello and good-bye songs every time provides continuity and is another way to ease anxiety. Next, we do a few stretches, jumps, and stomps to give some sensory input and settle our bodies.

Then we talk about the picture schedule. A picture schedule, as the name suggests, is a visual schedule that helps children anticipate what will happen next. Clip art images and words describing each activity are laminated and Velcro-ed to a foam core board. After each activity, I move the corresponding picture from the "to do" column to the "done" column. If children are uncomfortable reading the story or singing a song, they can see that something else will happen soon. That knowledge makes sitting through a potentially unpleasant activity more tolerable. (Consider the last time you were in a boring meeting and you kept checking the agenda to find out what to expect next.) Visual schedules are especially helpful because many children with autism are better able to process information visually than aurally (Knight, Sartini, & Spriggs, 2015).

After we discuss the picture schedule, we sing a name song to the tune of "Where Is Thumbkin," which we repeat for each child:

> *Where is [child's name]?*
> *Where is [child's name]?*
> *There she is*
> *There she is*
> *Say hello to [child's name]*
> *Say hello to [child's name]*
> *Clap your hands*
> *Clap your hands*
>
> (Klipper, n.d.)

The children take turns holding a small unbreakable mirror when we sing for them, and then they pass it to the next child. The mirror is beneficial because children might increase self-recognition when looking at themselves, and they work on social skills when passing the mirror from peer to peer.

Next come the first of two readings of the book. The first reading is a traditional read-aloud, and the next is far more interactive. I read aloud first so everyone can hear the rhythm and feel of the language. Before reading the book, I talk about the story to prime the children and help them connect with the book. Each child has a copy of the book to hold and share with his or her caregiver, who can point out things that interest the child.

Sitting still and listening to a story is challenging for many children. I always remind caregivers at this point that children can get up and wander if needed (I set this expectation in all my storytimes). They are probably still listening and learning. Children who don't appear to be listening often surprise me by offering answers to a question about the story. If they aren't attending, that is okay too. As long as they are having fun, they are building positive associations with the library that may serve them well in the future.

When reading the story, I ask targeted questions to help keep the audience engaged. Carrie Wolfson, who now leads Sensory Storytimes for older children at the Denver Public Library, explains, "A big challenge for me was adapting my training in dialogic reading. Open-ended questions like 'What do you think will happen next?' require a conceptual leap that doesn't fit with how these kids' brains process information. So, we focus on quick concrete questions and answers that relate to the text. For example, after reading 'The three billy goats crossed the bridge' ask 'What did the three billy goats cross?'" (C. Wolfson, personal communication, August 3, 2016).

Next we sing a few songs that encourage a variety of movement and sensory stimulation, because everyone is ready to move after reading the book.

Figuring out what types of movements and songs the group needs can be challenging. Some children become overstimulated while others seek more stimulation (Kranowitz, 2005). I try to balance movements like jumping, spinning, and stomping with calmer activities such as giving ourselves hugs, swaying slowly, and singing quietly. I pay close attention to each child so I can redirect the activity if someone appears upset.

Once the group seems ready to transition to the next activity, we revisit the book by acting out the story in a way that helps children connect to the story physically, instead of visually or aurally. The retelling involves lots of movement, turn-taking, and sensory input, including activities like tasting foods or climbing an obstacle course. As I introduce each new activity or element, I show the illustrations and read the book or discuss what is happening at that point in the story. The following are some of the most successful books and adaptations.

Chugga-Chugga Choo-Choo, by Kevin Lewis, follows a freight train through its busy day traversing mountains, bridges, and tunnels. First, I help each child put a ream of paper on her cube chair to imitate the train being loaded with freight. Then we make a line and push our heavy chairs around the room. This provides children with sensory input through "heavy work" (Kranowitz, 2005). Next, we abandon our chairs and climb mats that we pretend are mountains, crawl through a cloth tunnel, and walk across a balance beam like a train crossing a bridge. Finally, we retrieve our chairs, return to the station (our storytime circle), and unload the freight (we put the paper back into a box). Of course, we say plenty of "choo choos" along the way.

In *Dog's Colorful Day: A Messy Story about Colors and Counting*, by Emma Dodd, a dog gets covered in spots of pink ice cream, green grass, blue paint, and so on. Before I read the story, I hang a felt Dog on the flannel board and pass out different-colored felt dots for each child. As we read the story, the children put their dots on the board at the appropriate moment. This reinforces the colors in the story and encourages everyone to follow along and wait for their turn. Unlike some of the other story adaptations, this one can be easily reused and is good on short notice.

Feast for Ten, by Cathryn Falwell, is a counting book about a family shopping for and preparing a feast. Because the story heavily revolves around food, we taste and smell foods from the book. I put beans, collard greens, pickles, tomatoes, and potatoes into small individual cups and pass them out when the food appears in the narrative. Some of the participants are willing to taste; some are not, and some want to keep eating! I always have paper towels and a trash can available in case a child needs to wipe hands. I also ask caregivers about food allergies ahead of time via e-mail.

In *Go Away Big Green Monster*, by Ed Emberley, die-cut pages build on each other to create the face of a big green monster. The reader tells the monster to go away and it does, page by page and part by part. To adapt this story, I made a felt cutout to match each page. Then I put the felt pieces on top of each other in the order of the pages in the book, and I give each child a beanbag. As I tell the story, I carry the flannel from child to child on a portable flannel board (a pizza box covered in felt works well). Each time I tell a part of the monster to go away, one child throws a beanbag at the flannel and I take that piece off. The kids throw the beanbags enthusiastically; some of the verbal children yell "Go away," and hopefully everyone has a laugh!

The Snowy Day, by Ezra Jack Keats, is a classic story about a boy named Peter enjoying a snowy day. First Peter walks on the sidewalk. We act this out by taking turns crossing a balance beam. Then Peter makes footprints in the snow; we walk on cotton batting. Peter makes lines by dragging a stick in the snow, and we make lines, too, by drawing on butcher paper with markers taped onto pool noodles. When snow falls on Peter's head, the children put beanbags on their heads. Next, Peter makes a snowman and snow angels, and we lie on the floor and make snow angel movements. When Peter climbs a hill, we climb over mats. Then we feel warm water in a bowl when Peter takes a hot bath. Finally, each child receives a paper snowflake when Peter wakes up to snow again the next morning.

Once we finish acting out the book, we do our best to regroup and sing our good-bye song. After storytime, the school groups usually choose books, explore other floors of the library, or have a snack they provide. When we still offered the public storytimes, everyone stayed to play and interact with each other for as long as they wanted. Families enjoyed the opportunity to chat, and some parents were impressed that their child was interacting well with their peers.

Though following the same structure and repeating some of the songs every storytime is important, flexibility is essential, too. If something isn't working, I stop and move on. Conversely, if something is a hit, I spend a little more time on it.

With this flexibility in mind, the Central Children's Library has transitioned from a public storytime to a storytime for schools. We also adjust the content of the program to meet the needs of different classes. Most of our Sensory Storytime audiences are preschool aged. However, the students in one of our regular school groups are middle schoolers, and the books we share with preschoolers are too immature for them. Finding appropriate books for this group is a challenge. Carrie Wolfson, the librarian who provides their storytime, has had success experimenting with nonfiction books. Wolfson explains that she wanted to find something with subject matter and presentation mature enough for middle school students but without a complicated plot; following a complex narrative can be a challenge for children with autism. Nonfiction books allow children to focus on individual facts, providing multiple points of entry into the book. Wolfson has had success with *Elephants Can Paint Too!* by Katya Arnold and *Actual Size* by Steve Jenkins. She has even started to incorporate science, technology, engineering, and math (STEM) activities and tools and hopes to do more in the future (C. Wolfson, personal communication, August 3, 2016).

Most of the specific book adaptations we use in Sensory Storytime require small groups and therefore don't work for a large, mainstream storytime. However, many of the strategies do translate to other programs. In a training I led for storytime providers at the Denver Public Library, we discussed ways to make our storytimes more inclusive. Some easy adaptations included using a picture schedule and minimizing distractions by hiding props on a cart under a sheet. Another modification was to let children choose a scarf or egg shaker as they enter the program room instead of passing them out midway through storytime. This provided a transition cue and eliminated stress over choosing favorite colored props during the action.

We have also used some of the book adaptations as weekend passive programs that we set up and allow customers to interact with all day. For example, one Saturday I posted photocopies of the book and set up the cotton batting, pool noodle markers, beanbags, and everything else I used for *The Snowy Day* adaptation in Sensory Storytime. Children and caregivers followed the story on an interactive picturebook walk. Another librarian did a similar program with *We're Going on a Bear Hunt* by Michael Rosen. The most popular elements were white balloons hung from the ceiling to imitate snow and a sensory table full of mud made with baking soda, water, and food coloring.

Incorporating sensory experiences and strategies for children with special needs in all storytimes and passive programs is beneficial for multiple reasons. Disabilities aren't always evident just by looking at a child. According to data from 2006 to 2008, about one in every six children has a developmental disability (Boyle et al., 2011). Chances are good that there is a child with a disability in your storytime, even if you aren't aware. And I have observed in my classroom and library experience, strategies that work for children on the autism spectrum work well for their typically developing peers.

All children deserve the chance to experience a literacy-rich environment in the hopes that they will learn to read one day. Even children with significant cognitive delays may learn to read, even before they learn to talk (Kliewer, 2008). By providing accessible literacy experiences through inclusive mainstream storytimes and passive programs, or through a specific storytime for those with special needs, libraries can help children develop the skills they'll need to be successful and active participants in society.

Picturebooks Discussed

Arnold, K. (2005). *Elephants can paint, too!* New York, NY: Atheneum Books for Young Readers.
Emberley, E. (1993). *Go away big green monster!* New York, NY: Little Brown & Company.
Dodd, E. (2001). *Dog's colorful day: A messy story about colors and counting.* New York, NY: Dutton Children's Books.
Falwell, C. (1993). *Feast for 10.* New York, NY: Clarion Books.
Jenkins, S. (2004). *Actual size.* Boston, MA: Houghton Mifflin.
Keats, E. J. (1962). *The snowy day.* New York, NY: The Viking Press.
Lewis, K. (2002). *Chugga chugga choo choo.* New York, NY: Disney-Hyperion.
Rosen, M. (2007). *We're going on a bear hunt.* New York, NY: Little Simon.

Resources

Libraries and Autism and Fanwood (NJ) Memorial Library. (n.d.). *Libraries and autism: We're connected.* Retrieved from librariesandautism.org
Parrott, K. (2009, May 31). *Stories on the spectrum: Adventures in outreach, planning, and programming for kids with ASD* [Blog post]. Retrieved from http://www.alsc.ala.org/blog/2009/05/stories-on-the-spectrum-adventures-in-outreach-planning-and-programming-for-kids-with-asd/
Twarogowski, T. B. (2009, June 23). *Programming for children with special needs* [five-part blog series]. Retrieved from http://www.alsc.ala.org/blog/2009/06/programming-for-children-with-special-needs-part-one/

References

The Access Center. (2007). *Literacy-rich environments.* Retrieved from http://www.readingrockets.org/article/literacy-rich-environments
ALA Council. (2009, January 28). *Services to persons with disabilities: An interpretation of the Library Bill of Rights.* Retrieved from http://www.ala.org/advocacy/intfreedom/librarybill/interpretations/servicespeopledisabilities
Benish, T. M., & Bramlett, R. K. (2011). "Using social stories to decrease aggression and increase positive peer interactions in normally

developing pre-school children." *Educational Psychology in Practice,* *27*(1), 1–17. doi:10.1080/02667363.2011.549350

Boyle, C. A., Boulet, S., Schieve, L., Cohen, R. A., Blumberg, S. J., Yeargin-Allsopp, M., . . . Kogan, M. D. (2011). "Trends in the prevalence of developmental disabilities in US children, 1997–2008" [Abstract]. *Pediatrics,* *127*(6), 1034–1042.

Hume, K. (2008). "Transition time: Helping individuals on the autism spectrum move successfully from one activity to another." *The Reporter,* *13*(2), 6–10.

Kliewer, C. (2008). "Joining the literacy flow: Fostering symbol and written language learning in young children with significant developmental disabilities through the four currents of literacy." *Research & practice for persons with severe disabilities, 33*(3), 103–121.

Klipper, B. (n.d.). *Sensory storytime: Preschool programming that makes sense for kids with autism* [Webinar]. Retrieved from http://www.ala .org/alsc/edcareeers/profdevelopment/alscweb/courses/sensorystorytime

Knight, V., Sartini, E., & Spriggs, A. D. (2015). "Evaluating visual activity schedules as evidence-based practice for individuals with autism spectrum disorders." *Journal of Autism and Developmental Disorders,* *45*(1), 157+. Retrieved from http://go.galegroup.com/ps/i.do?id=GALE% 7CA408783750&v=2.1&u=denver&it=r&p=AONE&sw=w&asid=b4134 e321ddc9cec26f3732fd2a27c88

Kranowitz, C. S. (2005). *The out-of-sync child: Recognizing and coping with sensory processing disorder* (2nd ed.). New York, NY: Perigee Book.

3

Storytelling Strategies for Children with Intellectual/ Developmental Disabilities

Introduction

Sherry Norfolk

If you have ever watched a child's expression change from "Huh?" to "Aha!"—that magical moment when understanding is achieved, when the lightbulb goes on, and the connections are made—you know the joy of witnessing a small miracle.

That's what storytelling brings to the classroom, especially for children who have intellectual/developmental disabilities. Stories and storytelling are the ultimate instruments for differentiation, providing unlimited possibilities for integrating learning across modalities.

Exploring the storytelling strategies in this chapter will inspire you to create your own strategies—and small miracles.

My Story, My Voice: Storytelling with Nonverbal Students

Dr. Amanda M. Lawrence

Talking is hard, but I still have things to say.
—Duncan Lawrence, age nine

When my nonverbal son was in first grade, his teacher designed a wonderful activity in which students in his class shared their favorite stories with their peers. One at a time, each student was called to the front and sat in a special chair to share, and after each student finished, the others responded. My son was not called to the front; instead, he was given a seat in the back with his paraprofessional and directed to listen. When I asked his teacher about his exclusion from the activity, she insisted that it didn't matter because "it was just a fun day." Naturally my first thought was "Why doesn't he get to have fun, too?" My second thought was "What could have been done differently?"

Most of us think of storytelling as an oral art form, one that we may assume is closed to students who struggle to speak and who may have little ability to communicate beyond gestures or sounds. Because enabling nonverbal students to participate in basic curriculum can be challenging, the thought of involving students who communicate with pictures, gestures, or devices in advanced activities such as retelling stories and constructing original narratives may overwhelm even the most experienced, well-intentioned teachers, but it doesn't have to.

So, how can teachers, librarians, and storytellers engage nonverbal students in storytelling in meaningful ways? In the remainder of this essay, you'll find a variety of activities that you can use to create points of entry, reinforce emerging skills, break stereotypes, and teach empathy.

Creating Points of Entry

Nonverbal students may have a variety of conditions that affect their ability to produce speech. They may struggle with expressive language or receptive language as distinct disabilities, or with both. They may know what they want to say but be unable to get it out. They may be able to articulate words but may not understand how to construct an orderly sentence. They may face physical challenges with producing sounds or mental challenges with accessing those sounds at the right moment. But like all students, nonverbal children have a strong desire to communicate and to participate. Your first task is simply to create a point of entry, a place in which a nonverbal student can join a story.

One strategy for engaging nonverbal students in storytelling activities is to come up with a list of details that needs to be filled in as you tell a story. For example, is the main character short or tall? What color is the car? What did the children want to eat for supper? Did the dog get along with the cat? Where did the spaceship land? Depending on how they communicate best, nonverbal children can be encouraged to participate in a story by helping to fill in details like these, just by answering questions. They could point to yes or no cards, select from a variety of pictures, push buttons programmed with words, write down what they want to say, pantomime, or participate in some other self-directed way by indicating the choices that they would like to make. In this way, they can be encouraged and empowered to help create a story along with a storyteller without the pressure of telling a story from scratch. These same strategies can be used in retelling stories. The question "what happens next?" can be answered using any of the aforementioned communication mechanisms for choice making and any number of others that you can imagine.

Depending on the needs of the nonverbal student, the teacher could work with him or her on choice making in advance of the class in which the story will be told by having the student practice pressing a button, choosing a card, or pointing to something to make a choice. To smooth a nonverbal student's way into the activity even more, the teacher can lay the groundwork with the rest of the class ahead of time by saying something like "On Friday we're going to work together to tell a story. Johnny's job will be to decide what kind of animal the main character will be. Elizabeth can name the main character. Marcus can tell us its favorite food. Sondra can decide who the main character meets in the woods, and we'll see what happens from there." If everyone in the class is given choices to make, and all the students' choices are worked into the story, all students are included, regardless of how they express those choices. In other words, all are given an equal say in the narrative, whether or not they can "say" anything.

For verbal and nonverbal students who know or are learning parts of speech, Mad Libs can be another terrific point of entry to participate in storytelling. This game is very popular at my house, with my nonverbal son generating the list of words for a story by typing them or using an alphabet flipbook to spell the words he wants and my verbal son filling the words in the blanks and reading the story aloud. They love working together to tell stories in this way. This activity is easily adaptable for pairs of students or large groups working together to complete a story in a classroom, and it has the added bonus of reinforcing grammar skills.

Nonverbal students may also enjoy participating in turn taking or round-robin storytelling, with the teacher or storyteller starting a tale and students taking turns to continue it in pairs or in groups. Again, any method of participation that works for your nonverbal students can be used if it is planned ahead of time, and those students who aren't yet communicating in original sentences can still participate through choice making.

The point is this: Nonverbal students can feel silenced and unimportant in the classroom if teachers do not create points of entry for them to communicate in whatever form works best for them. When they are enabled to participate, even in seemingly small ways, they are empowered and taught that their voices matter. Because storytelling is a communal activity, it's especially important to enable nonverbal students to become storytellers so that they can have a voice and a role in their community.

Reinforcing Skills

When you are working with students who receive therapies to build needed skills, integrating therapy goals into storytelling sessions can be an excellent way to make therapy fun, increase student investment in working toward therapy goals, and break down barriers between typically developing and special needs students by engaging them in common activities.

For example, one of my nonverbal son's current speech therapy goals is to learn to blow bubbles off a bubble wand to strengthen his mouth and breath control for speech production. He has been working on this for several months, and along the way, he has learned to blow out a candle, which meant that he could blow out the candles on his birthday cake for the first time on his ninth birthday —talk about motivation! Even so, he began to grow tired of practicing every day, so one night, I told my children a story in which the main characters were standing on top of a tall building surrounded by thick clouds. They needed to move the clouds out of the way in order to see the path to the mountain where they would find their missing friend. The solution was for all the characters to blow and blow until the clouds moved. Everyone in my family participated in that part of the story, eventually falling into fits of giggles as we looked at each other's puffed cheeks and silly faces. It was so much fun that the kids wanted to do that part of the story again, meaning that my nonverbal son got in a lot of practice for speech therapy in a fun way that did not seem like work.

Almost any therapy goal can be worked into a story, from pressing buttons to standing on one foot to saying selected words orally or with a device. In many cases, these skills can be integrated into a story through universal design so that all the students in a class help a particular student to practice a skill without anyone being pointed to, pulled out, or isolated. A quick conversation with the school's therapy staff can provide a wealth of ideas for activities that can be woven into stories, and if you don't know which students are working on the skills, it won't matter, as you'll be involving the whole class. Imagine how much fun it could be to have a room full of kids practice stomping their feet up and down to represent a giant in your story or to have everyone look at a neighbor and say hello whenever a new character is introduced. By weaving students' therapy goals into stories, everyone wins.

Breaking Stereotypes

If you are telling stories to a class that includes children who are nonverbal or have other special needs and you want to include a story about someone with a disability, think carefully about the messages that your story sends. Being aware of the prominent stereotypes about people with disabilities in our society, and using your story to counter these stereotypes is a great strategy that educates and empowers all students.

One of our darker social narratives about people with disabilities is that they are a burden on society and have little to nothing to contribute. This narrative often makes people with disabilities the butt of jokes, denying them dignity and personhood, asserting that *different than* is equivalent to *lesser than*. At the other end of the spectrum lies the "hero" or "inspiration" narrative in which people with disabilities are valued only to the extent that they inspire others by smiling in the face of adversity. In this case, *different than* is equated with *more than*, as people with disabilities are depicted as having deep wells of personal strength, courage, and cheerfulness just because they have disabilities. Like the darker narrative, the inspiration narrative denies personhood, erasing the individuality of people with disabilities by making them symbols.

You can use a simple litmus test to make sure that your story doesn't fall into these traps: ask yourself whether the characters with disabilities are defined solely by their disabilities. If the answer is "yes," think more about the story before telling it, and consider using one or more of the following strategies for moving students away from stereotype-driven narratives and toward a more open, constructive viewpoint.

One idea is to tell a story about a character with a difference that enables him or her to do something that others can't. For example, one of my children's favorite stories is about a snail who is very brave. Because he is much smaller and slower than all the other characters in the story, he volunteers to sneak up on the evil genius and overhear his plans. He reasons that the bad guy will overlook him because of his size, and he is right. The snail emerges as a hero not simply because he is small or inspires others through his tenacity but because he knows how to use his size to his advantage. The African story of "Nonikwe and the Great Marimba" provides another example. In this tale, a blind girl comes to be valued in her village because she is able to look past external appearances and see people's true natures. Every culture has stories about characters that are different from others and succeed not in spite of but because of their difference. These can be a rich source of learning in your classes.

Another idea is to tell stories that highlight the interests and strengths of disabled characters that have nothing to do with disabilities. This can be fun and effective if you build the students in a class into a story as characters. Almost every night at my house, my husband and I tell the next installment of a sprawling adventure story that stars our children. This has gone on for a year now and has taken some unexpected twists and turns. Currently, they are members of a flying circus that jets from planet to planet solving problems. Although one of our children is typically developing and the other faces significant challenges due to having cerebral palsy and being legally blind, the story doesn't ever focus on who is able-bodied and who struggles. Instead, it depicts them using their individual strengths for the good of the other characters. For example, my nonverbal son is a terrific speller, so in one episode, he spelled his way out of danger. My typically developing child put his love of collecting things to good use in another episode by using the items in his pocket to save the day. The messages that come through these kinds of stories are subtle but clear: everyone has strengths and can make contributions, regardless of disability. Being disabled does not make you heroic, but using your gifts and skills to help others does.

To counter stereotypes in a more direct way, guide students through a discussion of a story that you tell featuring a character with a disability. You could, for example, have the students describe that character in as many ways as possible to enable them to see that disability is only one part of the character's makeup. Older students could be assigned to bring in a news article or story about someone with a disability. Have the members of the class share what they found, and together, analyze the messages that the stories send. Then tell a story that you have prepared, and have the class look at how it compares.

Using storytelling to break stereotypes can be as simple as showing that people with disabilities are just regular people. They can be heroes, villains, or tricksters. They can have the right answers as well as the wrong ones. They can be smart, silly, cranky, exuberant, confused, afraid, brave, or complacent, just like everyone else.

Teaching Empathy to Create Community

Telling a story about a central character with a disability of some kind can certainly evoke sympathy in an audience, but to teach empathy, try putting the students in the storyteller's role.

Showing and then teaching students how to tell a story without talking may increase verbal students' awareness and understanding of nonverbal methods of communication. Model the role of facial expressions and physical gestures in a story by telling a short story without speaking. Then have the students talk about what you did and what it showed. To get the students started, you can pass out cards with emotions on them and have students try to convey the emotions to the class without speaking, and then have everyone guess what was being shown. Another idea is to have pairs or small groups of students try to act out the stories without speaking, and then have students from other groups narrate those stories as they are being acted out. The students will enjoy seeing how close to (or far from) the narration is from what the group acting out the story was trying to show, and you can help the class unpack what happened afterward by leading them through a discussion of how we interpret and misinterpret nonverbal communication. Activities like these can open students' minds to think about communication as more than talking, which may, in turn, help them to become aware that their nonverbal peers communicate in many ways.

"What if?" or "What would you do?" storytelling activities can be used to teach empathy and promote inclusion more directly. Leading students in an activity in which they are asked to imagine, for example, how their day might be different if they could not speak can help them to better understand the lives of nonverbal students. In addition to having students think about what might be different, you should have them think about what might be the same. Would they have the same interests and needs? Would they still want to play with friends, to learn at school, and to ask questions and tell stories?

Students could be asked to tell stories about how they might solve problems or handle situations if they could not speak, such as how they might ask someone to play at recess or what they could do if all there was to eat for lunch was a food they hated. Students can also be asked to tell stories about how they would or would not want to be treated by their peers and teachers.

Through activities like these, you can empower all your students as storytellers. You can give your nonverbal students an avenue for sharing their experiences with their classmates, and, if you lead the class in a "What would you do?" story, you can enable nonverbal students to shine by showing off their own problem-solving skills. You can also enable your verbal students to become more adept at understanding nonverbal communication and hopefully more aware of communicators who use a variety of mechanisms to express themselves.

Although this article focuses on ways to use storytelling with nonverbal students, the strategies in it can be used with many different populations. For example, if you have a blind student in your class, you could assign everyone to engage in storytelling that draws on other senses. For example, what does the ocean sound like? How does sand feel under your feet? This will enable a nonsighted student to tell a story through his or her unique perspective, enable sighted students to experience the world in a new way, and enhance everyone's powers of description. The strategies for nonverbal students described here can also be used with hearing-impaired students and nonnative speakers.

By using storytelling activities to create common ground, you can promote empathy and inclusion in the classroom, with the ultimate goal of creating a strong sense of community.

Final Thoughts

My son's speech-language pathologist is fond of beginning sessions by saying, "Let's go find your voice!" Engaging nonverbal students in storytelling activities helps them to find not only their voice but also their place. Enabling them to become storytellers signals that their voices matter, regardless of the mechanisms they use to express them, and establishes them as equal members of the classroom community. Speaking to their experiences through stories acknowledges the fullness of their humanity and recognizes and celebrates their individuality. The work that we do as storytellers matters deeply in so many ways, and I applaud you for undertaking it.

The strategies in this article come from trial and error. As a teacher and storyteller, I have learned the importance of working and reworking a lecture or story to reach an audience in just the right way. As a parent of a nonverbal child, I have learned the importance of acknowledging and encouraging communication in all its forms and of taking a chance on something new when what is supposed to work does not. My son spent many frustrating years trialing communication devices that didn't meet his needs. He has cerebral palsy, is legally blind, and is astonishingly bright, so he needed something that didn't require vision or good fine motor skills and would enable him to say anything in the world he wanted to say. Traditional picture-based augmentative and alternative communication devices with 80–100 buttons per screen just didn't work. But through all the trial and error, he never stopped trying to communicate, and we kept looking for a way to help him. We finally found that way last year in a device called the Tandem Master that translates Morse code into text and speaks it out loud. He quickly learned Morse code, and now, through tapping dot and dash buttons, he can say whatever he likes. He is still working on learning to speak with his mouth too, and between the two approaches, he is getting out all the words that have been lodged inside him for years.

I encourage you to keep trying new ideas until you find the right way to unlock your nonverbal students' voices. The most important lesson I have learned for working with students with special needs is that the question is never *if*; it's always *how*. You can find a way. Being nonverbal in no way limits a person's desire to communicate, and with a little creativity, anyone can be enabled to tell stories, even students who can't say a word.

Making Meaning from Images: Predict and Infer

Sherry Norfolk

My students: nine students ranging in age from 7 to 10; their comprehension and linguistic skills ranging from ages 2 to 5; all diagnosed with severe learning disabilities.

My assignment: in three 45-minute sessions, help them learn to predict, infer, and create stories with a beginning, middle, and end.

My lessons: I decided on a variation of Cathy Ward's wonderful lesson plan "What Do You See? Visual Literacy and Story Structure" in Literacy Development in the Storytelling Classroom (Libraries Unlimited, 2009)—a process that was adapted by Annette Harrison in her article, "Yipes!" in this book. We began by looking closely at a print of Norman Rockwell's *Trumpet Practice*: a young boy sprawled in an overstuffed chair, blasting on a trumpet while his dog cringes below. I told the story I "saw" in the picture. Lots of laughs. Total engagement. Everybody in anticipatory mode, eager for whatever was going to happen next.

I explained that I created the story by thinking about what might have happened *before* the event in the picture, describing what was happening in the picture, and then thinking about what might happen *next*. This is inference and prediction, the essential comprehension skills with which these kids were struggling.

"You guys want to try it?"

Yep, they were ready to try.

Displaying another Norman Rockwell picture, *Boy on a High Dive*, I gave them time to observe carefully and think about what they saw. I asked them to describe everything they saw in the picture. They provided a good description of the boy in his yellow swim trunks, kneeling at the edge of a high-dive board and clinging to the edge with a terrified look on his face. I scribed their responses on the board. This would be the middle of their story.

Then I asked them to think about what had happened *before* the boy knelt at the edge of the diving board. Why was he there? How did he get there? Literally all of the responses were some variation of "He's on the diving board." No inference.

Before frustration set in (theirs and mine), I asked them to predict what was going to happen next. "He jumped!" "He fell off!" "He drowned!" We voted on the choices, and I added our choice to the description I had scribed on the board. This would be the end of the story.

We returned to the beginning. "How did the boy get up on the high dive? Why did he get up there?" They looked at me expectantly. I supplied some ideas; we voted on them; I added the beginning to the story on the board. Then, to model the process, I told them the story they had created. Lots of laughs.

The first session ended with all of the kids able to describe a picture (that's the middle of the story) and predict a possible outcome (that's the end). But nary a soul could infer what might have happened before the pictured event; they could not create a beginning for the story.

I went away to think. The thinking process goes something like this: If the lesson doesn't work, it's not the kids' fault; rather, the fault lies somewhere in the construction or delivery of the lesson. What would clarify this concept?

I needed to make it more concrete—to relate the lesson to something that they totally understood.

The next day, when I opened the door to their classroom, I waited until everyone was looking at me before crossing to a chair and sitting down. They watched with eager anticipation.

"Okay, everybody get out your cameras," I said, pretending to hold up a camera. They complied with alacrity. "Now take a picture of me." Click!

"What am I doing in the picture?" I asked. I received both a description and a prediction: "You're sitting down!" "You're going to tell us a story!"

I backed them up to the description. "Right, I'm sitting down." I rose and wrote on the board:

Ms. Norfolk sat down.

"What did I do *before* this picture was taken—*before* I sat down?" They had just watched me do this, so they had the answer. "You walked in." I wrote that on the board:

Ms. Norfolk walked in.
Ms. Norfolk sat down.

"What did I do before I walked in?" With some discussion (and a demonstration), we ended up with the following revision:

Ms. Norfolk opened the door and walked in.
She closed the door and walked to a chair.
Ms. Norfolk sat down.

"What did I do before I opened the door?"

Slowly, from the image of me sitting in a chair in their classroom, we worked backward step-by-step to the alarm clock awakening me that morning. My playfully indignant questions ("Wait! You mean I didn't get to eat breakfast?" "I came to school in my PJs?") provoked giggles and quick additions to the story. (The story ended as they had originally predicted: I told a story!)

When the story was complete, I read them their story, with lots of animation and sound effects. They applauded wildly. I grinned happily. We had inferred!

So, we did it again, moving backward from another Norman Rockwell painting. Then again, creating beginning, middle, and end—an entire story—about still another painting.

Now that the class was able to work together to create a story by inferring, describing, and predicting, we needed to move gradually toward doing this independently. Dividing the class into three groups of three kids, I gave each triad a new picture. Each student in the triad was assigned a job: one would figure out what happened before the picture was taken; another would describe what was happening in the picture; and another would predict what would happen next.

As the triads conferred, the teacher, teaching assistant, and I monitored, asked questions, and prompted. When the groups were ready, we arranged our chairs in a semicircle for the performances. Each group stood before the class while one of the group members walked around the semicircle, allowing everyone to see the picture. Then they told their story. Progress!

We did it again and again, rearranging the groupings and changing the assignments (a student who had been in the inference position would change to description, etc.).

Success! But would they retain the newfound skill, and could it be demonstrated individually?

On the third day—*yes!*—they did retain it and they could do it individually! We again sat in the semicircle, and each student chose a picture from a set of Mary Engelbreit images. The individual students were given instructions to create a story about their pictures, including what happened before the pictured event, what was happening in the picture, and what happened next. Again, the adults circulated, keeping the kids focused and providing suggestions as needed.

Finally, it was showtime! One by one, each student stood and showed his or her picture around the semicircle, and then took his or her place in front and told his or her story. The stories were brief but complete—every story was relevant to its picture and had a beginning, middle, and end!

Every face in that room was a happy face! But we had one more step to take.

I asked the students if they wanted to *write* a story, and got a resounding *yes*! I provided a new set of pictures from which to choose; again, students worked with the assistance of teachers, teaching assistant, and teaching artist.

Every student developed, then wrote or dictated, his or her own story with a beginning, middle, and end. The joy in that room was palpable—and only half of it was radiating from me! The other half was radiating from those triumphant kids, proudly reading their stories to their teachers and each other.

Beginning: Teaching artist and nine students trying unsuccessfully to infer what happened first.

The Image/Middle: Me, frustrated and worried that I could not devise a successful lesson plan.

End: Nine successful students, holding up their complete and wonderful stories!

Choosing Pictures

Pictures for this project must contain characters involved in a situation that is easily recognizable to the students, drawing on the students' prior knowledge. It's also useful to have a recognizable setting, although not having one provides another opportunity for inference.

Calendars are very useful for this purpose. The Mary Engelbreit prints in 365-day calendars are bright and cheerful, depicting multicultural children and adults doing mostly recognizable things. Cut out the useful ones, and mount them on card stock if you plan to use them more than once. Laminate them if you expect to use this lesson plan over and over!

It's also important to provide choices—there should be at least five more pictures than students so that everyone has more than one picture to choose from. Providing choices also means that students can identify something that they recognize and can make meaning of, rather than being assigned something that they don't understand.

Some picturebooks provide useful images as well. Ask your school media specialist for his or her discards, or buy paperback editions that you don't mind cutting up. I've used the pictures from Ezra Jack Keats' *Jennie's Hat* (HarperCollins, 1979) very successfully.

Graphic Organizer

Sometimes I use a graphic organizer for this lesson plan, depending on the students' reading levels. (If they can't read the questions, the organizer

Table 3.1   Graphic Organizer

Who are the characters?	What is the setting?	What happens before the scene in the picture?
What's happening in the picture?	What will happen next?	How does your story end?

provides more frustration than guidance.) The Graphic Organizer (see Table 3.1) allows students to draw their answers rather than write them and helps them visualize the story.

Another Option

If you have time to interpose an intermediate step between whole-class story creation and small-group story creation, try this:

1. Create a group story, scribing it on the board.
2. Determine with the class what the proper sequence should be (sentences tend to be dictated out of order).
3. Number the sentences.
4. Number and pass out a piece of "storytelling paper" or "story paper" (divided into equal areas for drawing and writing) to each student. Make sure that students who struggle with writing receive numbers corresponding to very short sentences.
5. Instruct students to copy the sentence that corresponds to the number on their page and to draw a picture that illustrates the sentence.
6. When finished, students line up in number order and read or recite the words on their page, thus performing their story.
7. Collect and collate the pages: Voila! A book!

Once students have a grasp of inference and prediction, try using this procedure when introducing a picturebook by having them describe what they see on the cover, infer what may have happened in the past, and predict what will happen next. Apply it to images in science, math, and social studies texts. Apply it to real life (look at the books scattered on the floor. Tell me what you see. Infer how they got there. Predict what will happen next.)

Making meaning from images is a giant step toward helping students develop the ability to infer, describe, predict, and conceptualize the world around them. Look around you—there's a story!

On-the-Fly Tales: Creating Stories with Young Children

Jeri Burns (The Storycrafters)

Nothing compares to the delight that a parent experiences when a child reaches a developmental milestone. The first words, the first steps, and the first bites of food are treasured moments of wonder at the unfolding of a new person. But when a child with developmental challenges achieves a milestone, this feeling of parental pride and joy is magnified with relief and exuberance.

But before I can tell a story about Molly and her mother, I must first provide context that circles back to our family.

We homeschooled our son from cradle to college. But he didn't sit at the kitchen table, alone with Mom, for 18 years. Zack's education happened on the road, through life experience, and at home, upside down and in motion on the living room couch. Our educational philosophy melded his personal interests with academic needs. Zack's overall education can be likened to eating at an organic foods buffet: it was exceptionally nutritious, deliciously satisfying, and had more diversity than all the offerings at multiple buffet stations combined.

A key component of Zack's education was his membership in homeschooling groups. Not only did he engage in numerous group-learning opportunities, but Zack also made deep and long-standing friendships with other children. Until the day that his high school academic classes moved to community and liberal arts colleges, the fabric of his educational life was woven with many educational threads, including homeschooling groups.

One group we participated in during Zack's active homeschooling years was a co-op—a group of families with varying educational, parenting, and political philosophies. With classes for different age groups held twice a week, students and even parents had opportunities to learn a variety of academic topics and life skills, together. Some classes were designed for specified age ranges, like for children aged seven to nine or for teens only; others could be taken by children of any age, all together. The multiaged nature of every class meant that a staircase of emotional and intellectual capabilities was always present. This element alone was highly valued by parents and children alike.

The diversity of the co-op was increased by another factor: our homeschooling group was inclusive. All children were welcome, including those with emotional, behavioral, or cognitive challenges.

Molly

Molly was a little girl in one of our homeschooling groups. Her face is unforgettable. With a smattering of freckles bridging her nose and cheeks, her expressive face communicated like language. The deep letter *u* of her smile to a small *n* of her frown were the volume control on her emotions. And when she smiled, her eyes blazed with joy.

Where the children in the homeschooling group had a wide variety of skills and educational backgrounds, Molly's cognitive and interpersonal skills were quite different from other young children. Though she was about five years old when I worked with her, she was minimally verbal.

Every family in our homeschooling co-op offered classes every semester. As professional storytellers, my husband and I sometimes offered storytelling, but not every semester. One fall, several families with young children asked for a storytelling option, and I offered a four-week block of weekly creative storytelling and writing classes for children aged four to seven. About 10 children attended the class regularly, along with some parents.

Molly was one of the students. As it happened, her mom was teaching a cooking class in the kitchen, so for the first time, Molly attended a class on her own.

Molly's mom worried that it wouldn't go well because Molly didn't like books or reading. She e-mailed me before the first class and said, "Jeri, it's okay if you need to send Molly out to the kitchen to be with me. She doesn't like stories, but I don't want to keep her from the class since it is the only one offered for kids her age this time of day. Is that okay with you?"

I was delighted to give it a try.

The Class

The class was designed to share stories, develop listening skills, and kindle beginner writing skills through oral expression (for more on this, please see later in this section). Every week I sang songs and told stories. As part of the writing component of the class, I cocreated stories with the children. "On-the-Fly" stories, my name for spontaneously created stories, are on-the-spot adaptations of a previously told tale with new content provided by the children.

When we met, I sat on a chair in front of the group. Some students sat on the floor; a few mothers held younger siblings on their laps, and a couple of kids draped themselves on chairs. Molly started the first class by sitting on the floor at my feet, front and center.

I have been advised to approach students with developmental delays by offering them physical opportunities for participation in storytelling. "That way, they can do simple things with their hands and work on fine motor skills" is how the advice often goes. In my experience, multisensory approaches to storytelling are often effective with special needs children. Given the age range of the students, all of this was appropriate for everyone, so I went full steam ahead.

I started the first class with an action-packed song with sound effects, participatory gestures, and refrains to sing. Everyone but Molly played along. She watched me a little; she studied the other students more. But she didn't attempt to join in or imitate.

I immediately scrutinized what I was doing. Was the participation too difficult for her? Was I expecting too much? I slowed down the later verses and simplified my movements. The others followed suit, but Molly still didn't join in. As the song continued, she inched away from her front and center position to the edge of the audience.

I considered carefully what to do next. I chose a longer-listening story that had a few simple repetitive hand movements should she or others want to join in; but there was little other audience participation. I did this despite the information I had received that she didn't like stories. I did this despite the oft-told advice to have many participatory options for children with special needs. I did this despite "common wisdom" that young children can't attend to long stories.

Why did I make that choice? Good question. The answer is a combination of an awareness of the other students in the class, instinct regarding

Molly, and experience. Although I wanted to meet her needs, I also had a responsibility to all the students. As to instinct, it was clear that physical participation did not meet Molly's needs that day; maybe something else would be in better tune with her. As to experience, in my work with The Storycrafters, we regularly tell long stories to young children.

As I launched into that longer story, the class was very attentive. For most of the tale, Molly watched them as much as me. Her face wore a concerned frown. But as we neared the story's end, the frown was replaced with a tentative, neutral look. She inched a little closer to me and even attempted one or two hand movements.

I told another story and Molly remained neutral. But when I explained that we were going to write our own original version of a folktale, she frowned again. (For specifics on the writing process, please see later in this section.)

When we moved into the oral writing portion of the class on that first day, the students offered many ideas for inclusion in the story. Molly's head swiveled as each hopeful child was called on. I told the tale featuring the children's ideas, pausing intermittently to ask for more suggestions. Toward the end, Molly raised her hand and made a halting suggestion about a color of an animal's fur. I included it in my telling of the tale. And did she smile! Every time that animal was mentioned in the story, I emphasized the color of its fur. And every time Molly heard her own idea in the new tale, her delight and pride grew. By the second class, it was hard to keep her suggestions out of the story. She bubbled with enthusiasm, and I never saw her frown again.

I was impressed with her recall of prior tales and songs. Her memory of every story I told was comparable to that of the other students. She also knew the first song I sang with the group, the one that she didn't appear to "get" when it was first taught. As the weeks progressed, her excitement about stories and language seemed to explode, and her willingness to try using her fine motor skills to participate also increased.

On-the-Fly Story–Creation Process

On-the-Fly Stories are created and told simultaneously, with content suggestions supplied by the students. The process is entirely oral and informal, which evokes an intimate storytelling feel instead of classroom formality. The decision to avoid classroom formality had nothing to do with their homeschooling status, however. While it is effective to acquire student suggestions first and then tell the new story, as I have done in storytelling workshops with older children, this project was different for several reasons. First, I wanted the children to experience the reward of hearing their ideas come immediately to life in a spoken story. Second, my sessions were an hour in length. Expecting youngsters of this age to listen to stories, participate in a formal brainstorming activity, and then tune in again for more formal listening was asking a lot. Finally, I developed this activity because I believed it would work well for the diversity of ages and abilities in my group, including Molly.

On-the-Fly story–creation works well with folktales because the structure of the traditional story is already known. One simply substitutes new images into a familiar, preexisting plot structure. The existing story structure guarantees cohesiveness for the new tale and helps the storyteller remember the new material better. The repetition of a classic folktale also connects children more deeply to meaning, develops their critical listening skills, and familiarizes them with story structure. Their contributions to the story-in-process also develop their vocabulary and oral expression skills.

Choose a Folktale That the Students All Know

I usually selected a story that was told in a previous class. In the first class, however, it was a tale I told earlier in the session. As we got more adept at this process, I allowed the students to have a say in what story we would adapt. By the end of the series, we even readapted previously adapted tales.

Example

One story that we adapted was "The Mitten," a traditional, cumulative, Ukrainian folktale.

Story Summary

A girl drops her mitten in the snowy forest one day. A mouse comes upon it and crawls in to escape the cold. Soon, a frog happens by. He asks and receives permission to move in too. They are later joined by a rabbit, a boar, and finally a bear. When the bear asks to move in, the animals say there is not enough room. But the bear squeezes in anyway. The mitten stretches to nearly bursting when a fly joins them. *Pop!* The mitten breaks completely. The animals scatter and find other places to stay warm. In spring, the girl finds her shredded mitten and shows it to her family as she tells the story to them.

Group Retelling of the Folktale as Remembered

Next, I asked them to tell me the story as I told it the first time. Since the children were young, I started telling the story and asked them to tell me what happened next. Sometimes we paused so I could ask them to elaborate on salient descriptions, details, or character information.

Review Story Elements

I provided simple explanations of the concepts of setting, characters, and objects. Next, we identified the setting, characters, and objects in the story we just retold as a group.

Example

In "The Mitten," the setting was a forest during in the winter. The main object was a mitten, and the characters included a little girl who dropped the mitten, a mouse, frog, rabbit, boar, bear and fly.

Prompts for the New Story

I began telling the On-the-Fly story. To model how to contribute to the rewrite, I offered the first new item—setting. Then I continued the story and stopped at the first character. I asked the group leading questions, such as "Who has an idea for a human character?" or "What farm animal should we use here?" These prompts helped me maintain story cohesiveness. By prompting student submissions, it opened the door to creativity that wasn't completely random. It fostered meaning and interconnection among all the story elements.

Example

I changed the setting of the story to our local, rural area during winter. I asked them to identify a different dropped object, a different character who dropped it, and all the creatures who inhabit it to stay warm.

Just Say Yes

Be inclusive. Accept everyone's responses. This process is about fostering creativity and fun. Like a puppeteer, you control the strings. By asking focused questions, you increase the odds that a student's response will fit into the story. Students feel good when their ideas are included and not modified.

Manage Adaptations

Be wary of the number of suggestions you include. Remember, you are working on the fly—without notes—to maintain orality in the tale. If you have too many adaptations, you won't be able to remember them all.

Sometimes you must stop students from calling out their ideas unbidden. If you accept some, others will quickly follow and you may find yourself at the mercy of an avalanche of ideas. While creativity is important, students stop listening to the story in a flurry of idea generation, and the literary experience of writing and listening to a new story is diluted.

Expanding Opportunities for Contributions

A story with numerous characters allows more students to contribute their ideas. However, not all stories have numerous characters. One way to expand the possibilities for student contributions is to ask for character description or for dialogue.

Example

In the On-the-Fly version of "The Mitten," I asked for more suggestions for animals than there were in the first version of the tale.

The Takeaway

It is impractical to make blanket statements about how to reach all children with stories. As we saw with Molly, advice about incorporating active physical movement and avoiding longer-"listening" stories was not right for her. Because each child's needs are unique, storytelling On-the-Fly works because flexibility is part of the package.

Storytellers are avid students of body language; it helps us adjust our stories and programs in response to audience cues. In response to Molly's sheer delight when her idea was included in a story, I repeated her suggestion more than I otherwise might have. However, reading body language is not a fail-safe strategy, and it was particularly confusing in Molly's case. During the first class, her body language sent me many signals that she was not engaged or paying attention.

But she was.

During the entire residency, there were times when Molly didn't appear to be actively engaged in story creation. I didn't pressure her. I asked the class for suggestions without singling anyone out. Molly was welcomed to contribute whenever she felt so moved. She had complete autonomy in her creativity.

In my estimation, this project was effective for Molly because it offered her the chance to participate in a group on her own terms. When she participated, her unedited suggestions were incorporated into each new story, which may have bolstered her self-esteem. By allowing her to participate in her own way, she connected to the stories all throughout the residency. My ability to be flexible "on the fly" allowed me to meet Molly where she needed to be met.

After her nervous start in the first class, Molly's face wore a bright smile that rivaled the curvy curls on her head for the rest of the sessions. Her mother was no different. She spoke to me in between classes. "I can't believe it! Molly really likes stories now. She lets me read to her and says some words. Sometimes she repeats phrases from your class stories." As she told me about Molly's newfound excitement about language, her smile was as curly as her daughter's, and her eyes burned with hope and joy. A door to literature was finally open.

Resources: Some Versions of "The Mitten"

Aylesworth, J., & McClintock. B. (2009). *The mitten.* New York, NY: Scholastic Press.

Brett, J. (1989). *The mitten: A Ukrainian folktale.* New York, NY: Putnam.

Bulatov, È . O. V., & Botting, T. (1989). *The mitten: A Ukrainian fairy-tale.* Moscow, Russia: Malysh Publishers.

Hill, T., & Pollack, Y. (1995). *The old man's mitten: A Ukranian tale.* New York, NY: Mondo Publishing.

Koopmans, L., & Vincent. J. R. (1992). *Any room for me?* Edinburgh, Scotland: Floris.

Southwick, J., Curnick, P., & Yeretskaya, Y. (2014). *The mitten: A classic pop-up folktale.* Mason, OH: Jumping Jack Press.

Stasiak, K. (1991). *The mitten.* Boston, MA: Houghton Mifflin.

Tresselt, A. Y., & Rachëv, E. (1964). *The mitten: An old Ukrainian folktale.* New York, NY: Lothrop, Lee & Shepard.

Sing Me a Story: The Language of Music for Students with Verbal Challenges

Cherri Coleman

My friend Jenny had plenty to say, but she couldn't speak. The words were there, but they tumbled out wrong, jumbled and stuttering; thoughts piling up one on top of the other with no means for release until she gave up with a sigh, frustrated and exhausted. But when all of us were marched from Sunday school into the sanctuary of our little country church, something miraculous would happen. The congregation would open its hymn books and Jenny would begin to sing, her rich vibrant soprano floating over the tiny congregation and dropping as if by magic, perfect, exquisitely formed words onto our listening ears. Each lyric so gorgeously enunciated that the pronunciation of words themselves seemed artful. I often closed my eyes and went silent, the better to listen. Jenny couldn't speak well, but Lord, could she sing.

"Where Words Fail, Music Speaks"—Hans Christian Andersen

Imagine the frustration of having a mind full of thoughts, ideas, needs, and emotions with no means to communicate them. Imagine the humiliation of having your intelligence and value underestimated and ignorance assumed just because you cannot express your intellect. Imagine appreciating the kind words and support of your champions without the ability to communicate your gratitude. Like people in a foreign land, those with brain-related language barriers live with these frustrations and discriminations on a moment-to-moment basis.

My dear friend Jenny has taught me many things, but the most important is that music truly has the power to work magical transformations. The word "enchantment" actually means "to be transfixed or spellbound by song," proving that the ancients knew of this power long before the technology came along to explain it with neuroscience. We read of David soothing Saul with lyre and verse, of King George III commissioning music as a remedy for memory loss and mania, and of an 18th-century villager who, like my friend Jenny, had lost the ability to speak except through hymns.

Modern studies show that students with autism, Williams syndrome, stroke damage, and other verbal issues have often preserved musical ability despite the loss of verbal function. The reason is that music is actually made and understood not in one area but all over the brain. According to the Cognitive Neuroscience of Music, when making music or engaged in song, the sensory cortex, auditory cortex, hippocampus, visual cortex, cerebellum, amygdala, prefrontal cortex, and motor cortex are all firing at once! Stimulating more parts of the brain than any other human function, music coaxes other portions to take over for the damaged verbal centers. This means that by combining the power of music with storytelling, we can literally *give our students voice*. The effects can be life changing.

Music, Like Story, Is a Multitasker

Multiple areas of stimulation in the brain result in multiple experiences and benefits for the student and his or her instructor.

Music Breaks Down the Word Barrier

- People with verbal issues often struggle with words both coming in and going out, but music circumvents those pathways, allowing the teacher not only to address Speaking and Listening Standards but also to access the student intellectually, socially, and emotionally.
- Rhythm can help filter and organize narrative information such as structure, sequence, and elements of character, which could otherwise be overwhelming.
- Singing provides the ability to express emotion on a level that is difficult for all of us to put into words.

Music Is Motivating

- Making and listening to music floods the brain with dopamine, the "feel good" motivational chemical, providing incentive to persevere, try harder, and stretch for goals.
- Songs are a great teaching tool both in school and at home, encouraging repetition and providing the opportunity to practice verbal expression and repeat therapeutic exercises in a fun and joyous way.

Music Is Multisensory

- Sound itself is *kinesthetic*, actually penetrating the body (think of the feel of a bass drum at a parade).
- *Auditory* skills engage with the act of listening.
- *Visual* senses are active as the students' eyes track the song leader.
- *Tactile* senses can also be stimulated by adding the use of instruments.

Music Is Social and Inclusive

- Group song provides meaningful opportunities for family involvement and creates a nonthreatening environment for the student to practice expressing verbally and participating socially.
- Song allows special needs students to join in regular curriculum activity and gives them the opportunity to excel.

In short, music can be the tool in the teacher's or storyteller's kit that unlocks the students' power of vocal expression.

Scaffolding Verbal and Narrative Skills with Story Song

The key component of both music and story that makes them beneficial is organization. The definition of music is "sound organized in time." Repetition, patterns of rhythm, pitch, contrast, mood, and variations of repeated themes in changing context work in harmony to maximize verbal potential and memory. It is for that reason that I love working with 18th- and 19th-century work songs and ballads. While on the surface, they are silly, whimsical fluff; in reality they are masterpieces of brain science made ingeniously simple. The older, more formal English lends itself well to modeling clear enunciation. Like verbal call and response, these folksongs promote focus, turn-taking, and paying attention to a leader; their kinesthetic rhythms were created to make repetitive, mundane tasks such as churning or raising a sail (or in this instance, repeating therapeutic speech exercises) joyous, team building, and goal oriented.

Without explanation, I place my fist at shoulder height and sing a loud "Heigh" and then punch the air with my fist over my head for "Ho." That gets their attention. Curiosity peaked, I repeat, "Heigh-Ho," punching the air and inviting them to join with a listening gesture of hand at my ear. I receive a weak experimental reply. Again a hearty "Heigh-Ho" and an invitation from me and then a louder response and they are ready to play. Some aren't. I playfully make my way around the room to a few students individually, making a game of repeating "Heigh-Ho" until I get enough students modeling to help the others to join in as they are able. They get it, so I make it a little harder "Heigh Ho, would a wooing go," swaying from side to side. Again we play with getting it right and then practicing both. I point to them, "Heigh Ho." They sing it back, "Heigh Ho would a wooing go." When I get the full-throated, amused kind of response I'm looking for, I launch into the full song and we are off on a silly, musical story adventure.

> *Frog he would a wooing go with a*
> *Heigh-Ho!*
> *Whether his mother was willing or no*
> *Heigh-Ho would a wooing go!*
> *He put on his high cocked hat*
> *Heigh-Ho!*
> *And out on the road he met with a rat*
> *Heigh-Ho would a wooing go!*
> *They rode down to Miss Mousie's Hall*
> *Heigh-Ho!*
> *And they gave a loud knock and they gave a loud call*
> *Heigh-Ho would a wooing go!*
> *They said Miss Mouse bring us root beer*
> *Heigh-Ho!*
> *That we may drink and have good cheer*
> *Heigh-Ho would a wooing go!*
> *They said Miss Mouse sing us a song*
> *Heigh-Ho!*
> *One that's pretty but not too long*
> *Heigh-Ho would a wooing go!*
> (See Resource list later for sources of complete lyrics.)

We applaud, we laugh, and we leave it alone. I start a different type of activity while they process what just happened. We get tactile and make some newspaper pirate hats and then try the song again, costumed in Froggy's "high cocked hat."

The next day I begin the same way. Usually a hearty and eager "Heigh Ho" is immediate. I have a precocious student stand beside me to model the response and the gesture while I hold up pictures at the appropriate point in the song: Froggy getting dressed to impress the ladies and his mother looking on; Froggy in his cocked hat meeting the rat on the road; the cats bursting through the door; and so on. When we finish, I mix up the pictures and ask them to direct me in putting them in order: "So Froggy went a wooing; then what?" Some students who are catching on quickly point out the correct pictures or sing part of the verses. I prompt them as we place the pictures in a line and celebrate by singing the song again with the pictures as cues.

Day three: We start as we ended on day two. I point to each picture we put in sequence as we sing. At this point several students are attempting to join me in the verse as well as the "Heigh Hos." We finish and settle in to discuss the story. I watch for nonverbal response from my students with the most challenging vocal issues, but several can handle two- to three-word answers.

Teaching Artist (TA):	"So what does Froggy want to do?"
Student (S):	"Goin on date."
TA:	"Do you think he's a young guy or an old guy?"
S:	"Old."
TA:	"Why?"
S:	"Likes root beer," and so on.

Day four: I split them into two groups. We take turns being the audience and the performer, supporting each other, prompting those who are learning the verses with cards. I sing where I am needed. Many are grasping the whole song. We split the two groups in half, and they try the song again with a smaller team of support. I continue to encourage them to divide as they are able. Leaders are emerging, and I am fading into the background.

This story song will go into our repertory; next week we move on to a more challenging one.

> *Scaffolding is the process by which someone organizes an event that is unfamiliar or beyond a learner's ability in order to assist the learner in carrying out that event. Learners are encouraged to carry out parts of tasks that are within their ability, and the adult "fills in" or "scaffolds" the rest. The scaffolding involves recruiting the learners' interest, reducing their choices, maintaining their goal orientation, highlighting critical aspects of the task, controlling their frustration, and demonstrating activity paths to them.* (Wood, Bruner, & Ross, 1976)

Essentially, *scaffolding* is modeling or demonstrating how to solve a problem and then stepping back and offering support as needed. Story songs almost scaffold themselves.

We entered into the song as an "event" that was unfamiliar and intriguing. Giving no verbal explanation and using only gesture kept the students from being overwhelmed with words and captured their focus and attention. The learners interpreted what I wanted from them as a group, and the song became a community activity. They mastered the first response, which was chosen because it was within their comfort zone, and then they were given a task slightly harder. As we sang, I watched, listened, and interpreted the students' verbal and nonverbal messages, letting them guide me in adjusting my instruction. As they mastered a piece, we went a little further, adding visuals and exploring narrative, sequence, and character.

After singing "Froggy" one time, students have followed a leader; watched for prompts and responded; taken turns; reinforced verbal exercise with gesture; reinforced a verbal exercise with rhythm; have been an active participant within an activity; participated socially; listened and responded actively to a narrative; repeated the therapeutic "Heigh-ho" speech exercise at least 20 times; and probably had a lot of fun in less than five minutes.

As a teaching artist, a single song has allowed me to employ all four elements of successful scaffolding:

1. Entering into an unfamiliar learning event with a common goal
2. Ongoing evaluation and adaptive support of learners
3. Dialogue and interaction
4. Fading and transfer of responsibility

Expanding to Performance

Both inclusive and individualized, story song, with its multisensory approach and different levels of verbalization, has the power to include all learners. Performance of these musical stories gives us the opportunity to celebrate many individual students' multiple achievements simultaneously. And these students, perhaps more than any others, have a need to be seen and heard.

Consider this work song:

> **Noah's Ark Shanty**
> In Frisco Bay there were three ships
> *Way hey aye oh (simple phonetic response)*
> In Frisco Bay there were three ships
> *A long time ago [simple phrase response]*
> And one of those ships was Noah's old ark
> *Way hey aye oh!*
> All covered about with hickory bark
> *A long time ago*
> *[Combining the skills in a shared chorus]*
> *It's a long, long time and a very long time*
> *Way hey aye oh!*
> *A long, long time and a very long time*
> *A long time ago.*
> They took two animals of every kind
> *Way hey aye oh!*
> They took two animals of every kind
> *A long time ago*
> *It's a long, long time and a very long time*
> *Way hey aye oh!*
> *A long, long time and a very long time*
> *A long time ago.*
> (See Resource list for sources of complete lyrics.)

This song allows us to include four levels of storytellers to perform simultaneously within the same piece: Level I, the simple phonetic response;

Level II, the simple phrase; Level III, the shared chorus; and Level IV, the text of the verse. Each performer can find his or her level of vocalization. The support of the musical structure and shared responsibility of the group alleviates fear, promotes confidence, and fosters a sense of accomplishment and community.

Can you imagine anything more moving than seeing an assembly of people previously denied the blessing of speech performing an entire musical story together, or a person not normally able to participate at all perhaps becoming the star and leading his or her family and fellow students in a celebration of story and song?

Music gives these students the power of speech. As teachers, it is a humble honor to wield that power, share the stories, and make our own lives more meaningful in the process.

Jenny's Song

My mother strongly encouraged voice lessons for my friend Jenny, and a well-known instructor took her on as a student. She progressed from hymns and folksongs to ballads and arias. Voice competitions give her ratings of "Superior," and comments have been made noting her fine articulation of the Italian language.

Because of her study of music, my friend Jenny gained the power of speech. Able to communicate her thoughts, she revealed herself to be one of the most ethical, sensitive, and fiercely wise people I have ever known. She now has a job and her own apartment, and she converses with my mother in long phone conversations. Music has given Jenny voice and allowed her to shine.

May her example light the pathway for others.

Resources

American Music Therapy Association. (n.d.). Special education: Music therapy research and evidence-based practice support. Retrieved from http://www.musictherapy.org/assets/1/7/bib_Special_Education.pdf

Kennedy, P. (1984). *Folksongs of Britain and Ireland.* London, England: Oak Publications.

Mannes, E. (2011). *The power of music: Pioneering discoveries in the new science of song.* New York, NY: Walker & Co.

Wood, D., Bruner, J., & Ross, G. (1976). The role of tutoring in problem solving. Retrieved from https://www.scribd.com/document/132906978/Woods-Bruner-Ross-1976-the-Role-of-Tutoring-in-Problem-Solving

Note: "Froggy" was chosen as an example because since it is centuries old and the "most widely known song in the English language," it comes in many forms, melodies, and variations that can be easily adapted to each classroom's needs. A quick search of "Frog, He Would a Wooing Go" or "Froggy Went a-Courting" will provide lots of choices. The melody of the version used here is available at https://www.discogs.com/Virginia-Company-Nine-Points-Of-Roguery/release/6723801.

The Noah's Ark Shanty is available in a slightly different arrangement at https://www.youtube.com/watch?v=BJHTaDJi3iM.

Storytelling to Improve Literacy Learning (and Self-Esteem!)

Sherry Norfolk

E-mail from teacher: "My class consists of 8 boys. Majority are mild ID disabilities. 5/8 are fluent readers on a 2nd grade level, the other 3/8 are still working on pre-primer sight words. All enjoy sports." Several also had behavioral disabilities; one was nonverbal. When I explained to their teacher that they would be listening to stories, learning and acting out the stories, and eventually composing and presenting their own stories, she warned, "Maybe you can get a *group* story out of them."

"No problem," I replied. "This is very flexible—we'll see what works."

I began to move slowly, step-by-step toward my objectives, employing the four teaching components that are generally acknowledged to be effective for teaching students with special needs: Modeling, Small steps, Multimodal, and Clues to facilitate recall. My goal was to enable every student to construct and share his own story.

Step One

Each student received a large page of manila paper. I asked them to copy the pattern (see Table 3.2) I drew on the board.

I explained that I was going to tell a story, and that from time to time, I would stop and let them draw what they thought was the most important thing that happened in that part of the story and then write a caption underneath that would explain what the picture was about. I assured the boys that we would help them with the writing. They nodded and waited for the story to begin.

The purpose of this exercise was threefold: I wanted to check comprehension, demonstrate that they could represent a story in pictures, and help them use words to make meaning. Not wanting the illustration process to be too challenging, I chose to tell *Baby Rattlesnake*. It's easy to draw a rattlesnake!

The boys howled with glee at the story and eagerly drew their pictures. The teacher, teaching assistants, and I circulated, helping with spelling or scribing as needed. The nonverbal student was an excellent artist, so we had no trouble interpreting his pictures with words that he accepted.

Step Two

I told a very simple version of the Cherokee/Creek/Kiowa story "Grandmother Spider Brings the Light."

Table 3.2   Graphic Organizer for Tell-and-Draw

1.	2.	3.

Grandmother Spider Brings the Light

Sherry Norfolk in David Holt's *More Tellable Tales*
(August House, 2001)

In the beginning, there was darkness, darkness, darkness.

The animals couldn't see where they were going, and they were always bumping into each other! "Ouch! Stop that! Get off my tail!"

Bear called a great council of all of the animals and tried to decide what to do.

"We need light!" said the Bear. "We can't see a thing in this darkness."

"That's right," the other animals said. "We need light. But where do we get it?"

"Well, when there is a thunderstorm, I sometimes see a crack in the sky, and light shines through. I figure if we send someone to the crack in the sky, he can bring back some light, and then we can see!" answered Bear.

"Great idea!" they all said. "Who will go? Who will go get light?"

"I'll go," said Buzzard. "I will go get light."

Buzzard was big and tough, with long, strong wings, so the others agreed. Buzzard spread his long, strong wings and started off toward the crack in the sky. When he got there, he broke off some of the light.

"Hmmm. Now how am I going to carry this light back to the other animals?" thought Buzzard.

"Oh! I know! I have all of these thick, beautiful soft feathers on my head. I will make a nest of the feathers to carry back the light!" And he put the light on his head.

Now Buzzard didn't know about light—he didn't know that it was made of fire. He didn't know that it would burn through the feathers on his head. So he started flying back, flapping his long, strong wings. Suddenly, the light began to burn through the feathers. It burned his head.

"OOOOUCH!" yelled Buzzard. He rubbed his head. The light had burned all of the feathers off of his head! He was *bald*!

And the light had burned out. There was darkness, darkness, darkness.

"Who will go? Who will go get light?" asked Bear.

"I will go," said Possum. "I will go get light."

Possum started out, heading for the crack in the sky. She broke off a piece of the light.

"Now, what will I do with this light? I know! I'll be smarter than Buzzard. I won't put it on my head. I'll put it in my nice, bushy tail!" So Possum put the light in her tail, and she started back. Suddenly, the light burned through the hair on her tail.

"OOOOOOO"WWW!" yelled Possum. She looked at her tail. The light had burned all of the hair clean off—her tail was *naked*!

And the light had burned out. There was darkness, darkness, darkness.

"Who will go? Who will go get light?" Bear repeated.

"I will go," said a tiny voice.

"Who's that? It's too dark to see. Who's talking?"

"It's me, Grandmother Spider. I will go get light."

"You're too small. And you're too old. You'll get lost and forget your way back. You can't go!"

"Well, I may be little and I may be old, but I reckon you oughta let me try."

"Let her try!" the animals said.

So Grandmother Spider started off toward the crack in the sky. She knew that she might forget her way back, so she spun a web all the way from where the animals were waiting, all the way across the sky to the light. When she arrived at the light, she remembered what had happened to Possum and to Buzzard. So she scooped up some cool, wet mud, and she placed the light into the mud so that she wouldn't burn herself.

> Then, she started back, following the web back to where the animals waited. On the way, the light baked the mud until it was dry and hard. It was the first bowl in the world!
>
> When Grandmother Spider got back to the animals, she flung the ball of light into the sky!
>
> Now, ever since that time, Buzzard has had a bald head.
>
> Possum has had a naked tail.
>
> Spider's web has been shaped like the rays of the sun.
>
> And there has been LIGHT!

After reviewing the story elements verbally and in writing (sequence, setting, characters, problem, solution, resolution), I led them in reviewing it visually and kinesthetically by mimicking the simple repetitive motions that I used in telling the story.

Then I asked the guys if they would like to act out the story together. Mixed response: yes, no, maybe. In the end, they all did, since the story has four characters, and we therefore needed two groups of four to enact it. This story can be told silently with actions, so it was no problem for our nonverbal friend to participate. Now everyone in the class knew a story that they could all act out and that had a simple, replicable pattern.

Step Three

I told them *How Snowshoe Hare Rescued the Sun: A Tale from the Arctic*. This folktale follows the same pattern as "Grandmother Spider":

What happens to the light in the beginning of the story?
Who knows where it is and tells everyone else?
Who goes first to get the light? Why does that character fail?
Who goes next to get the light? Why does that character fail?
Who goes last?
How does the final character get the sun back into the sky?

We reviewed the story, discussing how it followed the pattern. Then, I drew a rectangle on the board, divided into six sections (see Table 3.3).

I introduced the concept of storyboarding, and the students told me what to draw in the respective boxes. We now had a visual representation of this story, similar to the work they had done with *Baby Rattlesnake*. The storyboard was used as a reference tool as they acted out the story.

Step-by-step, we were using repetition to reinforce understanding of the pattern and exploring multiple modes of representation.

Table 3.3 Storyboard

What happens to the light in the beginning of the story?	Who knows where it is and tells everyone else?	Who goes first to get the light? Why does that character fail?
Who goes next to get the light? Why does that character fail?	Who goes last?	How does the final character get the sun back into the sky?

Step Four

I told still another story that followed the pattern ("Look Back and See," the title story of Margaret Read MacDonald's book). After reviewing the pattern, students were given large sheets of manila paper and asked to draw storyboards of the story. Some used words and pictures, others only pictures, but all storyboards clearly depicted the same story. When all of the storyboards were complete, some of the boys wanted to act out the story; others wanted to watch and provide sound effects.

Step Five

I told yet another folktale following the same pattern, this time a Mayan legend in which Possum steals fire for the animals (adapted from *The Myths of the Opossum*). This story is more complicated than the other three, and the dramatization is more difficult—also more rambunctious. By this time, however, the boys had internalized the story structure, and we were ready for the next step.

Step Six

Having learned and reenacted four folktales that fit a clear pattern, the students were ready to create a group story based on that pattern. I wrote the questions on the board again, and this time I asked them to generate a new story by coming up with new answers. Working together, they created a new story. I told them the resulting story, modeling how to add details, create character voices, and interpret the story through movements. They acted it out—hilarious! Those who didn't want to "act" joined in by making sound effects or becoming the "light" (it's a very unchallenging role!).

Step Seven

Now that they had experienced using the pattern to make up a story, I pointed out that they could do this themselves and asked them if they wanted to write their own stories. Yes, they did! I handed out sheets of paper, already divided into six equal parts to create the boxes for a storyboard. The questions were typed into the boxes (some of the boys could read these, and the remainders were helpful to the teaching assistant and teacher as well). Then, they were instructed to each create their own story by drawing the characters, setting, and details in the boxes (see Table 3.4).

The teaching assistants and I circulated, offering encouragement and brainstorming ideas. It wasn't long before stories began to emerge—and then students began to pair up to tell their stories to each other! Finally, everyone had a storyboard (and a STORY!).

Table 3.4   Graphic Organizer for LIGHT!

What happened to the light?	Who knew?	Who went first and why did he fail?
Who went second and why did he fail?	Who went last?	How did he get the light into the sky?

Step Eight

Several boys were eager to tell their stories independently, with lots of character voices and action; others enlisted their friends to act out their stories with them or for them. *All* of them had a story to tell!

So much had been accomplished in these lessons! We addressed the Common Core State Standards for English/Language Arts (and/or the language arts standards implemented in any state or region), especially those applying to writing narrative; we addressed the 21st Century Skills of creativity, communication, collaboration, and critical thinking. We addressed most of the multiple intelligences, including verbal/linguistic, logical/mathematic, bodily/kinesthetic, visual/spatial, interpersonal, and intrapersonal; we engaged auditory, kinesthetic, and visual learning styles.

The boys were very proud of themselves. They had each succeeded in creating and telling a story. They were *storytellers*!

Resources

Austin, A. L. (1993). *The myths of the opossum: Pathways of Mesoamerican mythology*. Albuquerque, NM: University of New Mexico Press.

Bernhard, E., & Bernhard, D. (1993). *How snowshoe hare rescued the sun: A tale from the Arctic*. New York, NY: Holiday House.

Holt, D., & Mooney, B. (2001). *More tellable tales*. Little Rock, AR: August House.

MacDonald, M. R. (1991). *Look back and see: Twenty lively tales for gentle tellers*. New York, NY: H.W. Wilson Company.

Moroney, L., & Te Ata (1996). *Baby rattlesnake*. San Francisco, CA: Children's Book Press.

Can Every Student Tell a Story?
Making Storytelling Accessible for Everyone!

Darlene Neumann

Learning stories and performing them can be challenging for many students, but for students in special education classes, the challenges are much more profound. In this article, I would like to discuss how special needs students successfully and happily participated in the Sherwood Annual Storytelling Festival and actually chose to do research.

I began teaching storytelling skills when I became the library media specialist at Sherwood School in Highland Park, Illinois. Four years later, we held our first ever Annual Storytelling Festival in which every fourth and fifth grader told a story. For 13 years, our school held this Annual Storytelling Festival. Each festival began with a professional teller who gave concerts and a storytelling workshop for the storytelling clubs, from second through fifth graders. Our regular education students, special education students, deaf and hard of hearing students, and bilingual students each participated in telling a story.

The Storytelling Festival was an outgrowth of storytelling that began with a pioneer unit in which every fourth-grade student told a story from the back of a "Conestoga wagon" in a back hallway to younger students. The following year, the students wanted to tell again, and they told stories outdoors under trees. When the principal asked if I would like to do a storytelling festival the following year, I was overwhelmed with excitement! The kids' rallying cry became "Let the festival begin!"

When our school district added 30 minutes to each day to provide more time for reading instruction, the librarian part of me was thrilled. The teacher part of me offered help for classrooms that wanted me to take a group of children who would be interested in an in-depth experience with literature. While I had been expecting a group that would delve deeper into mysteries or science fiction or high fantasy, the group that was assigned to me was a group of nine special education students from the fourth grade. I had known all of these students since they were in kindergarten, and I knew that I would need to come up with something new and different to make good use of the time we had been given while holding their interest and strengthening their reading skills. The teachers knew that I did not want to use the reading series or preprogrammed lessons, so the students and I were free to decide what we would like to do.

For purposes of this article, all names of students receiving special education services have been changed to respect students' privacy.

Group Storytelling with a Research Component

Coyote and Skunk Woman

A Navajo Story of the Trickster Coyote Who Meets His Match in Skunk Woman

As Coyote was walking in an arroyo, he called for rain to cool him and carry him to many prairie dogs. He asked Skunk Woman to tell the other animals that he was dead. She told Rabbit who told Porcupine who told the prairie dogs. They all went down to the river to see that dead coyote. After Skunk

Woman sprayed into their eyes, she and Coyote killed all the other animals. They built a fire, setting the prairie dogs to roast. Coyote suggested they race while they waited. Skunk Woman hid while Coyote ran by. She ate the prairie dogs, stuck their tails upright in the fire, and hid in her hole. When Coyote returned, he decided to eat the prairie dogs before Skunk Woman arrived. He pulled tail after tail out of the fire and went to find Skunk Woman, demanding that she share the prairie dogs. She told him his part was in the fire, but that he could have the bones, as well. Coyote had to be content with the tails and bones.

The fourth-grade social studies curriculum included an extensive unit on regions of the United States. Novels set in specific regions were integrated into the unit: *Holes* (Louis Sachar, Farrar, Straus and Giroux, 1998) or *Lost in the Devil's Desert* (Gloria Skurzynski, Lothrop, Lee & Shepard, 1982) were the choices. When I was invited to take the group of fourth graders, I decided to offer an alternative to the novels. I knew neither would be appropriate for my group of concrete, literal thinkers who were reading at the second-grade level. The challenge would be to find reading material to support the curriculum with differentiated content, while connecting with what the rest of the class was reading.

The group of nine children brainstormed what they "knew" about the desert. The challenge would be to reexamine their "facts" and to locate stimulating material at their reading level to increase background knowledge. I felt that nothing could be more interesting, entertaining, and instructional than Coyote stories. We discussed how the Navajo people, during long winter nights, used stories to teach clan history and to teach children right from wrong.

I handed out *Navajo Coyote Tales*. "Coyote and Skunk Woman" became their favorite. Although I had not suggested storytelling, the group decided they would like to tell this story for all the fourth graders. The copy of the tales that I used contains six stories, which are written on a first- to second-grade level. An updated version of this book is available.

Because this unit required a research component for regular education students, and knowing members of my group had been "reluctant researchers" since they were second graders, it was essential that they felt any research was their idea. They needed to practice the same research skills their peers were learning.

In a very conversational tone, I asked, "Do you guys know what an arroyo is? I'm not really sure what that is." They decided an arroyo must be something important and maybe they should look it up. Our school library yielded books containing descriptions and photos of arroyos. The group realized that if *they* didn't know what an arroyo was, their audience probably wouldn't either, so they decided to make a poster showing an arroyo. Their finished poster showed exactly what an arroyo is and explained why Coyote needed to be careful in the sudden rainfall.

The students began asking questions about characters. Why was the skunk called a spotted skunk? Didn't all skunks have stripes, like the ones that live in Illinois? Or did the Native Americans just have a different name for the skunk, or did they make it up? So they looked up the spotted skunk and were thrilled with what they found! Maybe the audience would need another poster to see what the spotted skunk really was and what it could do! They decided that Skunk Woman was a really neat character and wanted to find some more coyote stories with Skunk Woman in them.

The group realized that the other fourth graders might not know what a coyote or a porcupine really looked like. Did wild coyotes living in the desert look like the ones that roamed our suburbs? Was the rabbit like the ones that live in our backyards? Research began in books that were quite readable and then on websites written at a much higher level. As curiosity and enthusiasm grew, so did the level of understanding.

Because each student had told a story at our Storytelling Festival earlier in the school year, each of them knew they could tell a story because they had already done it. The hardest parts of telling this Coyote story had already been done because the story had been chosen, read, and reread, and research had strengthened understanding. Students divided the story into segments focusing on characters, and one lucky girl chose the Skunk Woman part.

Rereading increased fluency and boosted confidence. After considerable practice sessions, students were ready to tell the story and to share information while using their posters. They had become so excited about their research that some of their favorite facts made their way into the telling of the Coyote story. While local striped skunks just raise their tails, spray, and run, a spotted skunk stands on her front paws and aims her spray directly at her prey's eyes, so that's what Skunk Woman did!

Students invited parents, the principal, special area teachers, special education staff, fourth-grade peers, and second-grade reading buddies. After a confident group telling of the Coyote story, colorful posters filled with information about arroyos, coyotes, the spotted skunk, the jackrabbit, porcupines, and prairie dogs were shared with the audience.

Classroom teachers said that if they hadn't known these children required differentiated curriculum and accommodations, they would never have guessed from the storytelling and their well-researched posters. Parents said they couldn't believe their children had so much fun reading. A mother told me that her daughter had said, "The kids who teased me were wrong: I really can read, and I'm a great storyteller!"

Storytelling with Deaf and Hard of Hearing Students

At Sherwood, some of our students were in a regional program for deaf and hard of hearing students, and they came from a number of suburban cities and school districts. Most began coming to school at age three. It was a very long day for our little three-year-olds, but they became accustomed to school and enjoyed being able to learn communication skills.

The younger hard of hearing and deaf students came to the library weekly, as they said, to watch stories. With the help of the teachers, I redid my fingerplays using Signed English. While most of the parents used American Sign Language (ASL) at home, the program used Signed English. Older students taught me to sign a few fingerplays in ASL. The students loved folktales, especially ones with a great amount of exaggeration, which became even more exaggerated in their signs, followed by raucous laughter.

The year when Peter Cook, a well-known storyteller who is deaf, came to join the fun at our Annual Storytelling Festival, all of our students were excited, but our young deaf and hard of hearing students were especially mesmerized. At the festival, they performed a group story of "The Really, Really Big Enormous Carrot," their own interpretation of "The Great Big Enormous Turnip." One child signed the story, while a teacher did a voice interpretation for the hearing audience, as the whole group of hard of hearing and deaf students from age three to fifth graders acted out the story.

After the group performance, Shane, a first-grade student, signed a story while his teacher did a voice interpretation. Peter Cook was so thrilled with this performance that this professional storyteller did an almost unbelievable thing a few months later. At the Illinois Storytelling Festival in Spring Grove, Illinois, Peter was so excited to see Shane that he invited the boy up onto the stage and asked if Shane would tell his story to the Festival audience. While his mother did the voice interpretation, Shane signed his story, with great facial expressions and fluid signing. His mother made sure she was standing where Shane could not see her face, because her son was such a good lip reader that she was afraid he might stop and correct what she was saying if she changed any words.

Both Peter Cook and Shane beamed as the audience rose to their feet to thank the little storyteller.

One Special Education Student Tells His Story

The Little Rascal

Retold by Sherry Norfolk

Based on "The Rascal" in *African Tales of Magic and Mystery*, retold by Maria Kosova and Vladislav Stanovsky

Once upon a time there was a boy who loved to make trouble. Everyone called him "The Little Rascal," and they said that he was up to no good. They were right!

One day, the Little Rascal was rowing his boat on the river when he saw a dog lying at the river's edge. He rowed nearer, grabbed the dog, and rowed out to the middle of the river, planning to drown the poor animal. But when he leaned over to drop the dog into the water, it was the Little Rascal who fell into the water!

The Little Rascal yelled for help—he couldn't swim!—and he was just about to go under when the dog jumped in, grabbed the boy's shirt in his teeth, and swam with him back to the riverbank.

"You saved my life!" cried the Little Rascal. He learned a lesson that day: Repay evil with good.

Quinten was a child who had difficulty remembering sequences, and his sentence structures made sense only to him. He was one of my best story listeners and was eager to learn a story for the festival. Assuming it would be easy to work on and to learn, he wanted a very short story. He chose the story "The Rascal," after learning a rascal often played tricks on people. Quinten saw himself as one who liked to play tricks on others.

I read the story to him a number of times. I thought he would be upset at the idea of intentionally drowning a dog, but he had heard others talking about the story, and this didn't bother him. After all, no one he knew would do such a thing.

Next would come the process of breaking the story down into ideas. Normally, I would have students break down their stories into bare bones so that they could learn the structure of their stories. Consulting with the special education team confirmed what I had suspected, that Quinten would be unable to conceptualize what I meant by picking out the bare bones of the story. As I sat with him, we broke it down into ideas together. The first two sentences or "bones" were done by Quinten.

The boy liked to play tricks on people.
One day he thought he would try to drown a dog.
The dog was old and the boy decided he would be doing the dog a favor.
He put the dog into a boat and rowed out into the middle of a river.
The boy leaned over too far and fell into the river.
The boy yelled, "Help, help, I'm drowning!"
The dog jumped out of the boat.
The dog grabbed the boy's coat with his teeth.
The dog dragged him to the bank of the river.
The dog had saved the boy's life.
That's how it should be. Pay back evil with good.

Quinten drew pictures in a blank book to make a type of storyboard. He read the pictures to younger students and to as many teachers as he could find. He read the story at home and on his bus.

We told the story together with his storyboard. I would tell the story, leading up to the part of the boy falling into the river, and Quinten would tell about the boy drowning. I would let him go as far as he could and finish the story.

Finally Quinten was ready to tell the story to a small group, using the technique of my telling part, letting him chime in, and then I finished. At this point, he no longer needed to rely on the storyboard.

As the festival approached, Quinten was telling more and more of the story. The last day of the festival came. When it was Quinten's turn to tell, he decided that he wanted to tell the whole story himself. I couldn't talk him out of the decision, but I thought about how I might help him if he got stuck. Giving him a phrase wouldn't help because I had already tried that in practice.

I introduced him, and Quinten began to tell his story. He told his audience that his story was about a boy who played tricks. And then Quinten froze. He had felt so good about his story, but he was stuck on the first idea, and there was no going on. I didn't want him to fall apart and cry and lose control in front of his parents and the rest of the audience, and I knew I had to act fast.

I apologize in advance to those of you who know that there probably is no village in any country in Africa that tells stories in this manner, but since the story came from Africa, I did some emergency thinking. I had been sitting very close to Quinten, so I complimented him on the beginning of his story and explained to the audience that Quinten and I were going to teach them a different way of telling a story.

"There is a village in the continent of Africa," I told them, "where a master storyteller and the villagers tell a story together. Everyone in the village knows the story, and they all help the storyteller tell the story by asking questions. They all know what the storyteller will say, but the fun is in asking the questions. Since Quinten and I are the only ones who know the story, I'll be a villager and I'll ask all the questions this time. Another time some of you can ask the questions."

I began, "Oh, Master Storyteller, what story will you be sharing with us today?"

"I will be telling the story of the boy who played tricks and his name is Rascal," Quinten replied.

I continued, "Oh, Master Storyteller, what has Rascal decided to do today?"

This was Quinten's reply. "He wants to drown a dog. I don't know why. It isn't funny."

"Oh, Master Storyteller, what does Rascal do first?"

"He gets a boat. He puts the dog in it."

And so the story continued. At the end of the story, a smiling Quinten announced, "That's the best I ever told that story!" and the audience clapped long and hard. It was difficult to say who clapped the most—his parents, his classmates, his special education teachers, or maybe his librarian—but it was easy to find his mother after this set of stories. She was the one sobbing in the hallway.

Can every student tell a story? Yes! Yes, they can—with dignity, grace, a little bit of help, and the opportunity.

Resources

Note: The Coyote portion of the article was reprinted with the kind permission of Libraries Unlimited. This is an updated version of the article that first appeared in *The Storytelling Classroom: Applications across the Curriculum* by Sherry Norfolk, Jane Stenson, and Diane Williams. Westport, CT: Libraries Unlimited, 2006.

Hamilton, M., & Weiss, M. (2005). *Children tell stories: Teaching and using storytelling in the classroom* (2nd ed.). (Multimedia DVD included in the book.) Katonah, NY: Richard C. Owens.

Kosova, M., & Stanovsky, V. (1970). *African tales of magic and mystery.* London, England: Hamlyn.

Norfolk, S., Stenson, J., & Williams, D. (2009). *Literacy development in the storytelling classroom.* Santa Barbara, CA: Libraries Unlimited.

Thompson, H., & Morgan, W. (2007). *Navajo coyote tales.* Kaysville, UT: Gibbs-Smith.

Tolstoy, A. (1968). *The great big enormous turnip.* London, England: Heineman Young Books.

The Wide Mouthed Frog: Understanding Setting in Story

Sherry Norfolk

It was the first day of a mini-residency, during which I would spend three 55-minute sessions in the upper elementary self-contained classroom. The students varied in ages from 8 to 12 and represented a variety of disabilities: visual impairment, autism spectrum, ADD and ADHD, behavioral and emotional disorders, speech and language disorders, and developmental delays, to name a few.

During preplanning, I had consulted with the teacher about what issues/topics/standards she would like for me to address. The residency had been contracted and scheduled by an administrator; this teacher was not enthusiastic. She said that I could do anything I wanted, because it wouldn't make any difference—the disabilities and age range were so varied that there was no one approach to learning that could possibly work for everyone.

While it's true that the diversity within a special needs classroom absolutely demands differentiation, not *every* approach requires it every time. In this case, storytelling provided a means of reaching and teaching *all* of the students, with very little differentiation required.

Finally, "They don't understand setting," she said. "You could try to teach them about setting."

Hurray—a specific goal!

"I'm on it!"

I made some very, very, *very* simple "scenery" for my version of "The Wide Mouthed Frog." In this story, the overall setting is the swamp, but within the swamp, the characters are in subsettings: in a pond, in a tree, in the tall grass, in the river. My "scenery" was simply 8 × 11 representations of these settings, rendered quickly in construction paper (see Figures 3.1, 3.2, 3.3, and 3.4). I taped these around the room and then introduced the story.

"I'm going to tell you a story about a frog—a very special frog—called the Wide Mouthed Frog!" I said the name of the frog with a very wide-open mouth, of course. "Show me a big, wide mouth!"

All of the kids made huge, gaping mouths.

"Now show me a teeny, tiny mouth," I said, demonstrating tightly pursed lips.

They complied.

"Wide ... teeny, tiny ... wide ... teeny, tiny ... okay!" This silly little exercise helps establish the vocabulary, which will be essential to understanding the trick at the end of the story.

"So, who is the main character of this story going to be?" I asked.

They all answered, "Wide Mouthed Frog!" with very big mouths.

"Right! The Wide Mouthed Frog is the main character."

"And where do you think that the Wide Mouthed Frog lived? What do you predict will be the setting of the story?"

"*Outside!*" they chorused.

"Right, it will be outside, but *where* outside? In your backyard? In the ocean? On the playground?"

They offered water, pond, and river. I accepted all of those answers and then explained, "Yes, frogs live in water—like in ponds and rivers. And *this* frog lived in a *swamp*." We talked about swamps a bit.

"Okay, now we know the main character and the setting—let's find out what the Wide Mouthed Frog's problem is going to be!"

Then I told the story while physically moving from subsetting to subsetting as the story progressed.

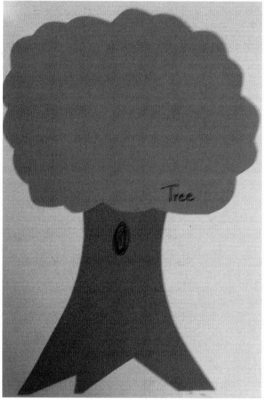

Figure 3.2   Tree

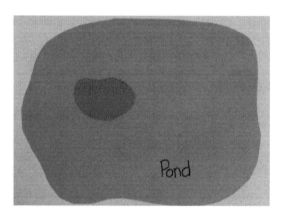

Figure 3.1   Pond

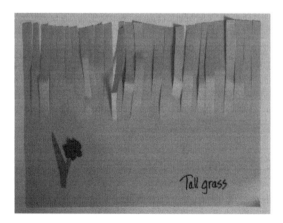

Figure 3.3   Tall Grass

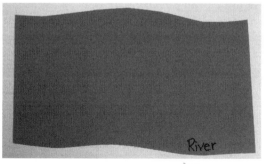

Figure 3.4   River

The Wide Mouthed Frog

Retold by Sherry Norfolk

Once upon a time, there was a Wide Mouthed Frog. Every day, he went hopping off through the swamp—boing, boing, boing—and every day he ate flies. Blah.

One day, he said, "I am a Wide Mouthed Frog. I don't want to eat flies—blah!"

But he couldn't think of anything else to eat, because that is all he'd ever eaten in his entire life. So he decided to go talk to his mama, because mamas know everything.

Off he went—boing, boing, boing—until he came to his mama, sitting on a lily pad in the pond.

He said, "I am a Wide Mouthed Frog. I don't want to eat flies—blah!"

"Well!" said his mama, "I am a Wide Mouthed Frog, too, and I eat flies. If they're good enough for me, they should be good enough for you. You had better go talk to Owl. Owl will tell you what to do."

So the Wide Mouthed Frog thanked his mama and went hopping off through the swamp—boing, boing, boing—until he came to Owl, who was asleep up in a tree.

"I am a Wide Mouthed Frog. I don't want to eat flies—blah!" he said.

Owl woke up.

"Hooooooo. I am a Great Horned Owl," he said, "and I eat fuzzy brown mice. Would you like a fuzzy brown mouse to eat?" He held a mouse out by the tail.

Frog sniffed. "BLAH!"

"Well, if you don't want to eat a mouse, you'd better go talk to Deer. Deer will tell you what to do."

So the Wide Mouthed Frog thanked the owl and went hopping off through the swamp—boing, boing, boing—until he came to the Deer.

Now the deer was a shy, timid creature, who was always hiding in the tall, tall grass. But Frog didn't care about that. He hopped right up behind the deer and said, "I am a Wide Mouthed Frog. I don't want to eat flies—blah!"

"AAAAAAH!" Deer screamed and jumped. "I can't believe you did that, sneaking up behind me and scaring me like that! Whew! Well, I am a Whitetail Deer, and I eat bark and grass and pretty flowers. Do you want a pretty flower to eat?" He held out a pretty flower to Frog.

Frog sniffed. "BLAH!"

"Well, if you don't want to eat a flower, you'd better go talk to Snake. Snake will tell you what to do."

So the Wide Mouthed Frog thanked the deer and went hopping off through the swamp—boing, boing, boing—until he came to the Snake.

"I am a Wide Mouthed Frog. I don't want to eat flies—blah!"

"I am a cottonmouth ssssssssnake," replied Snake, "and I eat rotten eggsssssssss. Would you like a niccccccce rotten egg to eat?" Snake pointed to an egg with his tail.

Frog sniffed. "BLAH!"

"Well, if you don't want to eat an egg, you'd better go talk to Alligator. Alligator will tell you what to do."

So the Wide Mouthed Frog thanked the snake and went hopping off through the swamp—boing, boing, boing—until he came to the edge of the river, where Alligator lived.

He called out, "I am a Wide Mouthed Frog. I don't want to eat flies—blah!"

He waited ... and he waited ... then some lumps and bumps appeared ... and two great big eyes ... and a great ... BIG ... **MOUTH**.

> "I AM THE KING BULL ALLIGATOR—AND I EAT **WIDE MOUTHED FROGS**!"
> The Wide Mouthed Frog gulped! Then he squeezed his lips into a teeny tiny knot.
> "Uh . . . I'm a Little Mouthed Frog! And I eat FLIES—buh-bye!"
> Then he went hopping off through the swamp—boing, boing, boing, boing, boing—and he ate *flies*.
> Buh-bye!

"What was the Wide Mouthed Frog's problem?"
"*He didn't want to eat flies! Blah!*" they yelled without hesitation.
"Right. And who did he go to for help?"
We reviewed the story, as I wrote the following outline:

MAIN CHARACTER—Wide Mouthed Frog
SETTING—Swamp
PROBLEM—He didn't want to eat flies—blah!
ATTEMPTS TO SOLVE PROBLEM—
    Mama Frog—flies
    Owl—mice
    Deer—bark, grass, flowers
    Snake—rotten eggs
    Alligator—Wide Mouth Frogs

"Now the Wide Mouthed Frog has a new problem—he has to get away from the alligator! How does he get away?"
The kids all made teeny tiny mouths or yelled "Boing, boing, boing!"
"Right—but how did that help him get away?"
As happens in general classrooms, some kids understood the trick, while others didn't. The ones who understood explained to the ones who didn't: peer teaching.
"And how did the story end?"
"*He ate flies!* Boing, boing, boing!" the class shouted.
The outline was complete.

MAIN CHARACTER—Wide Mouthed Frog
SETTING—Swamp
PROBLEM—He didn't want to eat flies—blah!
ATTEMPTS TO SOLVE PROBLEM—
    Mama Frog—flies
    Owl—mice
    Deer—bark, grass, flowers
    Snake—rotten eggs
    Alligator—Wide Mouth Frogs
    "I'm a little-mouth frog!"
PROBLEM SOLVED / END—he ate FLIES

As we reviewed the sequence, I again physically moved from subsetting to subsetting. "Who did Mama Frog send him to? *Where* did Owl live—what was the *setting*?" The "scenery" served as visual references, helping students recall sequences, characters, and settings.

Reviewing the story reinforced understanding of sequence, characters, settings, problem, and resolution of the story. The linguistic/print chart would serve as a reference for some students—but we had a few students who couldn't read, so we reviewed the story one more time as I added some quick, simple drawings to the information on the board.

We now had a print/image sequential chart to consult as we dramatized the story (the student with visual impairment was equipped with a camera that provided a magnified image at her desk). Time for *action!*

"Let's act out the story! I need someone to be the Wide Mouthed Frog!"

"Alright, where does the Wide Mouthed Frog live? What is the *setting* of the story?"

The class as a whole tended to answer, which was fine—it supported everyone's understanding. When everyone agreed that the Wide Mouthed Frog lived in the swamp, he or she was asked to stand in the appropriate *setting*.

"Who did the Wide Mouthed Frog go to for help first?"

"Mama Frog!"

"Right, we need a Mama or Daddy Frog. Now, where does he or she live?" The kids recalled that Mama lived on a lily pad in the pond, so the actor went to crouch in front of the "scenery."

Once all characters were in their appropriate settings, the group acted out the story, with the Wide Mouthed Frog hopping from place to place.

The kids begged to do it again, so we reassigned the roles and did it again.

Then I explained that we could use the pattern of this story to make up a whole new story. We would first have to decide on a new setting.

"Should our new story be in the forest, in the desert, in a haunted house . . .?" Providing some ideas helps the students recall exactly what "setting" means and gives them some ideas for directions to go.

"*Ocean!*" was the loud consensus. Let me mention here that "ocean" would not have been my choice, and it certainly wasn't one of the options I suggested. Developing the appropriate subsettings was going to be a real challenge, but we forged ahead.

I began a new chart. Once we knew the setting, we could choose characters appropriate to that setting. I reminded them of the pattern: the first character is a small animal that could (but wouldn't) be eaten by the last character. The second character should be a relative of the first character and so on. This is the outline that emerged:

> MAIN CHARACTER—*Clown Fish*
> SETTING—*Ocean*
> PROBLEM—*Clown fish didn't want to eat leftovers (I did some very quick Googling!)*
> ATTEMPTS TO SOLVE PROBLEM—
>   *Daddy Clown fish—leftovers*
>   *Mermaid—cookies*
>   *Pirate—pizza*
>   *Whale—krill*
>   *Shark—Clown fish*
>   *He puffed up his cheeks and said, "I'm not a clown fish—I'm a pufferfish!"*
> PROBLEM SOLVED / END—*he ate leftovers*

Okay, this was not a scientifically accurate story (although this is a great way to learn about habitats—see later). That was not the point. Moving on . . .

Once we had determined our overall setting, characters, problem, and solution, I posed a new question: Where do these characters live?

"Ocean!"

"Right, but let's think about the Wide Mouthed Frog. The story was in the swamp, but each character lived in a different part of the swamp—they lived in different settings. Just like all of you live in Knoxville, but you don't all live in the same house, right?"

Giggles and vigorous head shaking.

"So, if we told a story about all of you, the setting would be Knoxville, but each of you would have your own setting, too—the house where you live."

Ah-ha! They all smiled.

"Alright, the characters in our story all live in the ocean, but in different homes in the ocean. Where do clown fish live?"

Most of them had seen *Finding Nemo* and remembered something about coral reefs. They agreed unanimously that the mermaid lived in a sandcastle and that the pirate lived in a ship. We decided that the whale lived in a big underwater cave and the shark in open water.

"Excellent! Now remember, I had some scenery that I made with construction paper so that we could act out the story." I pointed out the scenery, reviewing the settings. "We're going to act out this story, so you're going to make the scenery for us."

Huge grins all around indicated that this was a really good idea. We divided into teams of two or three, and after each team chose the colors of construction paper they would need, they got to work designing, cutting, pasting, and drawing.

Once the scenery was complete, I asked them to help me decide where the scenery for each setting should be placed around the room. This not only reinforced the idea of setting and helped the spatial learners process the story but also reviewed the sequence of the story. I taped the scenery in place.

Then I told them the story they had created, complete with character voices, sound effects, and movement from setting to setting. The modeling prepared the kids for acting out the story, suggesting body language, tone of voice, phrasing, and so on.

Soon, we were acting out the new story—with much more fluency than the original one! The class *owned* this story and understood its structure more deeply than the original.

After dramatizing the new story several times, we reviewed the concept of Setting.

"What was the setting of our story?"

"*Ocean!*"

"What was the setting of the Whale's part of the story?"

"*Cave!*"

"If we wrote a story about having lunch at school, what would the setting be?"

"*Cafeteria!*"

Yes! By developing their own story; thinking about, conceptualizing and creating their own scenery; physically and visibly moving from setting to setting; and narrating that movement, students were able to comprehend the concept more fully.

The Wide Mouthed Frog had served a wider purpose!

Expanding the Impact

The lesson described previously was carefully focused on learning about setting and addressed not only setting but also a variety of standards in Listening, Writing, and Speaking—not least of all, collaboration. As noted, the resulting story was not scientifically accurate, but that can be changed!

After moving through the lesson plan earlier, use online or nonfiction picturebook resources to help the group research and develop a new, fact-based story. Choose a habitat and guide them in discovering what animals live there, what those animals eat, and where they live within that habitat. Help them understand that they can get lots of information from pictures as well as print. Use the resulting information to develop a new, research-based story! By embedding the information into a story that they create and dramatize, the information is made more relevant and retained longer because it is stored in multiple modalities.

Adaptations and Modifications

Pair a nonverbal kid with a verbal one. Both members of the pair will act out their parts, and everyone is more comfortable.

Accessible Aesop: Fables for the Best in Us

(Skill Levels: Grades Two through Five)

Lyn Ford

In order to communicate effectively through speaking, children must exhibit fluency, clarity, and an awareness of audience. Such verbal communication skills are learned through practice and observation of an effective speaker, such as the teacher.
—Yellen, D., Blake, M. E. & DeVries., B. A. (2004).
Integrating the language arts (3rd ed.). Scottsdale, AZ:
Holcomb Hathaway Publishers

Fables are short stories that often use animals as their main characters and shared to convey or teach a lesson.

Fables are an excellent tool for teaching or reinforcing lessons in critical and creative thinking and social behaviors. They are usually short and easily adaptable. The language is simple and, generally, easy to understand. Fables also provide opportunities to share narrative in dramatic storytelling format that models simple sentence structures and the basic elements of story: beginning, middle, end, protagonist, antagonist, problem, and solution.

Fables can become digital stories, illustrated posters, small books, free verse, songs, dances, and readers' theater—the possibilities are limited only by the time and space restrictions of one's location.

Aesop (pronounced *EE-sop*) is believed to have been a fabulist, a writer or teller of fables. He is said to have lived from around 620 BC to 564 BC and is credited with many stories that have become a part of the storytelling tradition, known around the world as *Aesop's Fables*, but whether he really lived is uncertain. If he did exist, it's possible that Aesop's stories are rooted in tales that began in Egypt or Ethiopia. Some of these well-known fables include the following:

- *The Ant and the Grasshopper*
- *The Cat and the Mice*
- *The Crow and the Pitcher*
- *The Dog and Its Reflection*
- *The Dove and the Ant*
- *The Fox and the Crow*
- *The Fox and the Grapes*
- *The Lion and the Mouse*
- *The Tortoise and the Hare*
- *Town Mouse and Country Mouse*

Note: In their earliest versions, fables were shared with no moral specifically stated. This provided an opportunity for listeners to develop their own concepts of the truths and lessons in the stories.

I have included the morals of the stories for educators' and storytellers' convenience. However, when I share fables, I ask students to tell me what each story teaches. I then write all their answers where they can be easily seen. We discuss all the proposed lessons. There are no wrong answers, only diverse opinions. This is a good exercise in critical thinking and thinking for oneself.

Most educators, storytellers, and students know *The Tortoise and the Hare*. Lesson plans for that fable are readily available on the Internet. Rather than share something that is already greatly in use, here are three fable contemporary variants, with accessibility adaptations.

The Hound and the Hare

A hound dog saw a hare on the hill. The hound ran toward the hare, who began to run away. But the hound said, "Don't run, little friend. I only want to play with you." So, the hare agreed to play and be the hound's friend.

The hound chased the hare. Sometimes the hound caught the hare and hugged it. But sometimes the hound caught the hare and growled and bit its tail or ears.

Finally, the hare stopped playing, and said, "I wish you would make up your mind, hound. Are you my friend, or are you my enemy? If you are a real friend, you will not bite me. If you are my enemy, you will not hug me. Which one are you? You can't be both."

(MORAL: Someone who can't be trusted to always treat you with friendship should not be called your friend.)

Questions for Research and Reflection (Overarching Social Studies and Biological Science)

- What is "friendship"? Give examples of friendship.
- Are hounds and hares usually "friendly" toward one another? Why?
- Do you think that different types of animals can become friends? Explain your answer.
- Do you think that different types of people can become friends? Explain your answer.
- Do some people do the same thing that the hound did? Give an example.
- What choice should you make when someone says he or she is your friend but treats you as an enemy? Talk about the possible choices.
- With a change of behaviors and different words, how might this story end?

To reinforce the action in this story, use gestures for each active verb. Examples: In the first sentence, the hound dog sees the hare. (Eyes looking this way and that. For those who can, hands up as ears as the student looks around. To include all students, including those students who do not see, include the sound of the dog's sniffing nose as he looks around and finds the hare. The dog's whimpering and quick barks add more to the characterization. The most important action is the hound "looking.") The hound runs and the hare runs. (Patting thighs with a rhythmic gesture for the hound can be contrasted with quicker pats for the hare. If this is too much action, the hound can bark and pant as he runs, and the hare can hold up his ears [hands on top of head and pointing upward]. Or the body can sway for the running hound and jerk up and down for the quicker running of the hare.)

As students become better acquainted with the story's actions, let them choose actions for seeing, running, stopping, asking questions, and so on. The story can also become a "partner play," with students in pairs, one becoming the hound dog and the other becoming the hare.

The Lion and the Mouse

Once, little Mouse, thinking he was on a hill, ran up and down the body of sleeping Lion. Of course, Lion woke up. Lion set his big paw on Mouse; then Lion growled, and opened his jaws to swallow the little creature.

"Oh, I am so sorry, great Lion," cried tiny Mouse. "Please, forgive me for bothering you this time and let me go. I promise that I will never do it again, and I will never forget your kindness. And one day, I will do a good deed for you!"

Lion was tickled at the idea of Mouse thinking he could help someone so large. Laughing, Lion lifted his paw and let the Mouse go. Lion thought the Mouse was a silly little thing.

But, not long after that, Lion was caught in a hunter's trap and found himself tied to a tree. Lion roared and roared, while the hunters went to get their wagon and carry Lion back home with them.

Mouse heard Lion's roar. Mouse scurried to the tree where Lion was tied up. Seeing that sad Lion was trapped, Mouse chewed and chewed at the ropes until he had gnawed them into threads and set Lion free.

Mouse said, "Lion, you laughed when I said I would do a good deed for you. Now you see that a little mouse can help a big lion."

(MORAL: A small kindness is never wasted.)

Questions for Research and Reflection (Overarching Social Studies and Biological Science)

- Why did Lion wake up?
- How do you think Lion felt when Mouse awakened him? How do you feel when someone wakes you up and you are not ready to get up yet?
- How do you know this story is fiction (made up; make-believe)?
- What do you think a real Lion would do if he caught a real mouse?
- What do you think the word "gnawed" means?
- What do you think a small kindness is?
- What small kindness can you do for others?

This is a good story for reinforcing the important ability to be still—Lion must be as motionless and quiet as a hill! For students who cannot move, this is a perfect opportunity to take the lead as the sleeping Lion. If the student doesn't have any issues with being touched, the teacher or mentor can then use gently running fingers on the student's arm for the little mouse's running up and down the Lion's body. Students can also pretend to be sleeping Lion and run their fingers up and down their own arms for Mouse's actions.

This story also includes two very distinct voices. For students who do not easily use language, the growl of Lion and the squeak of Mouse can be included whenever the corresponding character is about to speak. Students can also practice talking like each character, moving Lion's big paw, nibbling, and chewing like Mouse; let students decide on other actions.

The Ant and the Chrysalis

An ant enjoyed the sunshine as he crawled in search of food. The ant saw a chrysalis hanging from a low branch on a leafy bush; the chrysalis slowly moved its tail and squirmed a little, for it was about to change.

The ant had never seen this thing. He spoke to it: "Poor, pitiful thing! You are so ugly, and you can hardly move. While I can creep, and run, and climb the tallest trees, you just lie there, wriggling in your shell. How sad you must be!"

The chrysalis said nothing, so the ant crawled away. But a few days later, the ant crawled past the same leafy bush. On the low branch, the ant saw a broken shell. But where was the wriggly thing that had been inside it?

Suddenly the ant realized that something was hovering over him. Looking up, the ant saw a beautiful butterfly fluttering its brightly colored wings.

The ant asked, "Who are you?" The butterfly replied, "I am that thing you called poor and pitiful, the one you thought could hardly move. Run, ant, creep and run and climb. And as you do, know that *I* can fly!"

The butterfly flew higher than any tree in the forest, so high and far that the ant couldn't see it anymore.

(MORAL: Do not judge someone for the way he or she looks. Appearances can be deceiving.)

Questions for Research and Reflection (Overarching Biological Science and Social Studies)

- What are the stages of development of a butterfly?
- Does the ant go through different stages of development?
- Do people do the same thing that the ant did? Give an example.
- Talk about the way the ant treated the chrysalis. With a change of behaviors and different words, how might this story end?

We do all the movements of the chrysalis-to-butterfly metamorphosis and introduce the word "pupa" as another name meaning "chrysalis." Of course, the chrysalis initially is silent and motionless, which gives all students an opportunity to share in the "stage of being still." Then, gentle and still-silent wiggles and squirms are added; some students can do these actions while on the floor, while others simply move fingers or one finger. The butterfly's wing motions are a slow and sweeping movement of arms when possible, or a fluttering of fingers, or the American Sign Language gesture for "butterfly" (two flat hands crossed in at the wrists in front of you, with palms facing the body. Hands bend twice at the large knuckles). Any student can become a tree in the forest, with the teacher or mentor or gentle students fluttering around him or her as the butterfly.

I usually act as the ant, a rude and unfriendly character. In this way, all the students can be the quiet chrysalis and the butterfly that can fly.

Resources for Fables

Note: All fables adapted by Lyn Ford; permissions are granted for their use. For the Aesopic fables, go to http://www.aesopfables.com/aesopsel.html.

Aesop Fables.com. www.aesopfables.com/—656+ fables attributed to Aesop.
Karen Chace blogspot. karenchace.blogspot.com/—A wealth of stories and information from Karen Chace, the author of *Story by Story* (Parkhurst Brothers, 2014).
Read.gov. www.read.gov/aesop/001.html—The Library of Congress collection of Aesop's fables.

4

Storytelling Strategies for Children with Physical Disabilities

Introduction

Lyn Ford

Activist, author, and lecturer Helen Keller communicated when others thought she could not speak; she knew more of the world than many who could see. Keller said, "The marvelous richness of human experience would lose something of rewarding joy if there were no limitations to overcome. The hilltop hour would not be half so wonderful if there were no dark valleys to traverse."

Physical disabilities may limit a person's ability to easily function as they may impair everything from movement to sight; they may deter the ability to breathe, to hear, to speak, to rest, or to find the energy to perform, to sleep, to stay awake, and to let others know that one is truly aware and alive. But we should always remember a person is not a disability, and everyone deserves the opportunity to do more than just exist.

The gift of stories is an enrichment of life and a grand equalizer for all types of learners and all capabilities. Within the following articles, find ways to offer that gift.

Many of the articles in Chapter 5: Storytelling Strategies for Children with Multiple Disabilities and Chapter 6: Strategies for Inclusive Classrooms and General Audiences offer adaptations for those who have physical disabilities.

Storytelling with Children Who Are Deaf or Hard of Hearing

Erika Van Order and Geneva Foster-Shearburn

Storytelling makes language and reading come alive for children who are deaf or hard of hearing. How can we as storytellers and teachers ensure that they can access the language and appreciate the story? American Sign Language (ASL) storytellers, oral storytellers, oral and sign language interpreters, teachers, and parents must work collaboratively!

Walk into any early childhood and primary classroom for the deaf and you'll see teachers maintaining students' attention and involving them through various strategies during story learning and retelling experiences. Teachers and interpreters accentuate the story through changes in sign and vocal intonation, facial expressions, pantomime, props, drawings, and the use of book illustrations. Teachers match their students' language levels and explain new vocabulary or concepts. Students are involved though repeating lines, signs, sounds, or gestures. They also participate in hands-on activities to create the scene and characters.

Storytelling is rich with opportunities for language learning and social and emotional growth. For students who are deaf or hard of hearing to access, understand, and appreciate the story, many things must occur. Spoken-word storytelling is made accessible through sign language interpretation in the students' preferred modality, assistive listening devices, and explanations of setting, time period, and characters at the beginning of the storytelling experience.

The communication from the interpreting team and the storytellers may change depending on the developmental level of the student and type of story. Also, language levels vary; deaf-blind and low-vision audiences are growing; auditory and technology systems are ever changing; and a broad continuum of sign language modalities is utilized. Each venue and genre has its own demands, and each community has its distinct relationship; there is no single template that can address the needs of each setting and audience. However, there are specific items for consideration and adaptation.

Here are suggestions and tips from teachers and interpreters of the deaf for providing an accessible and successful storytelling experience.

Preparation and Planning

Start by conferencing as a team to discuss each other's expectations and roles. The goal is to work together to build a cohesive signed and/or spoken interpretation by analyzing scripts, assigning characters, and building team agreements to achieve a dynamic equivalence of the storyteller's performance. Whether the storyteller is a signer or nonsigner, it is critical to contact the teachers of and interpreter for the deaf several days before the performance, to provide them with the story/book/script. Teachers and interpreters will practice and preteach the basic storyline at the students' language developmental level. It might be taught utilizing real objects and props so that students can develop a mental "picture" or "movie" of the story before it is told.

Consider expectations for the audience. Will the children be asked to respond? What will they need to be able to say, sign, or do? Students can practice attending to the calls and also the expected responses.

The Storytelling Experience

Before beginning, make sure there is adequate lighting and space for both the storyteller and interpreter. Students will require preferential seating for both auditory and visual access. Assistive listening device microphones must be given to the storyteller or oral interpreter for optimal auditory access. Even if the storyteller has a "loud" voice, the assistive listening device brings that voice directly to the students' hearing devices and filters out most background noises. If two characters will be speaking, pausing during the turn-taking experience is important for the technology and the listener to process the information. There is often a slight delay in the transmission and processing with the various devices.

Sets, visual props, and illustrations can be explained to or experienced by students beforehand, especially if the set is an abstract representation. The interpreter can review the sign names for the characters and describe the setting and time period.

When everyone is in place, you are ready to roll!

Let the story unfurl! Good storytellers naturally use intonation, facial expressions, and body movements. The storyteller will want to enhance the experience with additional visual imagery through *pantomime*. Be mindful of difficult vocabulary and idiomatic phrases, and repeat it in another way immediately afterward. Example: His idea was a horse of another color. It was different indeed!

The storyteller should *check for understanding* and *monitor the engagement* of the audience by watching their expressions. *Eye gaze* to elicit participation and *hand gestures* to prompt responses are beneficial. If the storyteller plans to ask questions, he/she could provide a *variety of ways to respond* ("thumbs up if . . ., shake your head if you wouldn't . . ., nod your head if you would . . .") and participate through call and response or repeated lines students have practiced beforehand. *Visually prompting* the students on when and how to respond can be done with picture card, signs, gestures, and verbal reminders by the teller or a staff member.

Student Storytellers

As students master a story's concept and language, they can join in to retell. Primary students have also been successful in developing their own parallel stories from a previously learned story. Example: Instead of the "Three Little Pigs," students select new characters, like the "Three Little Antelopes." Later, they could change other components of the story and then retell it to an audience. Involving students in creating their own adaptations to a story builds confidence and ownership in their self-expression and communication skills.

Wordless books and comic strips are also good starting points for students to begin developing their storytelling skills. Also, show them deaf storytellers: The Texas School for the Deaf has developed an ASL Storytelling Library (https://texasdeafed.org/students/asl-storytelling-library), and PBS's *Between the Lions* has a cornerstone project with trade books that have interpreted into ASL and other sign language modalities and captioned (www.pbs.org/parents/mayaandmiguel/english/activities/aslsign.html).

Parents as Storytellers

Encouraging and teaching parents how to tell stories has been proven to increase hearing children's language and literacy development; it is even more critical for children who are deaf. Linda recalls her mother sitting down with her and telling her stories through children's books. It's critical that parents learn to "tell" the story and the pictures on the pages. If part of the story is not depicted in the pictures, it can be drawn or acted out for children who are just beginning to develop language.

If a storyteller is coming or a story is being practiced at school, teachers can send home a copy of the story/book/script for parents to read and sign to their child. Repetition of the language, hearing different voices, and seeing similar signs telling the story hasten the language-acquisition process. Sending videos of the teacher or paraprofessional signing and telling the story will help parents learn new signs and words to use with their children; students can also watch the videos to practice and gain a deeper understanding of the story. A shared reading experience is a natural way to enjoy and learn new language and vocabulary. It also deepens the parent-child bond and expands communication through a shared language experience.

Storytelling, teaching, and interpreting must be collaborative in nature in order to be successful. All team members must work together to provide the best learning experience for all students (see Tables 4.1 and 4.2).

Table 4.1   Preparation Checklist

Storyteller	Interpreter	Teacher of the Deaf
• provide the script, book, story, music to the teacher and interpreter • inform the team if any changes are made before the performance • notify the teacher of your expectations of the audience—that is, call and response items, repeated lines, and so on • if you have a video of the performance previously performed, share it with the team • inform the team if there will be a Q&A session (so a microphone for interpreter to voice for students who sign) • provide spelling and meaning for foreign language words/sayings	• review and practice the script • remind the team of positioning, space, lighting needs • share your expectations with the team • discuss the position (static or shadowing the storyteller)	• inform team of students' mode of communication, developmental levels, and if assistive devices are utilized • review the script • send the script home for parents • preteach vocabulary • practice attending to the "call" prompts • practice the responses • practice repeated lines that the audience is expected to participate in

Table 4.2   Performance Checklist

Storyteller	Interpreter	Teacher of the Deaf
• wear assistive listening device microphone (if utilized by students) • explain the setting, time period, and characters that will be encountered • watch the students' expressions, and use eye gaze to encourage participation • allow for various types of responses • be mindful of idiomatic phrases	• describe the characters and review the sign names that will be used for the characters • describe the setting if there are abstract depictions or time changes that will occur during the story • only fingerspell proper nouns • conceptualize all other words • be dramatic and exaggerate facial expressions to show different characters	• adequate lighting • adequate space for the storyteller and interpreter • provide microphone(s) • preferential seating for students

Advisors for This Section: Linda Whiggam, ASL storyteller and DHH paraprofessional; Terri Linhoff, preschool teacher of the deaf; and Chris Waldrop, preschool teacher of the deaf.

Additional Resources

Abarbanell, Alan. ASL interpreter, owner/producer of The ABABABA Road Tour. alan@abababatour.com

Bruce, Trix. ASL Storyteller, poet, actress. http://www.trixbruce.com/

Children hear better with FM: A starter guide for parents and teachers. Retrieved from http://www.phonak.com/content/dam/phonak/b2b/C_M_tools/FM/Children-Hear-Better-with-FM.pdf

The 15 principles for reading to deaf children—reading to deaf children; learning from deaf adults. Retrieved from http://www3.gallaudet.edu/clerc-center/info-to-go/literacy/literacy-it-all-connects/reading-to-students.html

Florida School for the Deaf and Blind. http://www.fsdb.k12.fl.us/

The March Wind: Interaction and Adaptation for Children with Physical Disabilities (Grades K through Four)

Lyn Ford

As a storytelling teaching artist, I have occasionally worked in classrooms with populations so culturally, intellectually, and physically diverse that all my story-sharing had to have the persistent source and continual fluidity and movement of an unobstructed river. The river's course relied on a deep spring of narrative material and remained aligned by standards that acted as riverbanks; stories joyfully flowed with rapids and ripples and curves of individual strengths and capabilities and unique situations that impacted its current.

Our classroom storytelling had to be like a river.

The standards were the guiding principles of Universal Design for Learning (UDL), as stated by D. H. Rose and A. Meyer:

1. Represent information in multiple formats and media.
2. Provide multiple pathways for students' actions and expressions.
3. Provide multiple ways to engage students' interests and motivation.

The rapids and ripples and curves were the different capabilities of the students with whom I worked and played. Sometimes I worked with inclusive groups of students at grade K through grade four developmental levels. Sometimes I worked with small groups of students in what were called the special education or student support or special needs classes (different school districts utilized different terms—I still try to respect the choices made within school districts and hope that parents, educators, all other mentors, and students have had the opportunity to weigh in on these choices).

We were usually in spaces that offered flexibility for room arrangements (one reason why it's important to contact teachers and visit a school before a residency)—larger classrooms, a part or all of gymnasiums, empty multipurpose rooms, and so on. The arts classroom in one school offered a space in which I could move tables and chairs and position students and their mentors in circles and horseshoe formations, rather than in rows, with the added advantage of the art teacher's involvement, support, and supplies.

In that arts classroom, we used a verse that lent itself to adaptations and arts extensions. It has become one of my favorite selections for inclusive interactive experiences:

The March Wind

I come to work as well as play;
I'll tell you what I do;
I whistle all the live-long day,
"Wooo—oo-oo-oo! Woo-oo!"

I toss the branches up and down
And shake them to and fro,
I whirl the leaves in flocks of brown,
And send them high and low.

I strew the twigs upon the ground,
The frozen earth I sweep;
I blow the children round and round
And wake the flowers from sleep.

—Anonymous

"The March Wind," as a teaching and storytelling tool, can enhance and increase students' awareness of:

- language and meaning;
- vocabulary and linguistic practice;
- self and others;
- body language and spatial relationships; and
- communal activity.

Before my presentation, I made myself aware of action verbs, onomatopoeic sounds, and descriptive words and phrases upon which we could focus. Examples: action verbs like work, play, tell, and whistle; onomatopoeic sounds like "Wooo—oo-oo-oo! Woo-oo!"; and descriptive words and phrases like "all the live-long day," "to and fro," and "flocks of brown."

I noted words that might need physical clarification through my own gestures and representations; additional "sidebar" explanations ("Does wind really sound like that? Give me *your* wind sounds." "Whirl. Spin. With your hands [or your body or your arms . . .], show me 'whirl.'" "Strew. If I throw papers all over the room, I strew them. I also get in trouble!"); searches through the dictionary or thesaurus; or the posting of definitions and synonyms as references and reminders. All this was dependent upon students' abilities.

I also prepped possibilities for sensory experiences. For example, to accompany or extend my initial narration of the verse, I could do the following:

- Bring in photographs of windy scenes to discuss after I had shared the poem for the first time.
- Carry a personal fan to make a "wind" for the students.
- As an arts project after one group's spoken-word experience, we made colorful paper-plate whirligigs that hung from strings; students could hold the string and make the whirligig spin by waving their hands or blowing as if they were the wind. These spun more easily than paper windmills or pinwheels. (For a simple whirligig tutorial, go to http://www.origami-resource-center.com/whirligig.html.)
- Use a series of photographs or illustrations for each stanza of the poem: Picture one showed a scene of wind blowing through trees; Picture two showed someone who was trying to walk, coat flapping and hair flying, against a blustering wind; Picture three showed trees with bare branches; Picture four showed autumn leaves blowing in the wind; Picture five was a close-up of twigs coated with frost; and Picture six was a close-up of flower buds in early spring (I found all of these images through several Internet searches, in the pre-Google and pre-Bing days).

Then I prepared for the best part of all, getting all the students involved in a very short play that recreated the verse. Yes, *all* the students. "The March Wind" seemed to have an outdoor setting. We discussed and listed what the poem stated, as well as what might be needed or found in its setting, and students selected or were directed (teachers, mentors, and the storyteller as directors of the play) to become:

- wind that worked (stomping or using fists in hands) and played (dancing or skipping or making silly movements and sounds) and whistled (or moaned when some students couldn't whistle);

- trees and bushes with branches and leaves (some firmly rooted with branches waving; some shaking like quaking aspens; some wiggling their fingers for the trembling branches and leaves);

- frosty and frozen grasses and dirt paths with twigs and leaves blown from trees and bushes (movement from some students; no movement from others; rocks resistant to being moved by the wind [these were students in wheelchairs or torso supports]);

- animals (forest animals and their actions in the wind were selected by students; I kept in mind the student's abilities to participate and facilitated choices) and children (holding their coats, shivering, spinning, rolling, shaking, freezing, and still);

- the buds of flowers still curled and crouched low in March weather (students wrapping their arms about themselves, curling their bodies or crouching on the floor, huddling together; eventually those who could would stretch and spread their arms for blossoms, but every flower didn't wake up in the same way);

- narrators with the accompaniment of teachers and other mentors, slowly sharing the verse in choral reading as the actors took their positions and created their characterizations.

When the last word, "sleep," was spoken, we all held our positions for a few seconds. Then we all applauded our fantastic play.

Because our list was extensive and our play was short, students could help recreate the poem even if they could not move. Every aspect of our March wind play was important. Everyone was a star.

When we had completed the play, in groups in which we could emphasize and discuss community, I facilitated participants' awareness of how their movements were similar or different. Examples: Show me "work," show me "play," and so on continued through the actions of the verse. We listed these responses on a chart to note how students' action selections were much more alike than different: "Look at what we all had in common when we shared this poem . . ."

That was the point of our work and play, what we all had in common.

The poem, "The March Wind," is now available from educators on Pinterest, in Creative Commons, and at other shared sites. We all love that wonderful author, "Anonymous," and her peer, "Unknown."

Resource

Rose, D. H., & Meyer, A. (2002). *Teaching every student in the digital age: Universal design for learning.* Alexandria, VA: Association for Supervision and Curriculum Development.

Storytelling with Children Who Have a Visual Impairment

Christine Moe

Most children who have a visual impairment attend their local neighborhood schools. They go to class with sighted peers and participate in all activities, classes, and assemblies alongside their friends. Children who have visual impairments can have a range of vision levels, from those who are totally blind to those who have considerable useful vision. Some children who are blind read and write Braille, while others use large print materials or even magnifiers to enlarge their materials. What these children have in common is a lack of easy access to visual learning.

Storytelling is often a great activity for children with visual impairments. Since this activity primarily relies on hearing rather than seeing, it is more accessible than traditional storybook reading. However, many storytellers add dramatic flair to their stories by using facial expressions to convey emotions, gestures to direct their listeners' attention, and body language to emphasize the personality traits of their characters. To capture and keep the attention of all children in the classroom, the story being told needs to be accessible to all.

One of the main challenges facing children who have visual impairments is the lack of visual learning they experience. Children who are sighted can simply turn their heads and observe the world around them. They can see the cows as their car drives past a field; they can see their classmates across the playground, and they can see what is written on the blackboard. They know the difference between a hippopotamus and a giraffe because they have seen pictures in books. Sighted children can see things too fragile to explore by touch, like spider webs and soap bubbles. They can see things that are too high to reach, like the tallest trees in the woods. They can see stars in the sky and that line between earth and sky that we call the horizon. They can see many things that children who have visual impairments miss. The incidental learning that occurs through vision is enormous, and for children who have visual impairments, this learning must occur using other senses.

Many sighted people assume that hearing is the main sense that children who have visual impairments use to learn about the world. While hearing is indeed very important, when used alone, it fails to convey enough information for a child who is visually impaired to make sense of it. For example, the sound of a ball bouncing on the floor lets everyone in the class know that someone is bouncing a ball. The sighted children can look over to see who is bouncing the ball; they can tell how big the ball is, what color it is, if it's heading toward them, and if they need to catch it. The child who is visually impaired misses all this additional information. Teachers and storytellers alike need to know what additional information needs to be shared through descriptions of the situation.

Children who have useful vision are often able to use visual information, but they need to see things up close. They should sit close to the action to catch the finer points and may need more time to examine something to grasp all the details. For children who are blind, the main sense they use for gathering information about the world is their sense of touch. Children who have visual impairments need to be able to touch things to learn about them; until they have handled and explored objects, they may not be able to develop a good mental image of the object. Some things are too big, too fragile, or too abstract to explore through touch. In this case, a tactile model may provide information that might otherwise be missed. This is why there are globes and maps in the classroom and models of atoms in science class.

A good model for children who are visually impaired is one that illustrates the story being told, whether it is "The Three Billy Goats Gruff" or a model of a dissected frog. Texture can provide more information than color and, in some cases, shape. Consider a set of plastic farm-animal models. While many of the animals have four legs and a tail, they are often roughly the same size and all have a similar texture. When the cat feels exactly like the cow and the horse and the dog are the same size, it can be difficult to develop accurate concepts about farm animals. Combining authentic textures with accurate relevant sizes and bringing them to life with sounds make it far easier for all of the children in the class to understand the characters that populate the storyteller's stories. Sensory learning, which uses all of the senses, is a great tool to use with children who have visual impairments. It offers them the opportunity for hands-on, ears-on—and in some cases—smell-on, and taste-on learning.

To capture the attention of the child who is visually impaired, stories need to have recognizable characters and themes, and the child needs to have prior relevant experiences with what the story is about. If you had never had an experience with an "octarine squinker," you might be confused, too, during the story. To ensure that all of the children in class share the basic concepts and ideas of the story, having the class help to define some of the key terms could help establish a foundation for understanding the story.

For sighted children, visual and sound effects are a delightful addition to the story. For children who are visually impaired, sound effects not only add interest to the story, but they can also be a way to understand the complexities of the story, keep track of characters, and build concepts about things they may not have explored in person yet. In addition to varying the pitch of the voice to indicate different characters, storytellers can change the speed of a character's voice to illustrate personality. Add in dialects or accents to increase recognizability, and make them as distinct as possible. Sounds that children would recognize, such as the whistle of a bird, the bark of a dog, the *vroom* of a passing car, or the swishing of the wind, help children connect the story to their own experiences and make it more interesting. Adding this kind of sensory detail allows every child in class to connect with the story.

Storytellers often use facial expressions, hand gestures, and body language to help illustrate their story. However, children who have visual impairments can easily miss this information. If the character is angry, ask the class how to show that. How should the characters sound when they are angry? Can they all make an angry face? What kind of body language does an angry person have? By asking the class to help describe the gestures and expressions of actions and emotions, every child can participate in the story.

Great storytellers add multisensory cues to their stories, painting pictures using sounds, words, and props. Instead of simply describing a beach ball as "yellow," the storyteller can add tactile dimensions to its description: "The yellow beach ball was so big, her hands could hardly meet around its middle. It was full of air and so light that unless she held onto it with both hands, the wind could pull it right out of her hands and whisk it away, going faster and faster until it disappeared far down the beach. When she tapped it, it made a sound like a hollow drum—thump, thump." When describing a puppy, the storyteller could add details like "this little black puppy was so small, she could fit inside one of his father's shoes. She smelled like one of his father's shoes, too, like grass on the lawn and dust from the back yard. The puppy was really soft, with a little round belly and floppy little ears that felt just like velvet. He knew the puppy liked him because her little tail kept wagging, back and forth and backandforthandbackandforthandbackandforth."

Occasionally storytellers use props to illustrate stories. If possible, bring two of each—one that can be passed from child to child in the classroom and one for the child who has a visual impairment so she can spend more time exploring by touch. The best props are familiar concrete items that reflect the main properties of what must be illustrated. While a set of wooden figures can be used to illustrate a story, it could be confusing to a child who is blind that the whole wooden family feels exactly the same as the dog, the cat, and the car—and are all roughly the same size. A great prop is one whose size and texture help illustrate the story being told. Beach balls, stuffed animals, an egg beater, and a train whistle make the plot and the characters immediately accessible to children who learn through touch and sound.

If the story is about a spider—a great big spider that was as black as the night, with eight long and hairy legs, a pair of fearsome pincers on her face, and a sharp stinger for a tail—try to find a good toy spider. It should have recognizable body parts, with eight legs and a front and back end that are distinctly different. When this story prop is going around the room, describe each part and invite the children to explore it. Count the legs, locate the front and back, and then continue with the story. This allows the children who have never handled a real spider to understand how spiders can catch their prey.

Don't be afraid to describe the color of a thing. All children need to learn that bananas are yellow, grass is green, and gingerbread men are brown. However, bananas can also be described as being long, smooth, and rubbery and tasting mild and sweet. Grass can be as tall as a person or mowed as short as a crew cut, and sometimes it smells like summer. Gingerbread men can be large or small, plain or decorated, and taste of sugar and spice, ginger and cinnamon, fall and Christmas. Yellow is the color of sunshine on your face; blue is the water you splash in the sink. White is the color of the milk that goes so well with cookies, while black is deep and dark and quiet as the middle of the night. Color is information, and for children who can't see colors, additional information can help them understand colors better.

Telling a story is a marvelous way to present information, whether it is a fairy tale, a grammar lesson, or a story about science. However, to ensure that all the children in class can access the information, storytellers may need to adapt the way they tell, to make all parts of the story accessible to all of the children.

Paths to Literacy: Adapting "The Three Little Pigs" for a Learner with Dual Sensory Impairment (Deafblindness)

Betty Braun

I adapted "The Three Little Pigs" for a 16-year-old student who is deafblind; he was functioning at a preschool level. My goal was to simplify the story and tell it with more of a teen perspective.

I used household items to help bring the concept of wolf, pig, straw, sticks, bricks, and so on to life and developed a book. For the pages, I used poster board, because it's stronger than paper and easier to cut than cardboard. Since the student sometimes shakes books, the book had to be sturdy.

I cut the top right-hand corner of each page so that my student would be able to identify and orient the tops of the pages. Instead of rings to bind the book pages, I used coated wire to enable easier page turning. I included both print and Braille on all pages.

The development of this book was more than a tactile activity. It was also an experience that created a personal connection to literature, since my student helped to make the book. This could motivate the student to learn and have fun at the same time. I hoped that, by using familiar objects in conjunction with Braille, this learning experience would be more meaningful for my student.

Materials

- Poster board (or cereal boxes)
- Cutouts from a cardboard box
- Felt
- Fur
- Beads
- Rubber bands
- Sticks
- Rocks
- Grass

Procedure

First, I decided to adapt the story's plot concept from an adventure with three pigs to a story with one pig as protagonist. This would make the plotting of the story an easier and more easily understandable task.

Drawing on the student's love of nature, we began by gathering some supplies outdoors. For example, we gathered sticks beside a tree, rocks from a rocky area, and tall grass beside bushes. I let the student feel all of these objects. I also put a rock by the school building so that we could engage in a description of "brick." The day happened to be windy, giving us an excellent opportunity to describe wind and to mimic the concept of huffing and puffing by blowing toward the student.

Once all our materials were gathered, we decided on which scenes should be illustrated for the book and then assembled three-dimensional pages for each scene. Our decisions included the following pages*:

Title page

Pig Needed a New House

Pig Built a Straw House

Wolf Blew the Straw House Down

Pig Built a Stick House

Wolf Blew the Stick House Down

Pig Built a Brick House

Wolf Couldn't Blow Down the Brick House

Wolf Felt Hot Water in the Kettle in the Fireplace and Went Back Up the Chimney**

Pig Lived Happily Ever After

Sharing the Story

I tactile-signed to the student and acted out the story while we read and experienced the book together.

Editor's note: This book was created as part of the online class *Accessible Literacy for Early Readers: Students Who Are Blind, Visually Impaired or Deafblind* at http://www.perkinselearning.org/earn-credits/online-class/accessible-literacy-for-early-readers.

---

*To see all of the 3-D illustrations for the completed book, please visit http://www.pathstoliteracy.org/strategies/adapting-three-little-pigs-learner-who-deafblind.

**Growing up as an older sister, I had already developed an understanding of modifications for this story. I felt that the topic of death was not suited to younger ears, and I did not like the idea of the wolf dying. So, when I was sharing the story with my student, I continued with the version I had created in my younger days. In addition, I felt that the student would enjoy the motion of physically moving the wolf down into the kettle of water and then back up again. This would encourage repeated readings of text, which is an excellent way to build reading fluency and comprehension.

5

Storytelling Strategies for Children with Multiple Disabilities

Introduction

Sherry Norfolk and Karen Young

The child is interested in the world, curious about it, keen to engage with it, but learns over and over again that it is out of reach. It is natural that they would eventually give up trying to find out about it. Children unable to process the world around them can turn inwards for stimulation, and become disengaged with the world. This limits their ability to learn and their desire to communicate.
—Joanna Grace, *Sensory Stories for Children and Teens with Special Educational Needs: A Practical Guide* (Jessica Kingsley, 2015)

Too often, people with multiple disabilities are isolated—not by their disabilities but by our inability to reach out to them; however, Patricia McKissack, acclaimed author and storyteller, reminds us that "the power of storytelling is to free us from isolation . . ."

Storytelling—especially multisensory storytelling as described in this chapter—provides vital stimulation for mind and spirit.

Karen Young, a storytelling teaching artist with Springboard to Learning (St. Louis, MO), wrote the following letter after her first residency in three self-contained classrooms of students with multiple disabilities. She makes several important points that all storytelling teaching artists can take to heart. (Emphasis added by author.)

I completed my residency with students [with complex needs] today. It was an honor and a pleasure to work with these wonderful students, dedicated teachers and paraprofessionals.

The changes I observed in the students from day one to day five were remarkable. Miss Meghan wouldn't look at me the first day and today she held my hand and walked with me. Students who slept while I told my first story now smile and laugh throughout the stories.

But the biggest change I saw was inside myself. *My experience with SSD students had been limited to performances only. After spending five sessions with these students I now see the richness in their lives. Much of that is because of the* talented and caring staff *and their willingness to* use all types of educational expressions— *including storytelling—to expand and enrich their students' lives.*

I am indebted to the librarian who created an entire set of educational applications for the three stories the students and I worked on. This included board maker versions of the stories displayed on the smart board and hand held pages for the students. *With my* puppets, *these gave the students one more reference point to use when they made their story* choices.

Thanks also go to the speech specialist who offered me valuable advice *on how best to work with the students and even spoke with the music therapist to give me* suggestions *for age-appropriate music choices.*

I am looking forward to my next storytelling residency with the middle schoolers at Ackerman. Because they are at a different level than the Northview students, I will be working with a new set of stories and lesson plans. And my third group will present another level of abilities. There is no "one size fits all" residency for these very special and endearing SSD students.

Thank you for letting them teach me as I taught them.

Karen

You'll see Karen's sentiments echoed throughout this chapter: there is no one guaranteed pathway to success—storytellers who embark on this challenging but rewarding journey must be willing to experiment, fail, evaluate, and try again. They must offer choices, working with the classroom teacher and aides as a team to serve the kids. Most of all, they must be willing and eager to learn and grow in order to help the students learn and grow.

Multisensory Storytelling with Children with Complex Additional Needs*

Ailie Finlay

"Once upon a time . . ." begins the storyteller and everyone gathers round for a story. Telling and listening to stories is one of our fundamental human experiences, so it goes without saying that children with complex needs should be included. My belief is that everyone can enjoy a good story well told; this includes children with even the most complex needs and sensory impairments. I would argue that it is particularly important that children with complex needs should be included in storytelling.

Children with complex needs often find that they are excluded from conversation because of their communication difficulties (often they will be nonverbal or have only limited language). A story can give us a way of having a conversation with a child who might otherwise struggle to communicate. This idea of the story as a conversation may be an unusual one, but it is this feeling I am striving for when telling a story, whether one-to-one or in a group. At a story session, I do not want to feel that there are a group of passive listeners and an active storyteller, but rather that we are all creating the story together. So there is a lot of to-and-fro between myself and the group members and lots of opportunities to join in. I am constantly reacting to the people present—to their comments, facial expressions, and body language. In this way the story session really does become a "conversation," and it is a conversation that allows people to take part who might otherwise struggle to join in with everyday conversations.

Furthermore, the story is a chance to have fun with language. When children have communication difficulties, a lot of time and effort is rightly placed in helping them with practical language—expressing when they are hungry, tired, or uncomfortable, for example. But storytelling can be an opportunity to enjoy other aspects of language—the flow and sounds and nonsense. We all remember the joy of chanting a rhyme over and over and very loudly in the school yard. Through storytelling we can offer children with complex needs a similar chance to revel in language.

Stories can also help people make sense of their lives. If they are told carefully and repeated often, stories can help us to see the patterns of our lives. This is particularly important for people who experience their lives as unpredictable because of their additional needs. Children who have difficulty understanding the world around them inevitably find that world less predictable then their peers. Stories can help with this, whether they are about the smaller patterns of life, like going on holiday, or the larger patterns of life, such as birth, illness, and death.

Choosing a Story

The first step in telling a story to children with complex needs is to catch the right story! I find that the stories that work best have a simple structure and lots of repetition. When a story uses heightened language and has a very strong rhythm and a clear climax, we can listen to it almost like a piece of music. We "get" the story without necessarily understanding all the contents.

*© Ailie Finlay, Flotsam and Jetsam Puppets and Stories, www.flotsamandjetsam.co.uk

When a story is well told, we get a sense of completion at the end; we give a little sigh of satisfaction. From my experience it is possible to get this sense of completion even if we have not understood all of the contents of the story. We all seem to have an innate sense of how the pattern of a story should go, and the satisfaction we get comes from the underlying pattern of the story as much as from the contents. For this reason it is important to make this pattern very clear when telling stories to children with complex needs. One way to check whether you have chosen a story with a simple-enough structure is to try to tell it to yourself as briefly as possible. If the structure is simple, it should be possible to retell the story in five sentences!

The Props

For some children, especially children with complex needs, the spoken word is not quite enough. The use of multisensory props is perhaps one of the most important ways that stories can be made accessible for children with complex additional needs. Props can be used to make the meaning of the story clear. But for me the props are not simply a sort of sensory dictionary added on for the children; they are an integral part of the story.

The props express the pattern, rhythm, and atmosphere of the story just as clearly as the words do. Indeed if we think about storytelling from the point of view of the child with very complex needs, we will see that the words themselves may be being experienced more as a sensory sensation than anything else. With this in mind, when I set about creating a story, I am not assembling a set of props that support speech, but rather a complete package of different sensory experiences that together tell a story. Each child will experience the story differently according to what is important to them and what their particular needs are. Some may be enjoying the meaning of the words, others the sensory experiences of the props or the heightened language and facial expressions of the storyteller. But every child should experience the story as a story, with continuity and a beginning, a climax and an end.

For this reason, it is important to choose the props as carefully as you choose your words. Think about the materials the object is made from, the style it is made in, and the color, feel, noise, and smell of the object. The props are your treasures. Make sure you love them!

When choosing a prop, I ask myself what it is I am trying to express. The most important thing may not be the usual meaning of the word but one particular quality. For example, in "Little Red Riding Hood," the most important thing about the wolf is not his "wolfishness." (It is perfectly possible to understand the story without knowing what a wolf is.) The most important thing we need to understand about the wolf is that he is fierce and dangerous. A soft toy wolf might say "wolf" to us, but in this context, it might not help a child with complex needs very much. Instead we could act out the role of the wolf, perhaps using some big furry mitts to show our "otherness" and playing at "catching" people with a large piece of see-through fabric: "I am the wolf and I'm coming to get you!" (We would start with the adults in the room and only "catch" the children if they were clearly enjoying the joke.) Through repetition of this, the children would come to understand the most important aspect of the wolf: badness! At this point we could continue with the story.

When I am expressing a concept, I am also trying to think about what part it plays in the structure of the story. Is the prop an invitation to join the story, the turning point of the story, or a calming object that appears at the resolution of the story? The role the prop is playing is as important as its meaning. For example, in the story of Jack and the Beanstalk, Jack usually steals three things. If we are "listening" to this story as a series of sensory experiences and the last thing that Jack steals is the climax of the story, then this particular prop has to make more of a sensory impact than the other two props that have gone before. I often make changes to traditional tales in order to take this kind of consideration into account. For example, Jack traditionally steals the singing harp last, but a honking goose that lays lovely shiny golden eggs is much more of a show-stealer from a sensory point of view than a gentle harp. So in my version, the goose would be stolen last.

Using props can have many other benefits as well. Most important of these for me is that the props can allow a child who is nonverbal or who has only very limited language to take more of a part in the "conversation" of the story. With careful thought and experimentation, props can be chosen that allow everyone to join in. Children can thump a squeaker to "be" the mouse, shake a bell bracelet to "be" Santa, or use a head switch to roar like a lion, and so on.

Some children with complex additional needs find focusing difficult, and for these children, props can be used to surprise or entice them into engaging with the story. The sound of a music box, the feel of velvet, or the smell of freshly ground coffee—sensory experiences like these can all be a gentle invitation to a child to come and join in with the story. Some children can find eye contact very difficult. Here again the props can be a help because they allow the storyteller to engage with the children without making eye contact, and as the story progresses, the props can give the children a little rest from listening. Listening is hard work, so it can be nice to take a break and do some looking, smelling, or touching instead.

Story Scripts

Here is a very old Scottish tale (often known as "The Sprightly Tailor" and found in many collections, including *Celtic Fairy Tales* by Joseph Jacobs [CreateSpace Independent Publishing Platform, 2014]). I've adapted to make it appealing for children with complex needs, including those with profound and multiple learning disabilities.

The Tailor in the Tower

Jack was a tailor.
A travelling tailor.
He stopped at every house and made clothes for all the people. *[Knock on different surfaces to indicate different houses.]*
And the thing he made best was waistcoats. *[Show everyone a waistcoat.]*
One day he went further than he had ever been before *[knock loudly]*— to the castle way up on the moor.
"Come in. Come in," said the king. "Come in. I have heard about your waistcoats. Make me a waistcoat and I will give you five golden coins. But only if you make it in the dark tower."
Now the dark tower was very dark.
And the dark tower was very windy. *[Make the noise of the wind by whistling.]*
And the dark tower was full of spiders. *[Make spidery noise by rubbing hands together.]*

And the dark tower was full of rats. *[Make rat noise by "scrabbling" fingers against the seat of your chair.]*

And the dark tower was full of ghosts. *[Make ghost noises.]*

[You could ask for other suggestions at this point and create sound effects to go with them.]

But the tailor didn't care. He didn't care one little bit.

He went pit-pat-pit-pat-pit-pat up the stairs to the top of the tower. *[Tap hands on knees to make going-up-the-stairs noise.]*

And it was dark.

And windy. *[Wind noise]*

And full of spiders. *[Spider noise]*

And rats. *[Rat noise]*

And ghosts. *[Ghost noise]*

But the tailor, he just sat down and began to sew.

Stitch, stitch, twist, button. Stitch, stitch, twist, button. *[Mime "stitching" and "twisting" with pretend needle in your hand.]*

[Bones noise]

"What was that? What was that noise?" said the tailor.

"It's my bones. Do you hear that tailor? Do you hear that?" said a voice from nowhere. *[In a monster voice.]*

"I do," said the tailor. "I do. I hear that very well. I hear that, but I stitch this."

Stitch, stitch, twist, button. Stitch, stitch, twist, button.

[Brains noise]

"What was that? What was that noise?" said the tailor.

"It's my brains. It's my brains rattling. Do you hear that tailor? Do you hear that?"

"I do," said the tailor. "I do. I hear that very well. I hear that, but I stitch this."

Stitch, stitch, twist, button. Stitch, stitch, twist, button.

[Teeth noise]

"What was that? What was that noise?" said the tailor.

"It's my teeth. It's my chattering teeth. Do you hear that tailor? Do you hear that?"

"I do," said the tailor. "I do. I hear that very well. I hear that, but I stitch this."

Stitch, stitch, twist, button. Stitch, stitch, twist, button.

[Feet noise]

"What was that? What was that noise?" said the tailor.

"It's my feet. It's my two muckle feet. And I'm coming to get you. Do you hear that tailor? Do you hear that? It's my bones *[noise]* and my brains *[noise]* and my teeth *[noise]* and my two muckle feet *[noise]*. And I'm coming to get you tailor. I'm coming to get you. Do you hear that?"

"I do," said the tailor. "I do. I hear that very well. I hear that, but I stitch this."

Stitch, stitch, twist, button. Stitch, stitch, twist, button. Stitch, stitch, twist, button. Stitch, stitch, twist, button. *[Getting faster and faster]*

The tailor finished the waistcoat, he ran down stairs. Pit-pat-pit-pat-pit-pat. *[Very fast hands patting on knees]*

He ran to the king:

"Here's your waistcoat, King. Here it is!"

And the king gave him his five golden coins.

And the tailor set off down the road. And never saw the monster again. And lived happily ever after.

Notes on Telling

Encourage your audience to join in as much as possible—for example, with the noises in the tower and the "stitch, stitch, twist, button." They can then help to create the monster using different instruments.

The "stitch, stitch ..." refrain can be tapped out on the back of someone's hand, if it seems appropriate. One finger taps for each "stitch"; the "twist" is a wee circle "drawn" with the finger and the "button" another tap: tap, tap, circle tap; tap, tap, circle tap. For people who are visually impaired, this will help to give the story continuity. Linger on the quiet "stitch, stitch" bits of the story to mark the contrast with the loud scary monster.

The "stitch, stitch ..." refrain should get fast and frantic as the monster approaches, and the running down stairs should get very fast. The breathless climax of the story is when the tailor flings the waistcoat to the king. Then there should be a wee pause before the king brings out the five gold coins.

Props

The instruments I use are as follows:

- Bones: a wooden "football rattle"
- Teeth: a wooden guiro
- Brains: a seed shaker
- My two muckle feet: drum

If you already have a music box, then you can use whatever you have and just improvise. Knees could jingle, toe nails might clatter, ears could flap in the breeze, and so on!

If possible, use a real waistcoat. Old waistcoats fit in well with the atmosphere of the story. Vintage clothes' shops usually have a good supply.

You could also add in the following:

- A wee jingly pouch of money for the "golden coins"
- A big shiny cloak and crown for the king
- A nice long measuring tape for the tailor. Lots of measuring tapes would be even more fun.

The Seed Pod

This story is also based on an old folktale, but I have adapted it to make it more interesting from a sensory point of view.

Once upon a time, there was a young boy. His mother told him it was time for him to go out into the world.

But she gave him nothing but a pod of seeds. *[Shake seed pod.]*

The boy didn't mind.

One, two, three, bumblebee
A wee pod of seeds just for me. [Shake seed pod.]

Well, after a while the boy sat down by the side of the path for a rest. And he fell asleep.

While he was sleeping along came a wee chick *[bird noise]* and ate his pod of seeds.

"Fair's fair," says the boy, "the chick's mine."

And he caught the chick up and put it in his pocket and set off down the road.

One, two, three, bumblebee
A wee little chick just for me. [Bird noise]

And after he had gone a wee way, he sat down for a rest. The chick jumped out his pocket and began to peck about on the road.

Along came a cat. *(Cat noise)* And the cat crept up on the wee chick and the wee chick ran away.

"Fair's fair," says the boy, "the cat's mine."

And he scooped up the cat and tucked it under his coat and set off down the road.

One, two, three, bumblebee
A nice little cat just for me. (Cat noise)

He was walking along when a knight on a horse came cantering up the road. The horse was snorting and the bridle jingling. *(Bells)*

And the cat got such a fright she leapt away and ran into the trees.

"Fair's fair," says the boy, "the horse is mine."

So the knight got off the horse and the boy jumped on. He trotted off down the road with the bridle jingling.

One, two, three, bumblebee
A nice white horse just for me. (Bells)

By and by the boy came to a wide moor. And as he trotted along on his horse, a great army came marching over the horizon—hundreds of soldiers marching, singing, and beating their drums. *(Drum)*

The boy's horse startled in fright and the boy fell off. The horse bolted away, running over the heather.

"Fair's fair," said the boy, "the army is mine."

And so he marched over the moor, leading the great army behind him.

One, two, three, bumblebee
A nice wee army just for me. (Drum)

He marched at the front, leading them over the moor and through villages and towns, with their drums beating. All the people came out of their houses and cheered the boy. What a great lad he must be, they thought, to be leading such an army.

On and on they marched. And then they came to a little farm all on its own. Instead of going around, the soldiers marched right through the fields and garden of the farm. Their big boots wrecked the crops and stamped on the flowers.

A wee old lady came out of the cottage, *(put on shawl)* shaking her fists at the soldiers:

"What are you doing, ruining my fields? What are you doing, ruining my garden?"

She was so fierce. She reminded the soldiers of their grandmas at home. And so they turned and fled, running away across the fields.

"Fair's fair," said the boy, "the grandma is mine."

And he went into the little farm house. And the old lady (who was fierce but very kind as well) made him a cup of tea.

One, two, three, bumblebee
A nice cup of tea just for me (rattle the tea cup and spoon)

And there he lived for the rest of his days, happily ever after.

Notes on Telling

Be sure to "ham it up" when saying the little rhyme. You can repeat it quite a lot and dance all around, really having fun and capturing the carefree nature of the boy. Then when you are "being" the army, you can be more serious and march around rather than dancing. Be nice and loud with the drum.

Props

- Seed pod shaker
- Bird noisemaker (these can be bought online)

- Cat noise toy (if unavailable make the noise yourself!)
- String of bells (for the harness of the horse)
- Drum
- Shawl
- Tin cup with teaspoon to rattle

Cinderella: A Tactile Story

This simple story is designed to be told to people who have both a visual and hearing impairment and experience the world primarily through touch.

Sweep, sweep, sweep (Gently "sweep" with the first brush on the back of the listener's hand.)

Little Cinderella sweeps the courtyard. *(Sweep more, with first brush.)*
Little Cinderella sweeps the stairs. *(Sweep with second brush.)*
Little Cinderella sweeps away the cobwebs. *(Sweep with third brush.)*
And Little Cinderella goes to bed.

(Repeat these lines and the "brushing" several times slowly and rhythmically.)

But one day her fairy godmother came and brushed Cinderella with star dust. *(Sweep with makeup brush, if appropriate on the "listener's" face as well as hands.)*

And warmed her in a velvet shawl. *(Lay velvet over hands and give velvet bag with heat pads.)*

And sent her to the ball.

Notes on Telling

This story should be told very gently and calmly and works best one-to-one. Use one hand for the props and keep contact with the "listener's" hand with your other hand. In this way they will experience the continuity of the story even if they are not hearing or seeing anything.

Props

- Three small brushes: natural wooden brushes are nice; the more varied the feel of the bristles, the better
- Makeup brush (as soft as possible)
- Piece of velvet
- Velvet pouch
- Disposable heat pads (sold as "hand warmers" in outdoor/ski equipment shops)

Scaffolding Learning for Children with Multiple Disabilities

Sherry Norfolk

I had worked with this class of seven- and eight-year-old students a year before. They were all on the autism spectrum, primarily nonverbal and functioning at pre-K level. It was wonderful to see how much the students remembered from last year and see how much progress we could make in just five sessions!

On the first day, M took one look at me and said, *"Muffet!"* His favorite activity last year had been acting out Little Miss Muffet: one child is "Miss Muffet," with a paper bowl and plastic spoon, and the other has a pom-pom-and-pipecleaner spider on a kraft stick. M loved to scream and run away when the spider "sat down beside her." He remembered!

We did it once, with M being Miss Muffet and me the spider. The teacher and assistants and I chanted the rhyme as M pretended to eat curds and whey; then I lowered the spider onto his knee. Ahhhh! He ran away giggling!

Then M was the spider while another child was Miss Muffet. We took turns until everyone who wanted to participate had a turn. This activity was repeated every day. On the first day, there was some hesitation or refusal from some students, but by the fifth day, everyone smiled and chose a role.

Each day, we repeated what had been done the day before, often scaffolding new interactive options.

Example: Hickory Dickory Dock

Day One

I produced a small, furry toy mouse and let each child feel it. Then I asked a student if the mouse could run up her arm. When she agreed, I used castanets to "ticktock" as I recited the rhyme and ran the mouse up her arm. On "the clock struck one" I rang a bell; then the mouse ran back down the arm. I used a large, colorful rainstick to accompany "doooooooooown he did run."

Every child allowed the mouse to run up an arm or leg.

Day Two

This time, I asked a teaching assistant to click the castanets, another to ring the bell, and a third to turn the rainstick.

Days Three to Five

I asked one student to use the castanets, another to use the bell, and another to turn the rainstick. Assistants helped the students follow their cues as the mouse ran up and down. The instruments were passed around so that everyone had a turn on each instrument and each had a chance for the mouse to run up and down his or her arm.

Watching the students go from wary to eager was fantastic! It was rewarding to see students begin to respond independently to cues, indicating that they had learned the poem as well as the proper response.

We also used 12" × 12" colorful scarves every day to help sing a song. Each student and caregiver received a scarf, and then, singing and demonstrating actions slowly, I led the class in "This is the way we plant the seeds," sung to the tune of "Here We Go Round the Mulberry Bush":

This is the way we plant the seeds. [Wad scarf into cupped palms.]
Plant the seeds,
Plant the seeds.
This is the way we plant the seeds,
Early in the morning.
This is the way the sun shines. [Wave scarf round and round in a circle.]
The sun shines,
The sun shines.
This is the way the sun shines,
Early in the morning.
This is the way the rain falls down ... [Wave scarf up and down.]
This is the way the flower grows ... [Hold scarf aloft, spreading it out like an open flower.]

Hand-over-hand assistance allowed all students to participate.

With repetition over the next four days, the students enjoyed this song and activity more and more! We noticed that A immediately smiled and balled up the scarf when she received it on the fourth and fifth days—she remembered what to do!

Every day, M would ask for a story that he had enjoyed on the previous day: "Hick'ry Dock!" "Ging'[erbread] Boy!" "Eensy Weensy!" "T'oll!" ("Troll"—his title for "The Three Billy Goats Gruff"). His request was always the very first story I did that day, followed by all of our favorites plus at least one new story every session. The new story was usually the requested favorite on the following day!

As the week went on, I experimented with adding stories that were less participatory but more visual and auditory—using puppets or props and lots of voices and sound effects. Having become accustomed to me and therefore more settled, they began to enjoy longer stories such as "Three Billy Goats Gruff" told with stick puppets, or "Are You My Mother?" told with finger puppets. They grinned and watched avidly as the story progressed.

They answered questions: "What did the cow say?" "Mmmmmmm!"—a very credible moo from a nonverbal student!

They anticipated the action: "Up jumped the big, bad ..." "*Grrrrr!*" roared several students as the Troll jumped up.

And they smiled.

Change in routine and change in personnel are difficult for these students to handle. Transitions are traumatic. My presence brought all of this chaos into the classroom; however, by slowly introducing new stories and carefully scaffolding options for interaction, we were able to overcome these obstacles and build rapport. According to Joanna Grace in *Sensory Stories for Children and Teens with Special Educational Needs* (Jessica Kingsley Publisher, 2015), "Individuals with ASD may benefit from the opportunity to encounter and become accustomed to sensory stimuli presented by sensory stories." This step-by-step approach served that purpose while allowing children to make choices about their level of interaction.

Every time I have an opportunity to work with these kids is a learning experience for me. They have taught me to go more slowly, repeat more often, and notice more fully. They have taught me to layer activities carefully, allowing time for acceptance, comprehension, response, and choices. They have taught me to recognize how each student demonstrates learning—a joyful smile here, an independent response there, a call for "T'oll!" there.

They have taught me to cherish their successes and to identify pathways to further success, building on-ramps to learning.

The Magic Tree: Creating Engagement through Interactive Storytelling

Sheila Wee

"I'm exhausted!" That was my constant refrain after finishing a story-telling performance for children with special needs. I didn't say it out loud; outwardly I smiled and said thank you for inviting me. But inside I was exhausted and disappointed in myself. The only way I could hold the children's attention was by upping my energy and being more dramatic with my voice and my body. As well as taking its toll on my energy, it also felt like a shallow experience for the children, a spectacle rather than something that touched their hearts and minds. I knew that there must be a better way; I knew these kids deserved better and so I started reflecting and researching how I could meet their needs more effectively.

While I was musing over these problems, fate intervened and gave me an opportunity to try to resolve them. I was approached by a special needs school in Singapore to conduct six one-hour workshops for four groups of 7- to 12-year-old children with mild to moderate intellectual disabilities (with a maximum of 16 children per group). I was told that the children had mental ages of between five and six years of age and that a few of the children selected for the workshops would be nonverbal and a few had difficulties with mobility. The aim of the workshops was to use storytelling to develop these children's language skills, listening skills, and their confidence in their ability to speak in front of a group.

As I was planning the workshops, I thought back to the days before I became a professional storyteller, to my early years as a preschool teacher and later experience as a creative drama teacher. When I was teaching creative drama, I reached out to those children who found it difficult to stay attentive by slowing down the action of the story we were dramatizing and giving them something to do. I began to look at how I could move away from a performance-listening model of storytelling to a facilitation-experience model. I thought about how I could slow down the telling of a story and move the children in and out of the action of a story. This would give me the opportunity to make the story experience more sensorial and interactive so that the children could engage on a more physical and emotional level. My aim was to make the storytelling experience both easily understandable and immersive for the children and to bring them into the world of the story in a safe and structured way and within that experience help them to develop language, listening, and speaking skills.

Choosing and Preparing the Stories

I looked for a warm-up story that could be used at the beginning of each session, before moving into the main story of the day. I chose "Two Goats on the Bridge," a simple and repetitive action story, which I had learned from Margaret Read MacDonald. I felt that a predictable introduction routine, with a predictable and simple warm-up story, would help the children feel safe. If they felt safe, they were more likely to participate fully in the activities of the main story and be less likely to show disruptive behavior. This theory was strengthened by my experience in the sessions. There were disruptions from some of the children but not enough to interfere with the flow of the session.

For the story that would be told and explored in the main part of each session, I looked for folktales that had:

- plenty of action;
- a simple storyline;
- a repetitive structure that would give opportunities for repetitive but engaging language;
- characters that would appeal to children. For example: animals, a child, a weak or vulnerable character that the children can empathize with;
- a problem that the children can give suggestions for solving; and values that clearly shine through.

One of the stories I used was my adaptation of an African folktale that I call *The Magic Tree*. I looked at *The Magic Tree* story and found places where I could include sensory experiences where the children could:

- see something;
- handle something;
- smell something;
- hear something;
- or even, if the circumstances were right, taste something.

I found places where I could make the story more interactive, where the children could:

- join in a song, refrain, or chant;
- contribute ideas for solving a problem; and
- do something physical.

I then broke the story into sections. To do this, I looked for natural breaks in the story, where I could leave the children wanting to know more and give them something to discuss with their class teachers between each session.

Because this approach involved slowing down the action of the story to add interactive, physical, and sensory activities, it was difficult to accurately predict how long things would take with each group, so my plans on how far we would get into the story in a session were provisional. Working with one story over several sessions meant that I had the opportunity to repeat the telling of the previous section of the story with the children at least twice. I believe that breaking up the story in this way and building in opportunities for repeating it aided the children's comprehension of the language and concepts in the story. For special needs teachers who may not be confident and experienced storytellers, working on a small chunk of a story at a time is much less challenging than telling the full story in one go.

Preparing the Environment

I thought about how I could prepare the room so I could:

- ensure the children's physical safety;
- facilitate class management;

- avoid distractions; and
- create positive anticipation.

I set up very clear seating and movement areas using small round plastic mats arranged in a semicircle for the children to sit on. I also set up large props to represent the settings and objects in the main story that we would be experiencing that day.

Beginning the Sessions

Each one-hour session began with me greeting the students individually at the door. Each student would then remove his/her shoes and sit down on one of the seating spots. Once every child was seated, I would give each a name badge. This allowed me to have some individual interaction with the children, to begin get to know them and to gauge how they were feeling that day.

Warm-Up Story

In "Two Goats on the Bridge," the children copy my actions and repeat my words. After hearing and joining in this story for a couple of sessions, I began to invite some of the children to come up and stand beside me and help lead the others in telling the story. The children gradually gained confidence in telling this story, and after the end of the six sessions (with some practice with their teachers), they successfully performed for the whole school.

The Magic Tree: Step by Step

Story Props

For "The Magic Tree," I created a set of story props:

- Mama Coco's cave out of a table draped in cloth
- The big rock out of a cardboard box wrapped in brown cloth
- "Magic" tree, with brooms and mops wedged into laundry basket and draped with colored scarves

I also had standing by:

- a long, blue, sparkly cloth to represent the rainstorm;
- a large soft, silky, blue cloth to represent the pond;
- a rainstick to make the sound of rain;
- sterilized dried leaves for the children to touch and experience what happened in the drought;
- a basket of common fruits for the children to identify and touch;
- a basket of fragrant flower heads to scatter to represent the blossom on the magic tree;
- a low table with puppets or soft toys representing the story characters on it; and
- a drum and various simple percussion instruments.

Pre-story Activities

I designed pre-story activities to familiarize the children with the characters and the setting of the story and to make clearer to the children the concept of a drought, by showing its more familiar opposite in tropical Singapore, an abundance of rainfall.

- I introduced each of the characters in the story using puppets. The children had a chance to interact and touch each of the animal puppets if they wanted to.
- The children were invited to choose an animal character to be and then come out individually and make their chosen animal's movement and sound.
- I introduced the forest setting of the story by getting the children to make tree shapes with their bodies.
- I put a soft, silky, blue cloth on the floor to represent a pond.
- I told the children that every day the animals came to the pond to drink water. I then invited them to come and drink water from the pond in role as their animal character.
- I told the children that in the forest it rained every day and so the animals were happy because they had water to drink and food to eat.
- I let them listen to the rain sounds made with a rainstick, and then we made a rainstorm by tapping and clapping our fingers and hands and stamping our feet from soft to loud.
- Using a long, sparkly, blue cloth to represent the rainstorm, the children, as their chosen animal characters, were invited one by one to come and sit under the "rain cloth," which was then wafted over their heads by a teacher and me. As this was being done, we all sang the song "I Hear Thunder."

I hear thunder, I hear thunder,
Oh, don't you? Oh, don't you?
Pitter-patter raindrops, Pitter-Patter raindrops,
I'm wet through. So are you!

It was only after doing all this groundwork that I began to tell the story.

The Magic Tree

Adapted by Sheila Wee

Tell the children that this is a story about Lion, Owl, Elephant, Rabbit, and Tortoise, showing them each of the puppets/soft toys in turn.

Lion, Owl, Elephant, Rabbit, and Tortoise lived together in the forest.

Where they lived, there were many, many trees and a pool full of cool, clear water. They were happy in the forest, because they had lots to eat and lots to drink.

(Repeat of hands and feet rainstorm and of singing "I Hear Thunder" under the sparkly "rain cloth.")

Every evening the rain came to fill the pool.

But then one day, it didn't rain. It didn't rain and it didn't rain and it didn't rain.

It didn't rain for a week; it didn't rain for a month; it didn't rain for a whole year!

Everything was dry and the leaves on the tree turned brown and fell to the ground.

[As the brown leaves are described, let the children look at and touch real dried leaves.]

The water in the pond began to dry up, and the pond got smaller and smaller and smaller.

One day there was no more water in the pond.

Only mud, dry mud.

[When describing the pond drying up, slowly gather in the blue cloth that represents it, making it smaller and smaller until it "disappears." Replace the pond with "the rock."]

There was no water to drink. All the plants died. There was nothing to drink and nothing to eat.

The animals were so hungry. The animals were so thirsty.

The Elephant waved his trunk and moaned, "Hungry!"

The Owl flapped his wings and moaned, "Thirsty!"

The Rabbit's ears drooped and she cried, "Hungry! Thirsty!"

[Encourage the children to join in with the animals saying hungry and thirsty with appropriate gestures.]

The Tortoise just kept very still, very quiet.

They didn't know what to do. What could they do?

[Ask the children for suggestions for what the animals could do to get water and food.]

None of the animals could think what to do.

[As the story unfolds, different animal characters will speak and go on a journey. At these times you may want to hold the corresponding puppet or soft toy, or you may just point out the character on the display table.]

Then Owl said, "I remember that my grandmother told me about a magic tree—a magic tree that grows in the middle of the forest. If you say the name of the tree, then fruit will appear on its branches. All kinds of fruit. Sweet, juicy, delicious fruit."

[Show the children and let them handle and name the different types of fruit you have prepared.]

"And you can pick and pick and pick the fruit, but no matter how many fruits you pick, there will always be more fruits.

Sweet fruit, juicy fruit. *[mime plucking fruit]*

Yummy in my tummy fruit." *[mime rubbing stomach]*

[Encourage the children to join in with the chant, repeating several times.]

So said Owl, "If we go to this tree and say its name, then all these sweet, juicy, yummy fruits will grow on its branches and we can eat them."

"Hooray," said Lion. "When we find the tree and say its name, we will never be hungry or thirsty again."

All the animals were very happy to hear about the magic tree.

They thought about the sweet juicy fruit and they cheered and cheered, "Hooray! Hooray! Hooray!"

And so Owl led them into the forest ... deep into the forest ... right into the middle of the forest.

[Encourage the children to line up behind you and move through the room to reach the magic tree.]

And there they saw the magic tree.

It was so *big*. So *tall*. So *beautiful*.

All the animals gathered around Owl and asked, "What's the name? What's the name? What's the name of the tree?"

But Owl said nothing.

So the animals asked, "What's the name? What's the name? What's the name of the tree?"

But Owl said nothing.

So the animals asked, "What's the name? What's the name? What's the name of the tree?"

And then Owl said, *"I forgot!"*

(Encourage the children to join in chanting "What's the name, what's the name, what's the name of the tree?")

Oh no! What could they do?

The animals sat down and thought what the name of the tree could be. They tried and they tried, but they could not think of the name.

[Ask the children for suggestions as to what the name of the tree could be. Together call out each suggestion and express in your face, physical expression and in what you say and how you say it, that none of these suggestions worked. This is a good place in the story to end the session, as you can ask the children to go away and think of more possible names and come back in the next session and try them out.]

And then Owl said, "I know who we should ask! Let's ask Mama Coco. She will know the name of the tree; she knows everything."

"But," said Lion, "Mama Coco lives in a cave right on the top of the mountain. We are all so tired and hungry. Do any of us have the strength to climb right to the top of the mountain?"

"I'll go," said Rabbit. "I am hungry and thirsty, but I can still run fast. I am the fastest runner in the forest."

"Alright, Rabbit," said Lion. "You can climb the mountain and speak to Mama Coco."

And Rabbit ran out of the forest and up the mountain.

At last Rabbit reached the top of the mountain and stood outside Mama Coco's cave.

Rabbit called out, "Mama Coco, speak to me. Tell me the name of the magic tree."

And from deep inside the cave, Mama Coco replied.

"Awongalema—the name is Awongalema."

"Oh, Awongalema! Thank you!" said Rabbit. "Won't they be so proud of me? I know the name of the magic tree."

And rabbit went running down the mountain as fast as she could.

Too fast! She ran *so fast* that she didn't see the great big rock in the middle of the path—she bumped right into it and knocked her head. *Bang!*

"Oww owww owww," cried Rabbit "I hurt my head, I hurt my head. Oh no! I forgot the name!"

And so Rabbit had to go back to the other animals and say, "I'm sorry; I forgot the name!"

And all the animals cried out, "Oh no! Oh no! Hungry! Thirsty! Hungry! Thirsty!"

(I narrated Rabbit's journey to the cave and back while holding the rabbit puppet. I then asked for a volunteer to be Rabbit and dramatize her journey, a volunteer to bang the drum when rabbit hits the rock, and some volunteers to create rhythm with the percussion instruments to express Rabbit's movement as she goes up and down the hill.)

Lion looked around and said, "Who else is strong enough to go up the mountain and ask Mama Coco for the name of the tree?"

(Elephant volunteers next and the same thing happens to him as happened to Rabbit. Then Lion decides that he should go, but again the same thing happens. After you narrate each animal making the journey, repeat

it again with a child (or two) taking on the role of the animal and others providing the sound effects with the drum and other percussion instruments.]

"It's no good!" said Lion. "Nobody is strong enough to climb up the mountain now. We should all give up and wait to die!"

But then a tiny little voice spoke up. "I'll go! I'm strong enough to climb the mountain."

All the animals looked around. Who was that? And then they saw it was Tortoise. And they laughed and laughed and laughed.

"You? You are too small and too slow! By the time you get to the top of the mountain, we will all be *dead!*"

But Tortoise said, "Let me go. Let me try."

And so Tortoise began climbing up the mountain. She was very slow, very, very slow.

But at last she reached the top and stood outside Mama Coco's cave.

Tortoise called out, "Mama Coco, speak to me; tell me the name of the Magic Tree."

And from deep inside the cave Mama Coco replied, "Awongalema—the name is Awongalema."

"Oh, Awongalema! Thank you." said Tortoise. "I must remember the name. How am I going to remember the name? I know; I will make it into a song.

Awongalema, Awongalema, Awongalema, Awong
Awongalema, Awongalema, Awongalema, Awong
Awong! Awong! Awongalema, Awong!
Awong! Awong! Awongalema, Awong!"

And so Tortoise made her way slowly down the mountain singing her song.

Awongalema, Awongalema, Awongalema, Awong
Awongalema, Awongalema, Awongalema, Awong
Awong! Awong! Awongalema, Awong!
Awong! Awong! Awongalema, Awong!

[Encourage the children to join in singing the song.]

And because she was travelling so slowly, she saw the great big rock in the middle of the path and went around it.

Awongalema, Awongalema, Awongalema, Awong
Awongalema, Awongalema, Awongalema, Awong
Awong! Awong! Awongalema, Awong!
Awong! Awong! Awongalema, Awong!

And slowly, slowly, very slowly, Tortoise reached the bottom of the mountain.

And slowly, very slowly, Tortoise reached the magic tree.

All the other animals were lying on the ground, moaning and groaning, "Hungry . . . Thirsty . . . Hungry . . . Thirsty."

Tortoise stood under the tree and said its name, "*Awongalema! Awongalema!*"

Then suddenly, beautiful, sweet-smelling flowers appeared on the tree. Then the flowers fell to the ground.

[Scatter the flowers in front of the children.]

And the fruit appeared on the tree.

Sweet, juicy, delicious fruit.

Sweet fruit, juicy fruit.

Yummy in my tummy fruit.

[Repeat the chant and actions a few times with the children.]

And the animals jumped up and picked the fruit and ate and ate and ate.

Each of the animals said thank you to the tortoise.

[Take the tortoise puppet around to each of the children so they can say thank you to it.]

> And the animals never forgot the name of the tree again, because every night before they went to bed they sang Tortoise's song.
>
> Awongalema, Awongalema, Awongalema, Awong
> Awongalema, Awongalema, Awongalema, Awong
> Awong! Awong! Awongalema, Awong!
> Awong! Awong! Awongalema, Awong!
> *[Sing the song together.]*
> And then one day, a little drop of rain came down, and another, and another.
> *And the rain came down! And the rain came down! And the rain came down!*
> *[End by making a rainstorm with hands and feet and then singing "I Hear Thunder."]*

After completing all the sessions, the class teachers (two for each group) gave their feedback. I knew the sessions had gone well. I had discovered I could hold the children's attention far better than with a traditional performer-listener model of storytelling. But I was surprised at how overwhelmingly positive the teachers' feedback was. The teachers observed that their pupils had:

- learned new vocabulary;
- developed their patience and turn-taking skills;
- increased their listening skills and their ability to focus;
- gained cooperative skills;
- improved their receptive and expressive skills; and
- improved their confidence to speak in front of others.

The teachers also told me that for some of the children, their gains in some of these areas carried back into their normal classrooms. I will never forget the little round-faced boy with Harry Potter glasses who spent most of the first two sessions with his head on his knees, who by the last session was hesitantly joining in and was now participating more in his regular classes. I may not have changed the world, but I had found a way to reach these children and the energy to go on and learn more—for I walked out of every one of those sessions not exhausted but very happily tired.

Resources

MacDonald, M. R. (2004). Two goats on a bridge. In *Three minute tales: Stories from around the world to tell or read when time is short* (pp. 46–48). Little Rock, AR: August House. For a video of the author telling this story, see www.youtube.com/watch?v=L0lz_u4—k4
Other versions of "The Magic Tree" story:
Lottridge, C. B. (2001). *The name of the tree*. Toronto, Ontario: Douglas & McIntyre.
Umansky, K. (1994). The Awongalema tree. In *Three singing pigs: Making music with traditional stories* (pp. 10–15). London, England: A & C Black.

Touching Stories: Connecting to Students with Cognitive Disabilities through Multisensory Storytelling

Gwen Bonilla

I'm a storyteller. I love words. I luxuriate in them. I thrill to a well-turned phrase. The unique challenge—and gift—of being a storyteller for audiences with special needs is that I have to develop my programs with the understanding that words alone may not be enough to bring my stories to life.

As humans, our first, and often most profound, means to experience the world is through our senses. What we see, taste, touch, hear, and smell impacts our understanding from the moment we are born. And for people with special needs, whose verbal language skills are limited, sensory communication remains primary much longer—for some, it is their primary communication all their lives. When I became a storyteller for audiences with special needs, I came to realize that for this audience, storytelling has the ability to be a whole-body interactive experience that allows people to learn about their world. I developed a "multisensory" storytelling program called Touching Stories. Touching Stories is geared toward children and adults with developmental disabilities that allows them to experience story, not just through words but also through manipulatives, scents, textures, and sounds that help the story come to life. The stories I tell are simple—many of them only about 8–10 sentences in length, short on plot and character, but long on sensory experience. Despite their simplicity, I still take care to ensure that every Touching Story I tell has all the elements of a good tale: drama, conflict, characters, and resolution. The following is a description of a typical telling in a special education classroom of one of Touching Stories' most popular stories, "The Monster on Grandma's Bed."

I always arrive at least 10 minutes early and make sure the room is set up for a successful telling. Seats are arranged in a wide semicircle that allows me access to every member of the audience. Next to the space where I will be telling, if possible, I have a table on which I can place the sensory elements for my story, in order. Fumbling around to find the right sensory items as I am telling is distracting and takes away from the magic of the telling. I chat with the teacher and paraprofessionals quickly to get a sense of which students may have particular sensitivity to noise, to smell, to texture. I give them a quick rundown of what might trigger dramatic responses from these students and ask them to support the students through anything that might be overly stimulating for them. I also plan for how I might adjust my presentation to prevent extreme reactions—for example, I always have a cloth or some foam or other way to muffle loud noises, or I plan to adjust how to offer something with a particularly strong smell. When everything is set up and I am prepared, I invite my audience to the story circle and we begin:

The Monster on Grandma's Bed

Sarah loved sleepovers at Grandma's house.
I have barely begun my first story and one of my audience starts to wail and rock back and forth. I see out of the corner of my eye that a classroom paraprofessional has eased in next to the distressed child and is calming her.
Sometimes, they made cookies. Sarah liked to stir the dough.

I lift aloft a bowl stuffed with a fabric "cookie dough" pillow. I demonstrate stirring the dough with a thick-handled wooden spoon. I walk to each child and, one by one, offer the bowl and spoon, as I repeat the phrase, "She liked to stir the dough." This is the pattern for the rest of the storytelling. At each new line, I offer the sensory item to each student one by one and repeat the phrase that goes with it. At this line of the story, audience members are asked to grasp a wooden spoon and stir. Some children stir just the way I demonstrated. Some audience members pointedly snub me, looking the other direction as I approach and pushing away the proffered props. Another child is visibly excited, bouncing in his chair. As I offer the bowl, he ignores the spoon and grabs the cookie dough with both hands—squeezing, yanking, and pulling. I note aloud how enthusiastic he is, as I gently loosen his grip. I don't make him try again with the spoon. On another day, I hope he'll try it that way.

Sarah loved the way the cookies smelled.

I offer a plastic bottle with a cotton ball soaked in vanilla oil as I repeat, "She loved the way the cookies smelled." This is a favorite. Almost no one turns me away when it is time to smell the "cookies." Inevitably, one or two tongues come out, wanting to taste. I have prepared for this by placing a gentle hand on the shoulder of each child. I guide each audience member's nose toward the bottle, keeping a good safe six-inch bubble between tongue and sweet-smelling goodness.

In this moment, I know it is working. I *have* my audience. Anyone who has ever told stories recognizes this moment—when the audience's energy mingles with your own and multiplies a thousandfold, until it becomes a presence in the room so palpable that you almost have to duck to avoid it. To someone new to telling with these audiences, my presentation may not look like a rousing success. One child appears to be sleeping. Many never make eye contact, and there are still those who shrink away at my approach. To a careful observer, though, it is evident that some cool things are happening.

After the cookies were baked, it was time to go to bed. Sarah had her own special bed at Grandma's house.

I walk the circle with a miniature bed—polyester foam covered in cotton percale and a section of an old quilt. The phrase here is "She had her own special bed."

This is a "touch" page of the story. Students are welcome to explore the folds and layers of the bed as they choose. Some pull back the blanket and explore each layer; some simply run their hand over the top layer, while others lay their heads on the pillowy softness.

The student who was wailing and rocking before continues to rock, but the wailing has ceased. One child, who has pushed away the other props, is craning his neck to watch intently as other students explore. His hand rubs the air, as though he is practicing for his turn. When I get to him, though, he still pushes the bed away.

In the middle of the night, Sarah was awakened by a terrible noise.

I stand in the middle of the circle and let loose a huge, loud, snuffling roar. This is the only sensory cue that I don't do one-on-one. The noise excites some and scares others. This is by design. One of the benefits of this type of storytelling is that it can help promote children learning to self-regulate. Self-regulation involves our abilities to use coping skills to keep on an even keel when faced with an uncomfortable, unpleasant, or otherwise stimulating experiences. Every Touching Stories story has at least one element that I know will provide some of my audience members an opportunity to practice self-regulation. My advance preparation with the teacher helps. I know who to be more cautious with, and the teacher and paras are prepared to jump in and provide assistance as needed.

Sarah looked to see what had made the noise, but the room was dark and she could not see a thing.

I take a piece of black fabric and drape it over my own head and the head of each audience member, placing us for a moment in a tent of darkness as I repeat, "She couldn't see a thing." I always check in with each audience member and ask permission before doing this. It is important to challenge my audience with their self-regulation skills; putting someone into close proximity with me in the dark, even for a brief moment, is something I would never do without permission. Some audience members decline, but most love this play with dark and light!

Bravely, Sarah reached out a hand to see if she could feel what was making the noise. She touched something big and furry! What could it be? Was it a monster? Was it a bear?

I walk to each audience member with a canvas board covered in thick faux fur for them to pet as I ask, "Was it a monster? Was it a bear?" Asking sparks participation. Children who are verbal will often respond with what they think. Some choose either monster or bear. Others suggest it might be a dog or an alien. One even suggested it might be grandma's hairy legs!

She grabbed her flashlight and shone it into the dark room.

I take a flashlight and a black canvas board around the circle. This is a tough prop. The flashlight itself is one of the more challenging items for the audience. Like the spoon in the cookie dough, it is designed for practice with fine motor skills. Exploring the bed with an open hand is a gross motor skill—one that encourages children to make broad motions with large muscle groups. Stirring the dough is fine motor. Some children with special needs may have conditions that make fine motor skills difficult, such as cerebral palsy that can cause the muscles in the hand to tighten and cramp. For this reason, I use a spoon with a very wide handle and often have to provide hand-over-hand assistance. The flashlight is even harder. I use a flashlight with a very large button that needs to be depressed to turn on the light, but even this requires more hand strength than some children have. When I was first telling this story, I just used the flashlight by itself, helping students turn it on and flash it around the room. In a well-lit room, though, the light didn't show, so now I place the black board on front of the flashlight's beam, which can be awkward to negotiate, especially for children who use wheelchairs. With one hand, I help push the button and with the other, angle the board into position so that the light shines on it mimicking a flashlight shone in a darkened room. It is interesting to note that many children with cerebral palsy are left-hand dominant. Whenever possible, I ask which hand the student would prefer to use, but if I can't determine that, I offer assistance to the left hand.

The magic of this story page is that it stimulates imagination. I started using the black board simply to have a surface for the light's beam to bounce off. To my audience, however, that board *is* the dark room. And I am always delighted to watch them peer intently into its depths, trying to find the source of the noise.

She turned the flashlight toward grandma's bed, and then she saw. It wasn't a monster. It wasn't a bear. It was Grandma's fuzzy bathrobe!

A terry cloth section of bathrobe, complete with pocket and sleeve, stretched over a canvas board is the prop for this one. The pocket and sleeve invite exploration. Students dig into this prop with their hands as I repeat, "It was Grandma's robe!" The child who was not willing to touch the bed or the fur or the bowl of dough, reaches out one finger and gently strokes the pink terry cloth. Then he grins.

Like the bed, the children want to lay their heads on the soft robe. It is important that items in a Touching Stories kit be washable. Germy hands and curious tongues are a normal part of a sensory storytelling process, and Scotchgard is a great defense against stains and bacteria. I try to make sure I have some way to clean and disinfect every item in a storytelling kit.

But then the sound came back, more terrible than before.

Again I roar (again, only one time—not repeated to each student), this time with a distinctive snuffle at the end. There is less extreme reaction as I roar this time. Some students will still respond by covering their ears; some will recoil. It took me a while to understand that I need not apologize or feel badly about these reactions but to recognize that for my audiences, for whom these stories are "life practice," these reactions are evidence of the story doing its work. Sensory stories are intended to be told over and over—at regular intervals. Ultimately, the goal is that the sounds, the smells, the sensations of a story that prompt a particular reaction encourage learning in self-regulation.

It was grandma! She was snoring!

One last roar—this time delivered with distinctly more "snore" than "roar." Many of the students laugh. Some make snoring noises of their own. Frankly, there is no therapeutic purpose to this moment. It's just for fun.

Sarah giggled and went back to sleep.

As with all storytelling with children, it is important to bring the audience safely home to a "happily ever after." The beauty of story is the ability to explore the things that scare us—in the case of this story, the things that literally "go bump in the night"—while in the safekeeping of a trustworthy storyteller whom we can rely on to bring us back to a safe place at the end. In addition to "The Monster on Grandma's Bed," there are Touching Stories tales that explore climbing a tall tree (and tangling with a wasp's nest), a middle-of-the-night thunderstorm, and a wild ride down a hill in a wheelchair. In each of these stories, audience members may experience fear and arousal, but they are always brought back to a safe and happy ending.

Thank you so much for being such a good audience member!

My last trip around the circle involves taking each audience member by the hand and making eye contact, to the extent that they allow me. Some people, especially those on the autism spectrum, actively avoid eye contact, and I never force the issue but merely offer invitation. I thank each audience member individually for participating. Touch that is not for an express, task-based purpose, such as feeding or hygiene, can sometimes be lacking in the lives of people with disabilities. This intentional touch, solely for the purpose of connection, is an essential piece of the multisensory story experience.

Sensory stories are so much fun to tell, and there is so much joy in watching an audience hear these stories for the very first time. The real benefit of sensory stories, though, comes from repeated and regular tellings. As the stories are told over and over, students learn to integrate the sensory experience with the words. Vocabularies grow. Sensory and emotional reactions become regulated. Students blossom!

Creating Your Own Sensory Stories

Making your own sensory story kits can be a fun, creative, and affordable process. The stories I share through Touching Stories come from a variety of places. Traditional folktales are a wonderful source—I have story kits for the stories of "Little Red Hen" and "The Six Blind Men and the Elephant," both of which offer rich sensory landscapes to explore. Other examples of folktales that could easily translate into sensory stories are "The Princess and the Pea," "Goldilocks and the Three Bears," and "Lazy Jack." These traditional stories will need to be simplified to accommodate an 8- to 10-sentence length and will need to be teased apart for their sensory element: Did the ladder shake as the princess climbed to get to the top of the mountain of mattresses? Was it rough to the touch? Did the mattresses squeak as she tossed and turned? Was her pillow scented with lavender? Any stories you create will need to be explored through the lens of touch, smell, sound, and sight.

You'll notice that I have not mentioned taste in my descriptions of sensory stories. The audiences I tell to are diverse in their needs. Some people I tell to have significant allergies; some are fed through tubes rather than by their mouths, so I don't use the element of taste in my story kits. Other sensory integration programs do choose to involve taste—carefully and being mindful of any health concerns. This can be done through the use of flavored lip balms applied to a cotton swab and rubbed gently on each student's lips.

In addition to folktales, you can create your own original stories for sensory tellings. "The Monster on Grandma's Bed" was inspired by nights spent at my own snoring Grandma's house as a kid. Memories from childhood are a rich area for sensory stories, as many of our childhood memories are ripe with sensory stimuli (which is what makes them so memorable). Create a story about flying a kite, about waking up on Christmas morning, or about taking the school bus for the first time. Finally, you can create sensory stories with your students, based on their memories and imaginations! Ask your students to help you write a story and then develop a sensory framework around it.

The props for sensory stories can be found in lots of places—the craft store and hardware or thrift stores are my usual go-to places. Items used in a sensory story kit must be accessible, easy to manipulate, durable, washable, and free of safety hazards. They must be interesting to touch, make a noise or produce a scent that replicates an element of the story, be visually engaging, or invite practice with fine or gross motor skills. The best stories use a mix of all these sensory elements. Don't limit yourself to what an item was meant to do—some of our best story props are repurposed items from other uses. Vacuum hoses make wonderful elephant trunks. Small foot massagers are terrific pint-sized rolling pins. Men's shoe trees (surprisingly abundant at the thrift store) rapped against a board can be used to create the sound of footsteps or a knock on a door. Build-a-Bear sells easy-to-use recordable sound buttons, and the Internet is rich with free resources for sound clips of everything from animal calls, to rolling thunder, to car horns. I prefer essential oils and other natural scents to alternatives such as air fresheners. First, essential oils are far less likely to bother people with sensitivities, and second, air fresheners and other artificial scents have more of a tendency to linger in the air, causing them to be a distraction from the story rather than adding to it. There are many online sites that sell essential oils, but choosing scents really should be a try-it-before-you-buy-it endeavor. My local metaphysical book store has a wonderful essential oil bar where I can get lost for hours putting together the scents for stories. Look into aromatherapy spas or retailers that sell essential oils in your local community for your scents. Essential oils are not cheap, but a couple drops soaked into a cotton ball will keep for a couple years in a story kit, so a little goes a long way. For a less expensive alternative, do some sniff testing at a tea bar or check out the spice aisle at your grocery store!

At Touching Stories, we attach all story-kit items to canvas boards so that they are easily identifiable as story pages and don't get misplaced in craft or toy boxes. Sensory stories are, by design, easy to tell and to use. Once you have invested time and effort in finding or creating a story kit, make sure you are taking it out and using it often.

Telling Sensory Stories for Diverse Audiences

My audiences are usually in special education classrooms. I tell stories to children with Down's syndrome, with cerebral palsy, and who are on the autism spectrum. These stories work well in special education classrooms for children of all ages, but this storytelling method is also good for virtually all young audiences, from preschool to second grade. In classrooms with older children with more advanced abilities, I use multisensory storytelling as an entryway to writing. I bring in a bin of sensory objects and help children develop their own kits based on stories they create themselves. In classroom with children with a wide diversity of abilities, I enlist kids with higher skill levels to become my storytellers, teaching them the stories and having them read as I pass around the sensory items or vice versa.

Ultimately, the school day is never as diverse in sensory experience as we wish it could be. For virtually all students, adding some smells, some opportunities to touch, some buttons to push, and interesting things to touch will enhance your storytime experience!

Stories in Motion: Creating the Path to Inclusion

Cassandra Wye

I have been creating inclusion for 45 years, both professionally and personally: as a child caregiver for my disabled father, as a researcher working to improve government policy for disabled people, and now, as a disabled storyteller working with marginalized communities around the world. I currently work with Arts Council England as a consultant on inclusion.

Championing inclusion is at the heart of everything I do. It frequently leads me into places I would not otherwise be able to go and to work with communities whom I would not otherwise meet.

In this article, I explain how my understanding of inclusion has developed over the years and how it has shaped my approach to storytelling. I will attempt to answer all the questions I have been asked about how to create inclusion through storytelling.

What Started You on This Journey to Inclusion?

My first experience of *exclusion*. I was five years old and was going with my father to attend a meeting with "an official." This woman refused to speak to my dad. Simply because he was blind, she completely ignored him. Bearing in mind that my dad was 6'5", that was an impressive feat. Instead, she turned to talk to me, a five-year-old.

It was as if he wasn't there.

And so, I realized that if you are disabled, *you do not have a voice*.

Even if you speak, *they will not hear you*.

And I thought, *that's not good enough*.

So I decided that when I got older I would fight, with whatever means possible, for the right for everyone to be heard.

Why Storytelling?

My belief in inclusion led me into becoming a professional storyteller in 1991.

Storytelling promotes people's right to be heard:

- It gives them the tools with which to communicate.
- It provides the opportunities to communicate.
- It allows communication in whatever form of communication they choose.

Storytelling *must* be for everyone, else it is for no one.

I started out thinking that my job was to make storytelling inclusive for disabled children—but *that's not good enough*. I was ignoring the needs of everyone else. There are many children who are marginalized, including street children, children in servitude, orphans, refugees—as well as disabled children—and are denied a voice. Aiming to make storytelling available to everyone has given me the chance to work with so many different communities across the globe.

What Is the Difference between Access and Inclusion?

Everyone has their own definition, but to me, as a disabled person, *access* refers to the physical environment. Accessible storytelling means that I, or any other audience member, can access the event.

There may be step-free access (ramps or lifts), disabled parking, public transport to the venue, or specialist transport available. This information is made available in advance so that people know how and where to access the site.

Inclusion means that I, or any other audience member, can be fully engaged in the storytelling experience. This could mean that the stories have been shaped to consider an audience's specific needs (e.g., using pared-down narrative for children on the autism spectrum), or that sign language interpreters for deaf or hard of hearing are available, or that audiovisual interpretation for visually impaired people is provided. This information is made available in advance so that everyone knows that they are welcome.

Access and inclusion are *not* the same. Creating accessible storytelling is fabulous. Well done. But once your audience has gotten into the venue, *how long do they stay*? If you haven't considered how to shape your storytelling to meet the needs of every individual, then the answer will be:*not for very long*.

Mainstream schools are increasingly encouraged to provide "inclusive" education; but how well do they meet the needs of children with special educational requirements? How many times have you been telling at a mainstream school and seen a bunch of children came in late, sit at the back, and disappear within five minutes?

The children with special needs have accessed the storytelling. The storytelling is available to everyone. But have they actually been included within the storytelling experience? No. *Is this good enough?*

My educational psychologist colleague calls this "the pot plant" approach to inclusion. The disabled children are there for ornamental purposes only, so the school is seen to be inclusive. Inclusion is merely a matter of being in the room, however temporarily.

Many of us have worked within this approach. It took me years to accept that there were children in the room who were not actively included—both in mainstream and specialist schools. It took me longer to admit that *it was not good enough* and longer still to fund the way and find the means to change.

Creating inclusion through storytelling is hard—it's a lifelong learning process. Becoming inclusive starts when you are able to admit that you need to change. So how can we make storytelling inclusive for everyone?

Inclusion is a process, not an end product. There is not one strategy that fits all. There is no one storytelling technique that will make storytelling inclusive to all. It depends upon the audience and the environment in which you are working.

Let's examine how I create inclusive storytelling in several environments.

Making Storytelling Inclusive within a Mainstream School Environment

I have worked as a storyteller for over 25 years, always with the aim to champion inclusion. My first storytelling project was working with a group of deaf and hearing-impaired unemployed adults to create a multilingual storytelling performance in sound and sign to tour local schools.

Schools in the United Kingdom are mandated to offer education to all their local communities. Within any school, I may work with children with physical, sensory, cognitive, or communication disabilities, including children with autism.

What Techniques Can Make Storytelling Available to Everyone?

I trained originally at Circus School in the United Kingdom, studying clowning, dance, and physical theater to create street theater performances. I learned to communicate both visually and verbally to work across languages and cultures.

I was further inspired by my training with a Bharatanatyam dance company. Bharatanatyam uses stylized movement to communicate a story, to create a visual physical language of story that can be universally understood.

I used my training to shape an approach to storytelling that would be accessible to everyone by blending movement creatively with sound, song, sign, and mime to create a style of performance that would engage every audience. But I didn't just want to tell stories *at* an audience—I wanted to tell stories *with* an audience through *interaction*.

How Can You Engage Everyone via Interaction?

Invite everyone to be actively involved—teachers and children. Interweave the narration with questions *for which there is no wrong answer*. At every decisive moment in the story, the audience must come up with a solution: How would you cross the river and outwit the crocodile? How would you solve the problem of the dastardly dragon stealing your food?

Weave these responses into the story so that no two tellings are the same.

Do You Choose Which Children Should Take Part?

I do not select children to play a certain part—we all act it out. A section of the audience might take one role, another section another role, or we might all play every role together. It depends on the size, age, and energy levels of the audience.

I found that developing the story collaboratively with the children leads to greater engagement and participation. The children's experience of the story is enriched by the opportunity to be physically, visually, emotionally, and creatively engaged within each twist and turn of the tale. They see that their ideas matter, that they have worth.

Doesn't This Type of Storytelling Become Chaotic?

Not unless you want it to! Do orchestras become chaotic when everyone plays at once? Of course not! Like a conductor with an orchestra, you guide the performance, tone it down when needed, and finish on a rousing or quiet note.

How Do You Interact with an Audience of 1,000 Children?

I manage the space, similar to a street theater performance. I seat the audience on four sides of a square and then perform in the middle, turning to face in each section of the audience in turn. Alternatively, I sit the audience on three sides and play to each section in turn. Working in this way, I can minimize the distance between myself and the audience and maximize the potential for engagement.

How Can You Ensure Everyone Is Included?

Preparation

Talk to the school prior to the performance or arrive early on the day. Find out who, in each class, has Special Educational Needs (SEN) and how they can best be included.

Set Up the Space

Request or recommend that children with SEN come first into the space and sit where it is comfortable for them. In large-scale performances, make sure they are at the front so they can see, hear, and engage easily. For those children who are nervous of being in large groups, create a cozy space slightly set apart from the rest so they can still engage but are not overwhelmed.

Use Multilingual Forms of Communication

Create a form of storytelling that is both visual and verbal, working with elements of dance and mime. Use visual props or story theater such as Kamishibai, and try to learn elements of sign languages ASL, BSL, and Makaton.

Use Collaborative Forms of Communication

Experiment with call and response techniques, sounds, chants and songs; use repetition: if the audience is seated on four sides, repeat everything to each section so they can see and hear you. Ask questions and weave their responses into the story

Create a Style of Storytelling That Is Fluid and Responsive to the Needs of Your Audience

Setting up the storytelling space with the audience on three or four sides so that I can easily see and hear them allows me to ask questions. I can take suggestions. I can simplify or make more complex my style of narration to suit the level of comprehension.

This approach has led me to work around the globe, crossing the barriers of languages and cultures. In Nepal, I worked with audiences of thousands on the streets, in the temples, and at market places—making storytelling accessible to everyone!

But Is It Inclusive?

I began to realize that there were children *present* in the room who nevertheless *excluded* from participating fully in the storytelling session. This applied especially to children with profound and multiple disabilities, who are not well served by conventional narrative approach, and to children with autism, who often found conventional storytelling sessions too stressful to remain in the room.

I knew I needed to change; but how?

Making Storytelling Inclusive for Children with SEN within a Specialist School Environment

I decided to work with the specialists—those schools that specialized in meeting the needs of those I found hard to reach.

In 2012, I secured funding to develop Tactile Tales—multisensory storytelling techniques for children with profound and multiple disabilities, including autism.

What Was the Idea behind Tactile Tales?

I had a giant sequined turnip prop created for a tour of "The Enormous Turnip" to Vietnam. Years later, I was asked to tell the story in an autism unit in the United Kingdom. A child picked up my sparkly turnip and held it up to the light. It created a pattern of light across the ceiling, which shimmered and sparkled as he turned the turnip.

He turned and smiled at me.

"The turnip sparkled," he said.

A boy with little verbal communication had found something new about my turnip that thousands of previous audiences had missed.

He had chosen to enter the space, to pick up the turnip, to experiment with how it moved, and to share his findings with me. It was his choice to participate, and he took it. And he created something unique.

I wondered, what if I commissioned a whole range of 2-D and 3-D props that children can manipulate themselves in whatever way they choose so that their ideas could input into the shaping of a story by empowering them to choose their means of communication? Maybe this could be a way to ensure that all of their voices are heard!

I designed a two-year research project, run in partnership with six specialist organizations.

Year One

Trailing my existing style of stories with existing props at each venue, I interviewed each staff at each session (and children where appropriate) to find out what worked and what did not work. What needed to change to fully meet the needs of their children?

I discovered that narrative-based storytelling—however enriched with mime, sign, and dance—can be very challenging for children with verbal processing difficulties. I needed to pare down the narrative to use the minimum of words with maximum effect and find ways of using 2-D and 3-D props to propel the narrative so that I was no longer reliant on the spoken word.

Year Two

I worked with a team of textile artists to design a series of specialist stories with over 90 handmade props that could be seen, heard, felt, and moved. I piloted these new stories and new props with our partnership venues, once again interviewing participants. My goal was to discover if my theories were right, what worked and what did not, and why.

I discovered that the props HAD to be interactive.

The children needed to be able to use them themselves, to choose how they engaged with them, and to choose how to use them to direct the development of the story.

The props HAD to be multisensory.

Each element of the story is first told to everyone and then repeated one to one with every child. This repetition of sound, movement, prop, and word enables those with sensory processing disabilities to engage with story at a pace that is right for them.

Each element of spoken narrative is *not* set in stone but changes depending on how the children are engaging with the props. The narration is improvised in relation to the children's ideas—no two tellings are the same.

Tactile Tales has proven so effective at creating inclusion through storytelling that it has traveled around the globe, working not only with children with SEN in specialist schools but also with all children, including those with SEN, in mainstream schools. Tactile Tales also provides specialist sessions for children with SEN within mainstream venues, creating inclusive storytelling sessions at festivals, libraries, and museums.

The success of Tactile Tales has led me further on my journey into inclusion.

Making Storytelling Inclusive for All Children at Festivals, Libraries, and Museums

Tactile Tales presents either specific storytelling sessions geared for a specific audience or inclusive sessions open to all.

How Do You Make These Sessions Inclusive?

For both these sessions, the planning is the same.

Setting Up the Storytelling Space

I make a site visit to determine where it is best to place the storytelling, making sure the site provides:

- ease of access for children in wheelchairs;
- little background noise;
- a signposted route for access.

I also arrange to seat the audience on three sides to maximize intimacy and ease of interaction and to offer a choice of seating so that everyone can be comfortable. I make sure there is plenty of room for those in wheelchairs.

Working in Partnership with Targeted Audiences; Working with Key Local Groups

For example: I contact groups for families with disabled children to ask for advice in designing the sessions and ask them for feedback on the day.

Targeting Publicity and Marketing

For example: If you are working with a sign language interpreter, make sure that every member of the deaf community knows that the event will be signed. This will build your audience for future inclusive events.

Conclusion

Inclusion is a process, not an end product. There is not one strategy that fits all, but as you can see, there are underlying elements of inclusivity that are the same, whatever the audience is:

- Preparation prior to the event
- Setting up the storytelling space to suit the audience
- Finding a multisensory form of communication that allows everyone to fully participate
- Working in partnership with venues and specialist organizations to get it "right"

Above all, I strive to create a style of storytelling that opens out the story to include everyone's contributions and to guide the audience through the process of storytelling from listening and observing, to participating, to directing the story to a satisfactory end.

It's the same process with everyone, on the streets of Nepal or delivering one-to-one sessions with children with complex autism in schools.

It stems from my childhood role as a guide to my visually impaired father. If you are a guide, you become attuned, learning to watch, listen, and respond to one another. You communicate through a shift in tone or body weight as well as through words. You ensure the visually impaired person leads and the sighted person follows, so you can go wherever you choose—*together*.

Inclusion is at the heart of what I do. I cannot imagine any other approach to storytelling.

Why would you?

6

Strategies for Inclusive Classrooms and General Audiences

Introduction

Lyn Ford

On the 4th day of the Litzsinger [School (Ladue, Missouri)] residency, we reviewed the stories we already had done with Magic Bag. Then Kelsey, the fabulous teacher, went to the board and we made a word web on storytelling. And Ellie, one of the students said, "Storytelling makes the rest of the world go away!" OMG! That may be one of the favorite descriptions of storytelling! I wanted to pass it on.

—Annette Harrison, storyteller and teaching artist, working
with students at the Litzsinger School; Litzsinger educates
students, aged 5 to 14 years, with a range of disabilities.

I would guess that Ellie's excitement about storytelling has to do with the fact that it can make "the world," the community of a classroom or school, a comfortable and comforting place that easily includes participants in communal narrative work and play, rather than excluding any of them from its social environment and practices.

Storytelling gives students opportunities they might not have previously experienced without difficulty, opportunities to get acquainted, to join in, to cooperate, to create as team members as well as individuals, to become the hero, and to rise up and stand out, not for any difference or disabling concern but for their abilities to become a part of the story.

The wonder and wisdom of storytelling is something they can share every day.

to children what is about to happen. Knowing that after the read-aloud, the next story will be told with puppets helps children channel their enthusiasm. The teacher or parent who knows that after the third story there will be an action song can gauge whether he or she should exit with Joey or Janie or hang in there another six minutes.

- Choose stories you love—and can tell from memory, even if you're going to show the pictures as you tell. Writing out the complete text and taping it to the back of the book allows you to hold the book open so children can see illustrations while you tell the story.

- If you are using picturebooks with older children, avoid books that look babyish. A child with developmental delays quite likely still knows his or her actual age. If he or she is eight, he or she wants to be treated like an eight-year-old, not an extra-large two-year-old.

- Know what can be left out of the story without sacrificing the gist of it. Paper-clipping pages together allows you to skip text that is too long and unessential for a particular setting. Just because you know all 27 verses and variations of a song does not mean you need to share all the verses—especially if your audience is antsy.

- Read the whole book before you use it with a group! Cute illustrations don't always make a good story. I once had to abandon a story midway because I realized it was insulting to my audience. The book, *Earrings*, by Judith Viorst was highly rated as an excellent example of persuasive writing (or whiny behavior?), with a refrain, "I want them. I need them. I love them. Beautiful earrings. Glorious earrings." Perfect, right? But her parents think pierced ears are "tacky." At that point, I realized all the little girls in front of me (and several of the boys) had pierced ears. Had I just labeled them all "tacky"? We stopped and talked about it.

- Similarly, a very good storyteller was reading a very simple board book about opposites (*Elephant Elephant: A Book of Opposites* by Francesco Pittau and Bernadette Gervais). Jane is usually able to hold any audience and is a master of adaptation, but she almost lost the group when the opposite of "dry" ("wet") was illustrated by an elephant peeing. It's a super clever book, so she still wanted to use it. In subsequent readings, she adapted her presentation to allow for the pandemonium that image caused—a combination of shock, thrill, and wild hilarity. Before turning to that page, she would caution the children, "Now the next one, you would *never* do." If the group was especially unruly, she just did an extra thick page-turn.

- Draw-and-Tell and Cut-and-Tell stories work especially well with children who need visual clues. Feeling clever when they figure out what you are making "right before their eyes" is an added bonus.

- Pay particular attention to transitions. Most of us aren't very good at waiting for the next thing to happen. Patience is a virtue we have to learn. Explaining what you are doing and what is going to come next can help children who have trouble processing information quickly. "Okay, George and Martha are going back in my story bag. Say bye-bye George. Say bye-bye Martha. Let's see what's next."

- Hide the props or puppets and the extra books. They can be distractions. Keep them in a bag or box, stacked in the order they'll be used, so you aren't pawing around in the bag. When you are finished with that item, put it in a second bag. Then all you have to do to get ready for your next program is reverse the order of the items in the bag.

- Assure parents or caregivers that if they need to step out of the room with a child, neither they nor the child have failed. They are respecting that child's attention span.

- Similarly, assure parents or caregivers that sitting still is not a requirement. Give children permission to participate. Often, the child who seems to wander during storytime is also the child who repeats the story verbatim, recites the poem, and sings the songs when back in the regular classroom or at home. Movement allows some children to process information.

- If a story has a refrain and you want children to join in, teach them their line(s) before you begin. Anticipating, and listening for when to call out their line, helps children focus.

- Ask the adults in the room to join in, too. I often tell audiences, "I don't sing solos." Asking adults to participate need not be awkward. We are the experts; parents and teachers sometimes need to be asked to participate and told how they can help. Encouraging them to model appropriate behavior will educate and empower them. When a group of parents or teachers are talking in the back of the room, I have sometimes asked the kids to turn around and shush them. Sometimes an adult will try to hush a child and cause more distraction than the supposedly disruptive child. It's okay to be direct: "Johnny's fine. I'll let you know if he's bothering anybody."

- If your stories are supposed to be funny, let the kids know it's okay to laugh. If holding their attention is a concern, give them a signal to watch for so they won't miss the next bit of the story: "When I do this, it's time to listen again."

- If you know sign language and can use it easily and accurately, add some to your repertoire. Teaching the whole group the signs for key words can help a child who relies on signing feel part of the group. This should be done matter-of-factly, as part of the story, not pointing out the signing child's "handicap" but as another bit of information. Sign language can be included in the same way that some authors incorporate Spanish, parenthetically, so the meaning is clear.

- Offer a tactile experience related to the concepts being discussed. For example, if the story is *Anansi and the Moss-Covered Rock*, bringing moss or lichen for each child to touch will help all the children understand the idea.

- Encourage varied ways to respond to the story. Often we expect a verbal response—but clapping to a beat, rocking in time to a song, or just making eye contact can be appreciated as participation.

- Be sensitive to touch. Even a reassuring touch on a shoulder or arm can be upsetting to some children. Respecting this difference can also help children whose personal boundaries are blurred to respect others' personal space. Use sit-upons or carpet squares to define each child's space. Don't require children to hold hands, even for a game or song. I often ask kids to move back from my space, "so I won't accidentally kick you when I get excited." It makes them laugh; it also establishes a boundary.

- Vary the pace. Sometimes keeping pacing slow and even is helpful for those who are easily distracted or excitable. When your audience is fidgety, you may need to speed up, cut out some dramatic repetitions, and cut to the chase.

- Similarly, vary the quality of your voice. Getting very quiet can build suspense and signal to kids that you and your story deserve their attention. That conspiratorial stage whisper can be intriguing. When you focus on distractions or disruptive behavior, everyone else does, too. Acknowledge whatever is distracting and then move on. "Andy seems to be having a rough time, but Miss Jones will take care of him. Let me tell you what Miss Frizzle did next."

- Sometimes kids need to move—that's why "Shake Your Sillies," "Head, Shoulders, Knees and Toes," and all those play-party songs persist, even in the age of YouTube. Free-form dancing allows everyone to join in, even if they have to stay in a wheelchair, can't hear the music, or can't see the pictures in a book. (Tip: Before you start the dance, establish what the cue for stopping will be: "When I move my hands like this, we're all going to freeze.")

- Choose stories with repetition, so children can predict what will happen next and participate.

- Choose stories with actions or motions, and encourage participants to make the motions.

- Demonstrate several ways to act out the same fingerplay. That famous spider can twist up the spout by alternating fingers and thumbs, walking your fingers up your arm, or simply pressing all your fingers against the fingers on your other hand while moving your arms above your head. Demonstrating both fine motor and gross motor skills gives children choices and allows everyone to succeed in their own style. You may even learn some new techniques.

- Vary your delivery method. Use puppets, flannel board stories, pop-up books, and masks. Sometimes telling the story more than one way—reading the book while simultaneously using flannel board pieces—provides more than one way to experience the story. How many times have you attended a concert or lecture and found yourself watching the deaf interpreter instead of the person who is singing or speaking? That's when I tend to remember the story—I have stored it in two different areas of my brain, which makes recalling its details easier.

- When the art in a picturebook is stunning, but your audience is large, a PowerPoint of the pages eliminates the chorus of "I can't see." My library did this in partnership with our PBS Television station and had 200, 300, and even 600 people coming for "Storytime in the

Commons." I'm sure there were kids with special needs in that audience, but they blended in with all the other distractions going on around them.

- Always, the focus should be on the story. If you aren't comfortable manipulating the props, cast them aside and rely on your voice. The power of imagination—making the pictures in their own mind—is what really gets the synapses firing.

Obviously these strategies are helpful for all children, regardless of their abilities. Kids with special needs are everywhere, whether they have been labeled and assigned Individualized Education Programs (IEPs) or not. As storytellers, as librarians, we need to be sensitive to each child's unique way of responding to stories. Give them a chance and they will respond.

Resources

De las Casas, D. (2008). *Handmade tales: Stories to make and take*. Westport, CT: Libraries Unlimited.

http://www.childs-play.com/teacher-zone/signed_stories.html. Part of ITV's Corporate and Social Responsibility initiative. Contemporary children's stories told in British Sign Language, text, animation, pictures, narration, and sound. American Sign Language versions told by Keith Wann, Pinky Aiello, and Peter Cook are available at http://www.signedstories.com/.

Kranowitz, C. (1998). *The out-of-sync child*. Cheltenham, England: Skylight Press.

Pellowski, A. (1988). *The family storytelling handbook: How to use stories, anecdotes, rhymes, handkerchiefs, paper, and other objects to enrich your family traditions*. New York, NY: Macmillan.

Pellowski, A. (2008). *The storytelling handbook: A young people's collection of unusual tales and helpful hints on how to tell them*. New York, NY: Aladdin.

Thompson, R. (1988). *Draw and tell: Reading, writing, listening, speaking, viewing, shaping*. Toronto, Ontario: Annick Press.

Thompson, R. (1990). *Frog's riddle & other draw-and-tell stories*. Toronto, Ontario: Annick Press.

Sensory Storytimes blog: http://www.ala.org/blog/2012/03/sensory-storytime-a-brief-how-to-guide/

Talking about Those Bears: Folktales for Social Considerations in the Special or Inclusive Classroom

Lyn Ford

Let's look at a story that most students in the United States will experience before the end of their elementary school years:

The Three Bears

Anecdotal Version from Lyn Ford

Once upon a time, there were three bears, a Papa Bear, a Mama Bear, and a Baby Bear, and they lived in a little house in the forest. One morning, Mama Bear made porridge, but the porridge was too hot for the bears to eat it, so they went for a walk in the forest, thinking they would eat the porridge when they returned. And they left their door unlocked.

A little girl went for a walk in the very same forest. She found the little house, whose front door was open. The little girl entered the house and found three bowls of porridge. The little girl decided to taste each bowl. The first one she tasted was too hot; the next bowl of porridge was too cold; the third bowl of porridge was just right, and the little girl ate it all.

Then this little girl found three differently sized chairs. She tried sitting in all three of them. The first chair was too hard; the second chair was too soft; the third and littlest chair was just right. But when the little girl sat on it, it broke into pieces.

The little girl wandered up the stairs and found three beds. Of course, she tried resting in each one. The first bed was too hard; the second bed was too soft. The third was just right; the little girl curled up in it and fell asleep.

Meanwhile, the three bears came home. They realized their front door was open. They discovered that the porridge had been tasted and one bowl was empty; that their chairs had been used and one was broken; and their beds had been rested upon and one held a little girl. The little girl awakened and was startled to see the three bears. She jumped from the bed and ran away as fast as she could.

Yes, sometimes that little girl is called Goldilocks, especially if the older variants of the tale are told. But in these days of respect for cultural diversity, to give any description of the little girl may diminish the possibility for students to imagine her as a fictional peer or acceptable protagonist. And, if you think about it, the story leaves out all the little boys in the classroom, unless they imagine that they are the bears.

This is an anthropomorphic tale, in which animals are given human characteristics. Such tales can be used to approach lessons about personal actions and social behaviors, pointing out inappropriate behaviors and responses, supporting and reinforcing useful social skills, and bringing critical thinking into play, without encouraging any student into self-consciously thinking, "Oh, the teacher is talking about *me*."

The story's theme is how the actions of one person or character can have a negative impact on others and how thoughtless action can cause harm to others, and, possibly, oneself. After I have told the story (or the teacher has read the story before my arrival and I retell it, comparing the printed work and the spoken word and pointing out their similarities and differences), and depending upon the knowledge base and levels of skills in discussion, we may talk about safety measures at home and criminal actions—trespassing, breaking and entering, vandalism, stealing—but foremost in any discussion is the act of doing something without thinking about its consequences.

First, and not only for fun but also for character recognition and reinforcement of the plot of the story, we recreate the characters through sound and movement in each scene. I'm usually the child who has done the breaking and entering so that no child is "the villain" or "the bad guy," and I model his or her behaviors in each scene. Then we become each of the Bear family members, first by talking about the ways each might sound, walk, or complain about damaged goods and strangers in the house, using the sentences each character speaks in the story: "Someone's been sitting in *my* chair!" "Someone's been sitting in my chair and broke it all to pieces! Wah!!!!" We do this for each scene. You get the idea.

In some story variants, the Bear family leaves their front door open, and that child walks right into their house. In others, the door is closed, the child knocks, no one answers, and the child walks right on inside. In that opening alone, we find points for discussion on remembering to close and lock doors when we leave our homes and why that's important; the danger of possibly walking into an unknown place; and the disrespectful action of walking into someone else's space (privacy in bedrooms is a real issue for some children, especially as they approach or reach puberty).

Add to these initial situations the chair-breaking incident, the porridge-eating incident, and the selection of a bed in which the discourteous child curls up under someone else's blanket and takes a nap—horrors! Then, the trespassing child runs away, and we don't know if she has really learned a lesson, or if she might do the same thing at someone else's house.

That's a cue for some critical thinking:

- Ask students about the trespassing child's behaviors and attitude:
    - Why do you think this child is walking through the woods alone? Is that a sensible thing to do? Why or why not?
    - Why do you think this child would walk into someone else's house without permission? Are there any reasons why this might be okay? What might those reasons be? Does the story say the child had any of these reasons to walk into the house?
    - Why did this child have to have a chair, a bowl of porridge, and a bed that were "just right"? What does "just right" even mean? Describe your idea of a "just right" chair or breakfast or bed.
    - Even if something looks or feels or tastes "just right," if it's not yours, should you take it or use it? Why or why not?
- Ask students about their own experiences of *trespass*:
    - Has it ever happened to you? Did someone use your belongings, something that belongs to you, without asking your permission? Did it bother you? How did you feel? Why do you think this bothered you? What happened to the person who used your belongings?
    - Have you ever used someone else's property without asking? What was it? Why did you use it without asking? How did its owner

react? How do you think its owner felt when you used something without asking? What happened to you because of this?

- o If someone is using your property and you want them to stop, without screaming or fighting or hurting that person in any way, what might you do?
- o If you have used someone else's property without permission, what should you do to keep that person from being upset?

- After our discussion, and guided by the suggestions of students, we model possible ways to face the consequences of our actions and make up for them:
  - o Sometimes the Goldilocks character simply says, "I'm sorry." Most of the time, he or she does more, by introducing herself and explaining why she did what she did (children always have great explanations, or excuses!).
  - o Sometimes he or she stays to fix the chair, wash the breakfast bowls and help make another tasty breakfast (menus are an additional activity), and make the beds. Then she usually becomes a friend and playmate for Baby Bear.
  - o We always write illustrated letters of apology to the Bear family. Sometimes we also write invitations for the Bear family to come and visit at the Goldilocks character's home. Sometimes this becomes a classroom party.

Whenever possible, our next activity is a rewrite of the story, changing the characters to the Three Bunnies and the Big Bad Wolf. The students give me ideas, which I develop into a story that we can act out together. From this model, the students gain ideas for their own story variant, which can include any characters they choose. Parents, student teachers, older students from other classes, and other voluntary scribes may help to get the ideas down on paper in written or illustrated format or a combination of both. These story variants can be published for their authors to enjoy and share in printed format.

When selecting a folktale or fairy tale to use as a stepping-off point for nurturing or reinforcing effective social behaviors, it is important to consider whether the story effectively approaches the intended concept, clearly identifies the behaviors that are the intended focus, is appealing and entertaining, with a touch of humor to temper serious events, and is something that you can prepare to share in both spoken and printed format. "Talking the story" breaks down any barriers that linguistic circumstances or reading for comprehension might have constructed.

A few other well-known and easy-to-find (and tell!) folktales, whose anthropomorphic characters' behaviors lend themselves to developing social skills, are the following:

"The Bremen Town Musicians"—Everyone has a "voice" and a way of being and doing. Everyone is unique and important. In a community, no matter who we are, we can find ways to work and live together.

"The Little Red Hen"—Helping someone bring rewards.

"The Three Billy Goats Gruff"—Sometimes we can't solve a problem by ourselves; perhaps it can be fixed if we walk away and leave it to the older folks (a good lesson on letting adults take care of a bully).

Resources

Cartledge, G., & Kleefeld, J. (1991). *Taking part: Introducing social skills to children, preK–grade 3* (2nd ed.). Champaign, IL: Research Press.

Cartledge, G., & Kleefeld, J. (2010). *Working together: Building children's social skills through folktales*. Champaign, IL: Research Press.

Spinning the Words: Deliberate Storytelling for Framing Vocabulary in the Minds of Scholars

Ken Wolfe

What we learn with pleasure, we never forget.

—Alfred Merciér

Your stories make the vocab words burrow into my brain!

—Connor H., seventh-grade scholar

Inadvertent (adj): Not Intended or Planned

"The sun was setting on the far end of the amber expanse of prairie. A cool, rolling night breeze had slipped under the hot prairie winds of the day, taking its place, and it gave a working man reason to stop and inhale with relief. The cattle were muttering to each other by the hundreds, and the cowboys, my brothers in the saddle, were muttering back over their shoulders as they sat, hunched and exhausted, facing the fire. Slim, our cook, emerged from the supply tent with an armful of raw dinner, ready to set above the flame. The tent, gray and patched, was left over from the War Between the States, what ended only a few years before.

"Most of our men had seen that war up close, and so had that tent. For some reason that Slim couldn't (or wouldn't) explain, the tent's panels were emblazoned on one side with the letters 'IN AD' and the other side carried 'VER.' A few of us, those that could read a Bible, thought it was Latin or some such foreign tongue. Some others reckoned it had to do with the unit or garrison that carried it in the war. I didn't care. It could have stood for the initials of men that Slim brutally killed, and I wouldn't have paid it mind. I was just hungry.

"Long minutes later, we shoveled in the usual brown, salty stew meat and some sort of gravy. It was hot enough that most of us chewed with mouths up and open to let out the steam; only a schoolmarm blows on a spoon. We weren't so dainty. Slim come up just then, said he had a treat for us. He said he'd been walking alongside the wagon most of the day, collecting, to give us this treat. He set out an iron skillet, poured some cooking oil in there, and let it sizzle. Then he hefted up a fair-sized sack and dumped the contents in the pan. It was grasshoppers. Big ones. Each with a snapped head, some of 'em snapped clean off. They sizzled and popped in the oil, bouncing around against each other. My brother cowboys and I were transfixed. We couldn't look away. We had to know what Slim's plan was. Sure enough, he lifted one of the bigger ones out of the pan with his huge calloused fingers and held it up high. Against the night's growing chill, the heat vapors rose from it like it was afire. With his free hand, he popped the lid off a jar of sweet molasses. He dipped the barbecued grasshopper into the jar and brought it out dripping. Slim lifted it to his lips like it was a dainty from a doily and said, 'They's just like candy when they's still hot.' And he chewed and he swallowed. 'C'mon, boys, and git you some eat!'

"We all tried one. Some tried two. They weren't bad, considering. Hayden picked one of them up and spiked it with skewer; he said he liked his toasted darker. But his attention slipped, like Hayden's always did, and his grasshopper soon caught flame. Well, he didn't know what to do. He tried to shake it off, but it didn't come. Slim yelled that he'd wasted one. In something like panic, Hayden flicked the skewer and the flaming crispy critter went soaring in an arc right toward the supply tent. It landed there in between the IN and the AD and rolled down to the edge where it began to light the tent on fire, too. Shoot, it was only moments before that whole panel was hosting flames. In no time 't all that tent and our supplies would be no more. We all leapt up and started throwing whatever we had on that tent: water, coffee, whiskey. Jeb stood there just a-spittin'. We put it out before it was destroyed utterly.

"We saved our supplies, sure, but Slim was mad as hornets. Hayden claimed that it was an accident. He didn't mean to have that happen. He swore up and down that it wasn't on purpose. I don't think that Slim believed him, though. I think he thought Hayden was just being a vandal. Slim couldn't stand to see a world where something accidental, not-on-purpose, and unintentional could happen like the burning down of the 'IN AD VER' tent!"

The Eclectic Audience Is Ready and Waiting

I have taught for 25 years at all the levels of secondary education, including the college and postgraduate levels, and I believe that seventh grade is the sweet spot on the bat. I have found that, if one is able to find and strike the correct chord with them, seventh-grade scholars are the most energetic and loyal group on the age spectrum. Striking that chord is the tough part sometimes, like contorting one's beginner fingers to hit a true-sounding F on the guitar. It's tricky. As with all grades, within each seventh-grade group are all manner of personalities and abilities, ranging from severely struggling scholars to severely gifted ones and all those who, at their respective places on the dial, wrestle internally with distractions, self-deprecation, and self-doubt. Into that mental mix fly social distractions and hallway politics, looming parental expectations, the draw of popular entertainment, and all the swirling chemicals that burgeoning puberty can provide. Specific scholars of mine have had the dubious honor of added challenges: dyslexia, ADD, fragile X, Down syndrome, Asperger's syndrome, ADHD, autism, ED, BD (way back when), ODD, deafness, diabetes, family trauma, and the like. It's somewhat foolish of me to assume that my lesson in grammar, vocabulary, literature, or composition is the primary focus of my scholars' lives. My classes, on the best day, have the attention span of a vapor. My attempts to gain and hold their corporate attention to introduce effective content that sticks in their minds can sometimes be a tenuous thing up against the clamor of these other aspects also wailing for their attention.

To that end, I have discovered that, in specific pursuits and especially for certain scholars, telling stories reaches where worksheets, activities, and group work cannot. The stories "unmount" the scholars from their immediate distractions, like a temporary bubble of a different reality, and create images and mnemonic devices that plant the knowledge deep into the scholars' memories and allow them to recall quickly and accurately. Think of your own life: you may not remember a list, or a group of facts, but you'll remember a story and all the intricate details that accompany it. I use storytelling most consistently as I present vocabulary. Doing so connects to the scholars' minds and imaginations, especially well for those scholars who deal with extra challenges. For those scholars, in particular, learning through story can be a fast, enjoyable avenue.

Telling stories to teach vocabulary is a little more intensive per word, ranging from 5 to 10 minutes (or longer if I really like telling the story). I view such time spent as an investment, though. Ten minutes of class time given now may equal a lifetime of retention. As a matter of fact, some of my scholars with whom I keep in contact through social media, now in their 30s, tell me that they still remember their vocabulary words (and the stories that accompany them), while all other middle school curriculum has long since faded into the gray.

Visualization and Mnemonics

One of the strongest benefits of telling stories to teach vocabulary is engaging and strengthening the scholars' ability to visualize. Many scholars who struggle with decoding or fluency have a weak ability to visualize the events as they read. Rather than seeing images with their "mind's eye," these scholars are stuck with a string of decoded words that carry little imagination with them. Our current culture of visual entertainment is little help. It allows the scholars to receive their mental images through films, computer, and gaming consoles, which is far more easily done than constructing their own. Given the option, most scholars will gravitate toward the easier option, which underscores for them the "boring" nature of reading. The telling of a good story can be a stopgap in that process. Storytelling to one's scholars lends itself to the construction of such mental images; the scholars picture the settings, images, and characters that I present to them. They connect those images, characters, and settings to the content at hand. Those images serve as anchors, as hooks for their brains to grab and hold on to the material. I describe this phenomenon to the scholars thus: "Your minds are like the fuzzy side of Velcro and, with my stories, I'm giving you the things you need to learn on the side that has the little hooks on it. One meets the other, and they stick."

While the scholars are simply listening (which seems to them like a passive thing, as watching TV is), they are connecting my words with images from their memory. If I say "a baby who can't sit up, but keeps falling over," they reach back mentally to baby pictures they have seen, memories of babies tumbling over while trying to sit up or stand. They hold that and other images in their minds like a mental hand of playing cards, and then I give them another, and they must arrange that image with the others they are already holding. They work mentally to make sense of it. They must reimagine the baby as I talk of her growing up into a girl of 13 years. In the scholars' minds, they morph that baby into a girl of their own age. It's only a short leap in visualization from the story told orally to the story told in text. The scholars review the vocabulary words with each other, telling each other the stories with great accuracy and recall, doing the motions, and using the voices, themes, and the mnemonics that each story features.

That's where the magic happens. The stories that accompany the introduction of these words are fabricated around a mnemonic that helps the scholars remember the spelling of the word. Most often it's a play on words (*meticulous*—"Me, T. I see you, louse."), a bad pun (*undulate*—"Uhhn, Dee! You late!"), a stretched phonetic (*evanescent*—"Evan's 'E' scent"), or something of the like (*immaculate*—"I'mma see you late!"). These phrases, all of which are the culmination of the story that precedes it, connect in meaning and sound to help them gain a foothold on their proper spelling. When the scholars take their vocabulary test and seem stuck, all I have to say is "Remember the stories." Then eyebrows lift, eyes roll up to the left in recall, lips move in silent remembrance, and smiles bloom while pencils scritch on paper. Alfred's maxim is proved right nearly every time.

Whence Come the Words

Most of the words that I present to the scholars are from an SAT prep flashcard set I bought years ago. There are some truly grand words in there: Perspicacity, Defunct, Indelible, Wizened, Venerable, Ensconce, Imperturbable, and Adamant. All are fine words and well used. Scholars have come back to me through the years claiming that they saw words from our list on the actual entrance exams. Likewise, as I travel through the everyday, I pick up words that come along and save them: Quaff, Fiasco, Fallible, Fortuitous. Sometimes it's a word that I find interesting: Obsequious, Inadvertent. Other times, it's a word that I think the scholars really need in their "toolbox": Ruminate, Sedentary, Impunity.

The words you choose can come from the same types of sources. Any word has the potential to become "sticky Velcro" and stay in the minds of your scholars. The key is to find words that offer themselves to breaking down into other words or associations. The following is a short list of SAT-level words that do so:

Meticulous	Jettison
Lackadaisical	Imperturbable
Fortuitous	Mollify
Indefatigable	Penultimate
Brouhaha	Volatile
Bellicose	Imbroglio
Apathetic	Truculent
Impunity	Ensconce
Somnambulist	Parsimonious
Indelible	Taciturn

As you read these words, looking for ways to break the words down, you might find some associations you can make. For example, the word "imbroglio" (n., a complex dispute or argument) could be broken down into "I'm Bro Glio." That's the first thing I see when I look at it. So, now I try to find a way to connect the definition to the association. *Could I come up with a situation where someone who calls himself "Brother Glio" causes or becomes involved in a complex dispute or argument? In what kinds of situations would this happen? A customer service desk? A line in a cafeteria? In a subway car? In the middle of a public street art fair? What kind of dispute could it be? A misunderstanding about a transaction? A mistaken identity? Being in the wrong place at the wrong time? A misheard phrase taken as an insult?*

So I choose to go with mistaken identity at an art fair. I remember what art fairs are like, crowded, full of strolling people, artists, collectors, and fans wandering through and among booths and in line for the food stands. I imagine an overfriendly man approaching me, calling himself Brother Glio, not understanding personal space, and expecting me to know him from a past to which he keeps referring. That's awkward but not complex. So, now I imagine Brother Glio as a large, intimidating man with wild eyes and a bushy beard and in a belted tunic and Birkenstocks. There. The addition of character traits makes the situation more complex, especially from the point of view of a kid having to explain to this big man, "I'm not who you think I am." Aha! I'll make the story happen to me when I was a kid. It would certainly be tough to negotiate out of this situation as an adolescent, especially if you could imagine this giant man turning from friendly to confrontational. *Why would I be alone at the art fair so that Brother Glio could corner me? When do kids wander without parents?* Aha. Maybe, it's the first time my parents let me wander without them for a while. Yes. *Why, though? What for?* I want a corn dog from the food truck, and they still want to make their way down the whole row of artists' tents. They tell me that I can go wait in line and cut through the tents to meet them on the next aisle over. *So, who does Brother Glio think I am?* Not a friend. Not a relative. A person would be sure enough of identity to not make an issue of that, unless he or she was unstable somehow. I'm not trying to get the kids to recall mental illness as part of the definition, just a complex dispute. So I won't add that part. He's not unstable, just mistaken but convinced that he's right. *What if I were mistaken for the nephew of a long-lost friend?* That's partially removed enough to be almost certain of someone but still unsure.

In short:

- I'm 12. I'm waiting in line at the corn dog food truck at the art fair; my parents trust me to be alone, finally.

- This big guy comes up and hugs me, calls me Li'l Freddy, and claps me on the shoulders, smiling broadly.

- He tells me how he knew my parents, gives history, and calls himself Brother Glio.

- I'm kinda scared, I try to dissuade him; he gets offended that I "don't remember" him; gets loud in his disappointment.

- People interact, asking questions, making demands; everyone who tries to help makes things more confusing.

- Everyone is frazzled; I'm scared; Brother Glio is trying to justify his behavior.

- My parents arrive, try to sort things out; Brother Glio calls them by incorrect names, claims they are the old friends.

- Parents whisk me away (with my corn dog) out of the fair to the car to go home; Brother Glio stands tall among the crowd, calling after us, shouting, "Don't you remember me? I'm Bro Glio! I'm Bro Glio! Sure, you remember me! I'm Bro Glio!"

Those are the "bones" of the story—the events in the story that move the story forward. The next step is to fill in the blanks with imaginative details—the meat on the bones, so to speak. The sensory details and the dialogue, the character traits and the emotions. I ought not change the bones once they are set, but the other stuff is negotiable and subject to the whims of my imagination. My knowledge of middle school kids (and my own remembrances of adolescence) will go a long way to bring life to this story. It's a situation to which the kids can likely relate a little, especially ones who know fairs. It's one in which the fear and confusion of a complex dispute would be palpable for the scholars. And, since I presented it as a situation that actually happened to me (which is what I tell them), the "No way! Really?" factor is high.

Now, I must admit that I tell my scholars that all my stories are true. My answer to them when they ask, "Wait. Did that *really* happen to you?" is "Yes, it did . . . as far as you know." It's a winking deceit, for we all know what's real, but the illusion makes the story "stickier" in the memory and they enjoy trying to call me out on it. I just shrug and smile and tell them that they may freely believe what they want. You may not be willing to follow that path and "lie" to your scholars. I understand. Still!

The Telling

In preparation for telling any vocabulary story, the crucial task for me is to convert fiction to memory. I take my list of bones, without all the fun details, and repeat them aloud to myself until I don't have to pause or refer to the list. I take each bone of the story and visualize it. I pick the settings from places in my memory, pictures, or films. I cast the characters with people and faces I know. I relive related events from my own experiences. I do my best to mentally put myself in the situation and imagine as many aspects and details that I can fabricate. I want to remember this story as if I had actually been there, seen it, heard it, felt it. Then I tell the story out loud, adding details as I gain the confidence of my fluency. Once I have done this, I can tell the story and connect with my scholars. As I do, I follow the bones. Those don't change. The details surrounding those bones add flavor and texture but are pretty negotiable and subject to time, audience, and my memory. The lovely reality is that the more I tell the stories, the better I know them.

The Benefit for the Scholars

In preparation for this writing, I asked my scholars what they found useful about the vocabulary stories. One of them, Connor, a young man with the desire to learn but whose attention issues often waylay his efforts, answered brightly with his hand waving in its customary fervor, "Oooh! It's 'cause your stories make the vocab words burrow into my brain." At the facial expression of the girls in the desks beside him, he realized the somewhat creepy sound of his contribution and rephrased, "No! Wait! They're *ensconced* in my brain!" "Ensconce" is a word of ours, and at the sound of it, the scholars all across the room said aloud and under their breath the mnemonic from the reptile breeding story I told, "*Every New Snake Cries ONCE.*" That scholar was right, of course. All this story preparation and thought benefit the scholars as they enjoy and absorb these vocabulary stories, these "sanctioned deceptions" that soak deep into their minds and cement in their memories. The information, whatever it may be, nestles right in his brain with all the other stories from life by which my scholars have learned to look both ways, to tell the truth, and to be kind to others. My material becomes immediately second nature. To some degree, every scholar comes to one's class struggling under nets of impediment to learning, from common adolescent angst and ennui to highly acute special needs. Storytelling, applied to almost any material or subject matter, can cut through those nets and seep into the scholars' minds.

Teach Them to Fly: Creating On-Ramps to Learning in the Inclusive Kindergarten Class

Sherry Norfolk

A Louisiana journalist named William Hodding Carter Jr. once said, "There are only two lasting bequests we can hope to give our children. One of these is roots; the other, wings."

This is a story about *wings*.

I met Jeremy when I was teaching a residency at his school, working with two kindergarten classes, plus Jeremy's special needs class, which was blended in with one of the other groups for the purposes of this residency.

During the planning meeting for the 10-session kindergarten residency, the teachers explained that we would be including a group of five children with special needs in one of the classes.

"Don't worry about them—they probably won't get much out of it, but maybe they'll enjoy the stories," their teacher told me. Well, wave a red flag in front of me—I love a challenge!

The teachers determined that the main objectives of the residency would be for children to recognize the beginning, middle, and end of stories; to understand and be able to identify story elements such as characters, setting, problem, and solution; and, to be able to identify the sequence of the story. My personal (but unspoken) objective was that the kids in the special needs group would get more out of our sessions than just enjoyment.

One of those children was Jeremy, a child with fetal alcohol syndrome. Among the many common symptoms of this brain damage are short attention span and difficulty organizing and retaining information. Yet from the very beginning, Jeremy paid attention. He made constant, unvarying eye contact, and his expression reflected an understanding of the story. When we retold stories through large- and small-group creative drama, he always demonstrated comprehension by doing what he was supposed to do when he was supposed to do it. He didn't have much language, but he used the few words he had appropriately. And during our reflection sessions, he was able to answer questions about the characters and sequence correctly.

Each day, the students heard and learned to retell a more complex story, and each day, the groups were reduced: the first day, the whole class retold a story together through creative drama; the second day, groups of six children worked together to tell a story; the next day, groups of four children performed, and so on. Eventually, we arrived at the day when students would retell a story individually, demonstrating their ability to use their math/logical intelligence by correctly sequencing and their linguistic intelligence by using complete sentences and story structure.

Our story was a very simple version of "The Turnip," a cumulative Eastern European folktale found in many picturebooks (see Resources). For teaching purposes, I tell it with repetitive, rhythmical phrases, distinctive character voices, and stylized body language to help visual, auditory, and kinesthetic learners succeed. Each character is represented by a specific gesture (the Old Man grabs his suspenders; the Old Woman holds her apron; the Little Boy has a baseball bat; the Little Girl cradles her doll; the Dog begs; the Cat licks her paw; and the Mouse has big round ears). Yes, these are stereotypes, but that's why they work!

The Turnip

Retold by Sherry Norfolk

Note: The actions are described only the first time they are used but should be repeated with every repetition of the relevant phrase. Feel free to use American Sign Language, create your own actions, or have the students determine the actions—just be sure to use them uniformly throughout the story!

Once there was an Old Man who always wore overalls, *(hook your thumbs into imaginary overall straps to indicate the Old Man)* and he loved to eat turnips.

So he got a turnip seed *(hold up imaginary turnip seed between thumb and forefinger)* and he dug and he dug and he dug and he planted the seed *(pretend to dig and plant)*. Then he covered it up, *(pat down imaginary soil)* and the sun shone down and the rain fell down *(make rays of sunshine and rain showers with hands)* and that turnip grew, and it grew, and it grew. *(Hands indicate a turnip shape getting larger and larger.)*

The Old Man said, "I think it's time to pull up my turnip."

So he took hold of the turnip and he pulled and he pulled and he pulled and he pulled, but it wouldn't come up. Hmph! *(I sing the phrase "and he pulled and he pulled and he pulled and he pulled, but it wouldn't come up"—any rhythmic melody will do! Grab imaginary leaves and pull and pull and pull—then hold hands flat and palm down, crossing them in rhythm as you sing "but it wouldn't come up!" Hmph! is said with hands on hips and an annoyed expression.)*

The Old Man got the Old Woman. *(Old Woman is indicated by holding the ends of an imaginary apron or skirt.)* She took hold of the Old Man and the Old Man took hold of the turnip, and they pulled and they pulled and they pulled and they pulled, but it wouldn't come up. Hmph!

The Old Woman got the Little Boy. He was out back playing baseball, but he put down his bat. *(Hold imaginary bat.)* He took hold of the Old Woman and she took hold of the Old Man and the Old Man took hold of the turnip, and they pulled and they pulled and they pulled and they pulled, but it wouldn't come up. Hmph!

The Little Boy got the Little Girl, who was playing with her doll. *(Cradle imaginary doll in arms.)* She took hold of the Little Boy and he took hold of the Old Woman and she took hold of the Old Man and the Old Man took hold of the turnip, and they pulled and they pulled and they pulled and they pulled, but it wouldn't come up. Hmph!

So the Little Girl got the Dog *(hands up in begging position, pant with tongue out—lots of giggles!)*. The Dog took hold of the Little Girl, the Little Girl took hold of the Little Boy and he took hold of the Old Woman and she took hold of the Old Man and the Old Man took hold of the turnip, and they pulled and they pulled and they pulled and they pulled, but it wouldn't come up. Hmph!

So the Dog got the Cat *("lick" paw and smooth whiskers)*. The Cat took hold of the Dog, the Dog took hold of the Little Girl, the Little Girl took hold of the Little Boy and he took hold of the Old Woman and she took hold of the Old Man and the Old Man took hold of the turnip, and they pulled and they pulled and they pulled and they pulled, but it wouldn't come up. Hmph!

So the Cat got the Mouse *(cup hands to make mouse ears above head)*.

The Mouse squeaked, "Hey wait a minute! I'm very little—how can I do it if you big strong animals and people can't?"

But the Mouse took hold of the Cat, the Cat took hold of the Dog, and the Dog took hold of the Little Girl. She took hold of the Little Boy and he took hold of the Old Woman and she took hold of the Old Man and the Old Man took hold of the turnip, and they pulled and they pulled and they pulled and they pulled, and...

POP! *(clap)*—it came up!

The Old Woman took it and she washed it *(roll hands)*, and chopped it *("chop" with sides of hands)*, and cooked it *(holding hands palm-up, wiggle fingers to simulate flames)* and they all ate it—slurp!

And they lived Happily Ever After!

As I told the story, the repetition and patterning allowed the children to begin to tell along with me, repeating the phrases and mimicking the actions. After the first telling, we identified the characters and listed them on the board (unsurprisingly, the children produced them in perfect sequence). We talked about what was happening at the beginning of the story (the Old Man wanted a turnip, so he planted a seed); what happened in the middle (the turnip wouldn't come up when pulled, so the Old Man got help from all of the other characters); and what happened at the end (the Mouse pulled it up, the Old Woman cooked it, and they all ate it because they all helped). We identified the problem and the solution.

Having reviewed the story logically/sequentially and linguistically, we reviewed it for the visual and kinesthetic kids—retelling the story using only actions. This allowed the linguistic learners to retell it in their minds, the kinesthetic learners to review the sequence through their body language, and the visual kids to watch the action.

We also determined the pattern of the story—from largest to smallest—and I drew simple stick figures to help them remember that pattern. In addition to reinforcing the pattern, the stick figures provided an easy reference point for kids who couldn't read.

The next step—dramatizing the story collaboratively—was the kids' favorite! We counted the number of characters (seven) and the number of kids in the class, and I explained to them that we would have to act out the story several times so that everyone got a chance and *no one would be left out!*

I started by taking the role of the Old Man, and beginning to narrate the story, and then chose an Old Woman to take my hand. "Who did the Old Woman get?" I asked her, and when she answered correctly, she got to choose a Little Boy and so on. We did the play three times—once, in order to use all of the kids, we had a child be the Turnip and get pulled up; another time, we had two Mice. No matter, we all had a chance to participate! Best of all, everyone heard and saw the story told three more times.

Our final review was Round Robin telling: we sat in a circle and I started the story and then clapped and stopped, turning to the child beside me to continue. She told until I clapped again and so on. We went around the circle a few times. If a child had trouble remembering what came next, I provided the visual cues to help her remember. For children with no language, we provided picture cards or three-dimensional objects for them to point to or hold up, or they could simply indicate the next character using the simple hand movements we had been using.

Repetition is crucial, of course, but doing it in a variety of ways keeps kids engaged and provides multiple points of entry into learning (visual, aural, kinesthetic). It also engages all ways of knowing through linguistic, logical, kinesthetic, rhythmical, spatial, interpersonal, and intrapersonal strategies.

When it was clear that everyone had a good grasp of the story, they paired up to practice telling it to a partner.

At this point, I noticed that no one paired up with Jeremy, so I asked him if he would like to tell me the story. He was sitting directly at his teacher's feet, but she shook her head, rolling her eyes. Let me say here that she was a very good, caring teacher. She wasn't being cruel—Jeremy had been diagnosed as unable to learn and she simply did not believe that he could do this. I figured that whether or not he could do it on his own, he could at least do the actions with me or listen to me tell it again. I sat down.

"So, Jeremy, what happened?" I asked him. Long pause.

And then, "There was Ol' Man," he began. "He wanted Turnip. He planted sheed. It grew. It grew. He shaid time to pull. He pull, he pull, it wouldn't come up. He got Ol' Woman. She pull, she pull, it wouldn't come up ..."

He told the whole story in perfect sequence.

The teacher was agog; I was thrilled; Jeremy was unmoved. He had always known that he could do it.

When the practice session was complete, I gathered all of the children and asked who would like to tell the story to the whole group. Hands went up, and a little girl got up and told a very elegant version of "The Turnip." We all clapped (we had learned our audience manners). But before the applause ended, and even before I asked for another volunteer, Jeremy stood up and walked to the front of the group.

"Onsh there was Ol' Man. He wanted Turnip. He planted sheed. And the sun came down and the rain came down. It grew, it grew, it grew ..."

He told the whole story in perfect sequence, adding details. Everyone cheered. Jeremy grinned from ear to ear—he liked applause, and he rarely got to hear it for himself. All four teachers were in tears.

The next day, the teachers and I met to discuss plans for our grand finale, which was scheduled for four days later, complete with video cameras, special guests from Young Audiences-Woodruff Arts Center, and the principal. I asked the teachers to decide which of the several stories that the children had learned would be featured in the performance. Nobody mentioned Jeremy and his story.

"I'd really like for Jeremy to tell his story," I said hopefully.

"Oh, no, let's not put that kind of pressure on him," his teacher replied quickly. "It will have been five days by then—he won't remember it."

So we agreed to let the whole special needs class act out the story with me as narrator, thus removing any pressure but allowing everyone to participate. We practiced it that way before the finale.

Grand finale day arrived, along with all of the promised suits and equipment. The children performed with lots of giggles and impressive stage presence. Then it was time for "The Turnip." I gathered my troupe and quickly reviewed our roles: "Who is the Old Woman? Who is the Little Boy?" When I reached Jeremy, he said matter-of-factly, "I de Ol' Man."

Well, the Old Man is the narrator, and that was supposed to be my role. So what? I moved Jeremy to the front of the line and stepped off-stage. I could narrate from there if necessary, but maybe it wouldn't be necessary.

"So, Jeremy, what happened?" I said.

"Onsh there was Ol' Man. He wanted Turnip. He got sheed. He dug, he dug, he planted. And the sun came down and the rain came down. It grew, it grew, it grew. He shaid time to pull. He pull, he pull, it wouldn't come up. He got Ol' Woman—" at this point he turned, grabbed the child playing the Old Woman, pulled her into position and continued, "she pull, she pull ..."

He not only told the whole story, in perfect sequence, with some new language, but he also *directed* it!

When the story was finished and the children had taken their bows, the teacher came over to me.

"Jeremy's life has changed as of today. He was tested and diagnosed as unable to learn, but he obviously *can* learn and remember what he's learned. I'm going to have him re-tested. His IEP (individualized educational plan) will change and his whole educational future will be different." She was delighted by the discovery—and so was Jeremy. He had been given his wings.

There are only two lasting bequests we can hope to give our children. One of these is roots; the other, wings.

Expanding the Impact

The Strategies, Step by Step:

- Tell the story with expressive voice, repetitive actions, and sound effects.
- Review orally, linguistically, and logically (discussing the elements and sequence of the story and writing the sequence on the board).
- Review kinesthetically (using only the stylized movements to review the story).
- Review visually (drawing or diagramming the story, or using three-dimensional objects to tell the story).
- Dramatize collaboratively (acting out the story in groups of seven or eight).
- Retell in small bites (Round Robin).
- Practice individual retelling in pairs.
- Individual students tell for entire group.

You can use these strategies singly or in combination to teach children almost any story, but they work especially well with other cumulative stories. Some teachers have expressed surprise that I use them all in the same lesson plan—and even more surprise that the kids don't get bored! But the variety seems to keep them engaged while successfully addressing a multitude of learning needs.

You'll notice that in this process, we have addressed the Common Core State Standards for English Language Arts (or any other state ELA standards) as well as the 21st Century Skills of creativity, communication, collaboration, and critical thinking. We have also employed the "Four Effective Teaching Components for Children with Special Needs": modeling, breaking the lesson into small steps, making it multimodal, and using a variety of sensory clues to facilitate recall.

Of course, "The Turnip" is a useful story when you are teaching about the parts of plants and the way plants grow; its pattern employs the math concept of relative size and requires counting; and, it teaches the lesson that everyone—no matter how big or small—is important. English/Language Arts, Science, Math, and Character Education—that's a lot to unpack from a short story!

You can also help the children use the pattern of any cumulative story to make up a new story! This process requires that we apply our understanding of "setting" and "characters" and that we comprehend and use the story pattern to make a meaningful new story.

To build a new story on the pattern of "The Turnip," ask the students to think of a new setting. Alternately, you could choose a setting that you have been studying, such as an ocean or a swamp, or explore the community and how various community helpers help pull up a tipped-over bus—the possibilities are endless! Let the kids decide what will need to be pulled up in that setting, and then assist them in creating a largest-to-smallest sequence of seven characters. When the pattern is complete, *tell the resulting story* with an expressive voice, sound effects, and movements, and then let the children dramatize it collaboratively. This story-composition step helps students recognize and use the pattern (a math skill) and encourages them to apply prior knowledge about a place or setting while reinforcing the relevant vocabulary.

Resources

Amoss, B. (1999). *Cajun gingerbread boy*. New Orleans, LA: Cocodrie Press.

Aylesworth, J. (2009). *The mitten*. New York, NY: Scholastic.

Brown, M. (1972). *The bun: A tale from Russia*. San Diego, CA: Harcourt Brace Jovanich.

Burningham, J. (1970). *Mr. Gumpy's outing*. London, England: Jonathon Cape.

Galdone, P. (1984). *Henny penny*. Boston, MA: HMH Books for Young Readers.

Ginsburg, M. (1974). *Mushroom in the rain*. New York, NY: Macmillan.

Lobel, A. (1978). *The pancake*. New York, NY: Morrow.

Peck, J. (1996). *The giant carrot*. New York, NY: Dial Books for Young Readers.

Sawyer, R. (1978). *Journeycake, HO*. London, England: Puffin.

Tolstoy, A., & Niamh, S. (1998). *The gigantic turnip*. Brooklyn, NY: Barefoot Books.

Or visit "Cumulative Tales" at https://www.pinterest.com/ircaulibrary/cumulative-tales/ for more titles!

To Boo or Not to Boo: Spooky Stories for Middle School Students as the First Step on a Path to Prereading, Reading, and Writing

Lyn Ford

Why and How the Day-Long Spooky Storytelling Residency Happened

I was invited to share stories and facilitate a storytelling/story-writing workshop with students in a middle school for alternative learners. Their English teacher, new to this classroom but experienced in working with similar populations of students with ADHD, autism spectrum disorders, and related disorders, told me her goal was to increase the number of and interest for reading and writing experiences her students engaged in and completed. Working with them during the first days of the school year, she and her assistants discovered they all shared an interest in television shows and stories about paranormal events; their favorites were about ghost hunts and supernatural creatures. There were many of these programs available for them to watch and carry into classroom discussions the next day. The teacher wanted to catch the excitement in their chosen curiosity and use it to light a fire of interest in ELA studies in their classroom.

The teacher informed me that, according to the prior year's records, these students had not completed a single novel listed as reading exemplars for grades 6, 7, or 8. She wanted to make the students' interests the focus of their reading material, discussions, and reflections and, possibly, a field trip. So, this teacher and her assistant teachers developed a very special reading and resource list for the beginning of the school year.

Student Reading and Resources

Stoker, B. (1897). *Dracula.* London, England: Archibald Constable and Company.

Shelley, M. (1818, c. 1992). *Frankenstein or the modern Prometheus.* New York, NY: Knopf.

Stevenson, R. (1886, c. 1986). *Strange case of Dr. Jekyll and Mr. Hyde.* Canongate, Edinburgh; Chester Springs, PA: U.S. distributor, Dufour Editions.

"Hair-raising" short stories and novels, such as Edgar Allan Poe's "The Tell-Tale Heart" and "The Black Cat"; Ray Bradbury's book, *Something Wicked This Way Comes* (Avon, 1999), and his short stories, "Homecoming" and "Uncle Einar."

Contemporary fiction about paranormal entities, such as the Twilight series by Stephanie Meyer and The Wolves of Mercy Falls series by Maggie Stiefvater.

Local ghost stories, such as "The Phantom of the Music Hall," about a music hall built in 1878 on top of a "potter's field," a mass grave for those who died without money for burial and for unidentified bodies; "The Cemetery," about a cemetery constructed in 1844, where the legend is that a bust with glass eyes may watch you or rise and follow you, and two otherworldly dogs may growl and chase you; "The Gazebo," about a haunted structure in a city park, visited by the ghost of a woman murdered by her gangster husband.

Folktales dealing with characters such as ghosts and other paranormal creatures. One example, available in picturebook and recorded formats to support its telling, is the Appalachian spooky story, "Taily Po" (also known as "Taily Bone"):

Taily Po

A man goes hunting with his three dogs, in search of an evening meal. He manages to find a rabbit, but that isn't enough to fill his belly. Still hungry, and with the sun going down and casting shadows that make it difficult to see in the woods, the man eventually perceives a creature with red eyes and a long tail. The man can't catch the creature, but, skilled with his hunting knife, he manages to quickly cut off its tail. The creature shrieks and runs into the darkness, and the man takes home the rabbit and the creature's tail and makes a stew for himself and his dogs. With his belly full and the cabin warmed by the fire sparking in the fireplace, the man prepares to go to bed.

Soon, the man hears a scratching sound at his window. He sees the creature's red eyes peeking in at him and hears a voice calling for its lost tail: "Taily-Po, Taily-Po, where is my Taily-Po?" The man shouts for his hunting dogs, which awaken. He sends them out to chase away whatever is at the window.

The dogs return, but now there are only two of them. The man lets them back into the house and tries to go to sleep, but the creature returns, scratches at the window on the other side of the little cabin, and again moans for its Taily-Po. Once again, the man sends the dogs out to chase away the creature he now thinks of as "Taily-Po." Only one dog returns.

Now the man is too afraid to sleep. He makes sure the door and windows are locked. He makes sure the fire is stoked and burning high in the fireplace. He crawls into his bed and covers his head with his blanket. He keeps the dog at the foot of the bed. But the door creaks open ... something crawls across the floor, the dog yelps and is silent, and from the foot of the bed comes a snarling voice: "Taily-Po, Taily-Po, who has my Taily-Po?"

The man trembles as he pulls the blanket down from his head. There are the red eyes, glaring at him. The Taily-Po leaps on the man and growls, "Taily-Po, Taily-Po, who has my Taily-Po? YOU do!"

Now, in some variants of this story, the man yells, "I haven't got your Taily-Po!" And the creature responds, "Yes ... you ... do," turns him upside down, shakes the undigested tail from his belly, snatches it up, and runs out the door, leaving the man alive and packing to leave and never return to that cabin. In other versions, the horrible creature tears the man apart to get his Taily-Po, and the man's ghost haunts the woods, where the voice of the creature can still be heard calling for its Taily-Po.

There are many variants and many endings for this story. I choose to tell the one that fits the apparent sensibilities of my audience and my venue.

Other ELA Common Core Standard exemplars appropriate for grades 6–8 are above. I'm sure the first three books were selected with consideration of their various contemporary formats as novels, graphic novels, and films, a factor in offering the material for diverse types of learners at various skill levels in reading, writing, speaking and listening. The dates of their original publications also coincide and connect with some of the historical periods that may be a part of the Social Studies curricula for these grade levels. Other literature was selected to provide opportunities for discussions of comparison and contrast, as well as to initiate research into the realities behind the stories.

I did some research on whether these books were acceptable material for the students' studies and approach to academic content standards and discovered that there were already several lesson plans on each book available on the Internet. However, most of the lesson plans recommended the books for reading and work in honors classes.

When I arrived to provide a day of stories, discussion, and writing and a school assembly, the students had already read *Dracula* and *Frankenstein* and were looking forward to beginning *Strange Case of Dr. Jekyll and Mr. Hyde*. They had already earned a field trip, which they would take in the spring. This was in their first grading period!

The Prewriting Exercises We Used

The stories and our discussions were prewriting exercises; they required attentive listening and responses to the shared material. Using dictionaries and thesauri, we also made personal lists of descriptive words that could enhance our writing; some of these words were also shared on a classroom list.

The Writing We Did and Shared

Fiction

I modeled stories such as "Taily-Po" in spoken-word format. Prep time for story development was no more than 10 minutes. Some students told stories; some wrote stories and read them. Some worked with scribes to develop their stories from spoken word or illustration into written format. Every student received well-deserved applause. Students were reminded that all our writing was "rough-stuff," rough-draft formatting of our ideas so that they would be available for developing into more exciting tales (revision).

Nonfiction

I shared local ghost stories, some already known and some that were new to the students. We discussed historical details of the stories and whether the events might have happened. We also discussed why paranormal stories had grown from the events and offered opinions on whether these stories were people's truths (what people believed) or a reality. These discussions led to short opinion pieces offered without judgment or critiquing of any kind and for which each student was thanked for sharing.

One student walked around his table saying, "This is too hard. I don't want to do it. I just want to listen." I asked him if he could write about his feelings instead of the stories. He wrote, "This is too hard. I don't want to do it. I just want to listen." The teacher told me that was the first time that student had put any language on paper.

Descriptive Anecdotes

I made a clear distinction that these might be useful to set a scene or build tension in a story, but these writings or tellings weren't complete narratives, since they did not contain many of the important elements of an effectively developed story: beginning, middle, and end; a distinct protagonist;

and a problem and solution or conflict and resolution. One student described the haunted gazebo, including its surrounding landscape. Another told about a bad dream that was prompted from a scary movie. Still another shared his conceptual drawing of "Taily-Po," with gestures and lots of verbalization. The anecdotes drew oohs and uh-huhs and nods of understanding and were kept for further writing after my visit.

Why did both the teacher and I think this approach to literature might work for her students? We both recognized that presentations of "spooky" or "creepy" stories approach education standards in ELA (and, depending on what, how, and with whom you share, social studies and critical thinking in natural/biological science). They also support literature studies in higher-grade levels; reading lists, particularly for middle through high school students, include fantasy, science fiction, and the works of such masters as Edgar Allen Poe.

But there were also other reasons to use these stories, stated best by two authors:

1. ... *scary tales serve an important purpose, say psychologists and children's literature specialists ... [providing] great entertainment [and helping] kids through key developmental stages ... fairy tales actually help kids face the fears they already have—and vanquish them.*

—Originally published by Patti Jones in the October 2001 issue of *Child* magazine

Every student in this class, regardless of emotional, social, and intellectual development, reading levels, or writing capabilities, had a distinct and expressed interest in ghost-hunting "reality" programs, fictional plot lines about the paranormal, and the spooky stories of their own city, Cincinnati. These students were already sharing a knowledge base ("I saw that show, too!" "Did you see the one where ...?") and emotional reflections ("I *hated* that show!" "I loved when ..." "My favorite character is ... because ...") about their shared interest and sometimes offered empathetic responses to the similarities and differences in their reactions to that interest. This focus could be utilized to further develop a burgeoning community unified by its members' interests, where the teacher and her assistants could nurture and utilize teachable moments and facilitate discussions that guided participants through critical thinking.

2. *Technology does nothing to dispel the shadows at the edge of things.*

—Neil Gaiman

Although the students had cell phones and access to television, computers, and diverse sites for social media, they seemed to believe that they rarely, if ever, did personal reading or research through technology on their chosen favorite topic. Only in conversations with their teachers, their mentors, and one another did they realize that they had already been doing some information gathering. Technology provided them with stories viewed or heard; classroom conversations and group compilations of what they had seen and heard gave them a connection to both prewriting research and prereading interest. These collective moments also helped them to assess what they had seen or heard and present their own opinions on a topic. Now that they understood that research was an exploration of what they wanted to know, their excitement led to a desire to do more of it.

How well did our day go? I was told that, for this diverse group of learners, who had never had an assembly, a 20-minute program of gently spooky stories would be fine, and I could go longer if they seemed interested. Forty-five minutes later, we had to stop so that the students could get ready to go home. But they wanted to ask questions and share comments. Total time: 50 minutes, which included two standing ovations.

One student stood and walked along the wall as I told. His mentor was concerned that this would be a distraction. I told her that it was fine with me, if he was comfortable with that. After the assembly, he approached me, and again, the mentor seemed concerned. But the student said, "Hi, remember me? You were in my class. Can I give you a hug?"

After the hug, with tears in her eyes, the mentor told me that this student had never permitted anyone to hug him.

Thanks to some attentive educators' flexible thinking and support of student interests, the day went very well for everyone.

And what was the field trip going to be in the spring? One student told me they were going to a theater to see a play. "A horror story!" he excitedly told me.

"Really? That's wonderful!" Then I asked, "Which horror story are you going to see?"

The student grinned, "Romeo and Juliet."

I wasn't sure what to say. I hesitated, and then I asked, "Is that a horror story?"

The student rolled his eyes. He responded, with appropriate gestures accentuating his reply, "Knives. Poison. They die . . ."

"You're right!" I laughed. "That's a horror story!"

Critical thinking. Connections between genres. Articulated opinion with supporting evidence.

To boo, or not to boo.

Four Elements of Our Spooky Storytelling Day and How You Can Play with Them

The Environment

- Work indoors or in a sheltered area, if you can. This helps to provide a close environment and control some distractions.

- If possible, use a single source of light that highlights the storyteller, especially face and hands. At the least, dim the lights, and make the brightest corner of the room the stage area.

- Arrange the room, if possible, so that the storyteller is the center of attention in this stage area.

- Request that the audience turn off technology, and tune in to the telling.

The Participants

- Make eye contact whenever possible. If there are segues or asides, scan the audience and make them a part of this "insider" info, and then touch on the last sentence of the story to provide re-entry.

- As the model storyteller for students, direct energy first toward the people who are reacting to the story and then toward the rest of the audience. The response of and rapport with the "fan club" guide others into the story and facilitate their participation.

The Narrative(s)

- Stories that cause an emotive response in the storytelling mentor are the ones he or she will most effectively share.
- The story must feel "true" (see "The Teller") even if it never really happened. This creates a connection with participants.
- Foreshadow. Hint. Suggest. Creepy stories and ghost stories build on the imaginations of those who experience them. Blood, gore and guts aren't essential—that's the stuff of horror stories, a darker genre of the dark tale.
- Explanations and elaborations distract from the overall mood of a good ghost story. Mystery, illusion, impression, a touch of misdirection, or hidden information—these are tools that enhance the telling.

The Teller

- The storyteller is the narrator, set builder, director, characters, illusionist, and the story itself. A teller must be fully invested in the selected story so that audience participants will also invest in it.
- Comfort is more important than costuming. Simple, dark clothing helps to highlight face and hands. If the storyteller wants to wear colors, consider colorful tops with dark pants or skirts; the brighter top will draw the viewers' eyes toward the teller's face. Bold patterns in clothing draw attention away from the tale and away from physical, empathic storytelling tools—voice, facial expression, gesture, nuance, guiding movements.
- Gestures should be natural and comfortable, unless the characterization calls for affectation. Example: Rumpelstiltskin having his temper tantrum but only if physical expression is natural for the teller or practiced until it seems natural.
- Deliver the story as a gift. Tone, pacing and pauses, and the volume of voice impact every aspect of the spoken-word process. Remember and respect silence as well as sound; two or three soundless seconds after an active scene or a revelation help the listener to process and personally experience what just happened.
- If telling "spookers" for children at the elementary level of skills, silliness and humor are important and fun tools to share; short stories, rhymes and rhythms, and participatory tales work very well. When telling for teenaged through adult learners, it's possible that they don't intend to invest in "scary" tales (which can cause snickers when creepy moments are overdone), but they'll listen to and enjoy any well-told tale, particularly if it is set in contemporary times and places, or the protagonist is a young person, or the adventure is a kind of hero's quest.

When the story (or the last story) is over, it's over. Again, no revelation or explanation is necessary. Exhale. End gestures and movement. Wait for applause. If the storyteller has done what he or she intended to do, the story has crept into the audience's minds and chilled their bones.

Inclusive Embodied Storytelling Strategies: Power Words

Arianna Ross and Suzanne Richard

The activities that this article will give you a brief peek into are generally geared at pre-K through eighth grades. They can also be used to tie into STEM, language arts, writing, and socioemotional learning. Specific inclusion adaptations are provided throughout our packets used in Professional Development workshops (PDs) and residencies as well as pages in our supplemental material on inclusive language and other guidelines to help teachers make the culture of their classrooms accessible to all. These activities were developed for the professional development programming of two organizations in empathetic collaboration, Open Circle Theatre (OCT) and Story Tapestries (ST).

Through the efforts of Suzanne Richard, artistic director of OCT, and Arianna Ross, storyteller and executive director of ST, as well as their artists and partnership members, OCT and ST developed an educational, inclusive arts integration and storytelling development tool called "Embodied Storytelling." This educational tool is inherently accessible to multiple types of learners and consciously inclusive, regardless of students' developmental or physical abilities.

Embodied Storytelling is an art form utilizing the body and voice to tell, analyze, and create a "story." Its process directly leads participants into comprehension of the material they have embodied. In its presentation in the classroom, a teacher will use a combination of dance, storytelling, drama, and visual art elements to teach various subject matters.

Embodied Storytelling

- Brings the content and word choice of a story to the forefront of understanding by engaging the whole child: voice and body
- Allows teachers to assess knowledge and students to demonstrate their ability to communicate clear, creative ideas, both verbally and nonverbally
- Helps students become better readers by having them tell the story with their body and then their voice and finally demonstrating their understanding by answering questions about the story in written responses and visual images
- Provides an effective tool for increasing the ability to comprehend and effectively use vocabulary
- Builds self-confidence, body awareness, and vocal strength by having students move and speak in front of their peers
- Builds teamwork, spatial understanding, and decision-making skills through its collaborative group dynamics

Accessibility Highlights

- When calling the students to a plenary session, students are asked to "come to a circle," rather than being invited to "stand in a circle," so that students who may use a wheelchair or have difficulty moving for any reason are easily included. We refer to this as Instructions with Open Possibilities. When an adaptation is needed to keep an instruction open, the whole class is given the option, with no particular attention to any students needing adaptations.

- In cases where students may have difficulty following directions such as "Move to the large circle," careful attention should be paid to breaking down each step with as much detail as needed. In between each instruction, students should be given suitable time to move, and instructors should clearly express one step at a time.

Example:
On my cue: Move out from your desk and slide your chair in; move to the aisle by your desk; come to the gathering part of the room; get into a circle; put your body in mountain position and so on.

- For students who find it difficult to move, we have found it valuable to employ a gesture partner who serves as a director who models and speaks to his or her partner about how to move to reflect the meaning of a word; if this partner is comfortable with being touched, the director partner can move the partner's arms for them. Likewise, students with difficulties in speaking can use a voice partner to verbalize ideas. This partnership can be employed in games that provide exercises in mirror imaging, body or voice sculpting, and puppet play (in which one person is the marionette and the other is the puppeteer).

- For students with disabilities, it is important that you consider introducing one step or one exercise per day. For example, spend a day using your voice to play with a word. The next day, ask students to turn off their voices and show the word, and, finally, on the third day, practice putting word and gesture or movement together. Once students have broken it down into pieces multiple times, they will be able to do all three activities at once. Also, it is helpful to draw a picture of the word so diverse types of learners have a visual, kinesthetic, and audio demonstration of the meaning of the word.

A Four-Step Embodied Storytelling Activity

Building Vocabulary

Power Words are any words that empower students to feel more confident about their vocabulary. A strong vocabulary is of great importance to the development of readers and writers.

Through Power Words exercises, students explore the nuances of word meaning through body and voice. They explore vocal range and inflection while saying the words and use gestures and facial expressions to demonstrate their meaning. Students also gain a simple arts and drama/theater vocabulary: nonlocomotor movement; levels; personal space; whole body expression; facial expressions; voice control; solo tableau; point of focus.

Our goal is to begin by meeting the students where they are and work toward expanding their vocabulary. These exercises empower students with limited vocabulary to learn complex words at a faster pace. Additionally, the meanings of simpler words are reinforced as they are being physically and mentally learned. These exercises also challenge students who have a more prolific vocabulary to think about and more effectively express the meanings of words.

Guidelines for Success

The students will:

- stay in their personal space bubble;
- use different levels;
- turn their voices on and off as requested; and use their faces and bodies to express emotion.

Brainstorm

There are many ways to create a list of words. One way is to engage the students in brainstorming the list. Another approach is to preselect a list of words and encourage the students to add a few words to that list; one possible way to do this is as follows:

Select a category of Power Words that fits the needs of your lesson. If your goal is to improve or enhance reading skills, you might say:

Our goal as strong readers and writers is to be able to understand the words in any story. However, if we break the words down with our body, then we will understand the words more clearly. Additionally, we will be able to use the words in our writing to create clearer images in the reader's or listener's mind.

Then share your predeveloped list with the students, and ask them to brainstorm a few more words to add to it.

Vocalize from the Power Words List

Gather students into a circle or have them move behind their desks. Select one Power Word from your list.

You could begin by saying the following: *Today we will start by choosing the words from a list from the story we have selected.*

Ask a volunteer to choose one of the words on the list. Encourage students to do the following: *First you will say the word, connecting your voice to your body. Use your hand like a wave to simply sound out the word phonetically the first time. Play with the word with your voice beginning the word at a low pitch and ending on a high pitch, as if you are singing out the word.*

Remember to wait for my cue to begin: "1, 2, 3 Action."

Sounding out the word phonetically in this step helps students to correctly spell the word when they write.

Continue: *The second time, as you are saying the word, think about what the word means. What kind of voice will you use as you say it? A miserable voice will sound very different from a compassionate voice. Allow your voice to demonstrate the meaning of the word.*

Guide students to say the word a second time, this time using vocal inflection to demonstrate the meaning of the word. Tell your students that this strategy can help them understand new words more quickly.

Teaching Tip

The purpose of vocalizing the words before acting them out is to help the students understand how to spell the word phonetically. Speaking and hearing the word can influence their spelling when they go to write, but some students might consider this silly and become too playful.

Physicalize Selections from the Power Words List

You will model and use tableau (a grouping of motionless figures, representing a scene from a story, painting, or from history; also, known as a "tableau vivant") to teach a specific concept, in this case, vocabulary. It is important to model one Power Word before you have students create their tableaus alone. Tell them that although a tableau is a frozen picture, they will be moving into their tableau from mountain (tall) position. Their movement should not be robotic but should illustrate the meaning of the word just as the tableau does. Once they do freeze, their tableau should clearly demonstrate the meaning of the word.

Before modeling the concept, you could say, *I am going to create a tableau to show the meaning of the word "excited." However, I will not begin in my frozen tableau. I am going to begin in* Mountain position *and move fluidly into* tableau, *all the while thinking of the meaning of the word. You will notice how my body expression, face, levels, and shape demonstrate the meaning of the word. Please give me the cue.*

After the students say, "1, 2, 3 Action," model moving into tableau. Follow up by reflecting on what you did: *Did you notice how my eyes were fixed on a point of focus? Do you see how my body was open and my face reflected my emotion? All of these physical choices helped you understand my story. Now it's your turn. On my cue, move into a tableau that shows the word "excited." 1, 2, 3 Action.*

After they have done this exercise at least once, you can skip the modeling. This is a good time to employ Gesture Partners and Voice Partners.

Putting It Together

When students have performed this exercise several times, you can begin with Step 3, asking them to demonstrate the meaning of the word through their voice and body.

Choose another word from the list. Ask the whole group to vocalize and physicalize the word at the same time when you give the cue. Once students are comfortable, spotlight students who are demonstrating strong Power Words.

Power Words: The Review Strategy

This is a perfect complement to the previously discussed activity.

Prepare ahead of time all the words on your list, on separate slips of paper; put these paper slips in a hat. Select a student to start the process of reviewing the vocabulary. Each student will have a turn to either perform or help another student explain a word.

Teaching Tip

The students could also use the basic movement language that they came up with in Power Words to review other new words that they must learn to be successful. Students with limited movement abilities can tell someone else how to move or draw a visual image that demonstrates the word.

The first student draws a word from a hat. That student does not speak the word. Instead, he or she uses any words, movements, or visual images to help the class to guess the word. If the class cannot guess the word, the student can make an agreed-upon sign for help. Another student can then join in, coming forward and helping demonstrate the remembered movement. For younger or more challenged students, a list of the words being reviewed should be visible to all on a basic word wall.

After all the words have been guessed, they are put back into the hat and students again come up one at a time and choose one. The students then turn off voice and can only use motion and a frozen tableau to get the class to guess the word. Again, help can be requested.

Call and Response

This exercise allows the teacher to have the students learn how to use the words with accuracy in the context of a story

Teacher needs to select a passage that contains action and movement. As a class the group should read the text at first in a boring voice. Guide students: *"We're going to read the text in a slow and boring voice. Enunciate each word clearly. Don't drop a single sound."*

Next, students should read in a dramatic voice, pausing at the important words to build understanding.

Afterward, the class should read through the story line by line and *bold* the important phrases/words with the students. This exercise can be done by the teacher. However, it's more effective if students have an opportunity to participate in this step. Identifying important words when they read helps them in their writing process.

The voice partner reads the passage dramatically, and the gesture partner acts out the passage as it is read. The class mirrors this adaptation.

Both partners need to pause at the specific words to have the class repeat those embodied words with both voice and bodies.

When the class finishes, they should have a strong understanding, not only of the vocabulary in the story but also of the sequence of events.

Teacher Adaptations

For our students with Intellectual Disabilities (ID) or autism, it is important to read through the story one section at a time, repeating it using multiple strategies. For example, spend a day using your voice to play with the words. The next day the teacher could ask the students to turn off their voice, and finally on the third day, they could practice putting them together. Then they can break the story into the beginning, middle, and end of the story. Also, it is helpful to draw out the story so that these students have a visual, kinesthetic, and audio demonstration of the meaning of the work.

These Power Words strategies can be applied to any word list and any passage of writing; the key is to make each section feel action packed by using your voice and body. As you explore more topics—whether fiction or nonfiction—the students and the teacher can create lists of words and phrases. The more the students embody the words by acting them out, the easier it will be for them to understand them when they encounter them in other texts and to use them in context in their writing. The more you use Power Words, the easier it will be for the students.

Oral Communication and Narrative Formatting: Five Everyday Ways to Share Storytelling* in the Special Needs or Inclusive Classroom—Show, Tell, Read, Reflect, Share

Lyn Ford

In order to communicate effectively through speaking, children must exhibit fluency, clarity, and an awareness of audience. Such verbal communication skills are learned through practice and observation of an effective speaker, such as the teacher.

—Yellen, D., Blake, M. E. & DeVries, M. A. (2004). *Integrating the language arts* (3rd ed.). Scottsdale, AZ: Holcomb Hathaway Publishers

1. **Show *and* Tell:** In the past few years, the concept of "Show, Don't Tell," or using our written words to provide important details in a sensory manner, has been introduced. The statement's meaning is sometimes misconstrued, and perfectly good (perhaps not great but utilitarian) sentences are being corrected. For example:

Tell: It rained this morning.

Show: I was awakened by whispers of raindrops from a dull, sunless sky.

Okay, the second sentence is a bit flowery, but I wanted to make a clear distinction between the "tell" and the "show" sentences.

Of course, we want to encourage effective writing from our students. But one prewriting skill is the ability to choose effective descriptors and action verbs. The key to making such selections is acquisition of and experience with vocabulary. As a storyteller, I know that many of the characterizations, scenes, and actions in my stories will be set up and offered through other tools besides the emotional flow of the spoken word; my facial expressions, gestures, and body language will add adjectives and adverbs and recognition of motion to the telling, showing what I do not say. The audiences, including those with limited understanding of the English language or limits in the ways they can personally share a story, comprehend my narrative's path and travel it with me. In other words, in some way, they get it. And after I have told, they ask questions or repeat parts of the story or make statements that let me know they get it, and they'll carry the story's gifts with them.

This leads me to the premise that, to help students at every age and skill level acquire vocabulary, basic grammatical form, and an understanding of effective communication in both spoken and written format, I must encourage them to tell *and* show. As their skill levels increase, I encourage them to use what they have learned to revise, making word and phrase and sentence choices for more effective

---

*Oral communication and narrative formatting as skills used every day.

communication. At its most basic level, that's what a story should do: communicate.

The daily communication of sharing what in kindergarten is called "Show and Tell" is a structured way to begin.

Why? Some gifts of showing and telling in spoken-word format prior to writing exercises are as follows:

- Students practice the important skills of speaking in their turn and attentively listening. This translates into those wonderful classroom and audience behaviors we want to nurture and encourage.
- Students learn to more confidently introduce themselves to others, a primary skill for any potential social relationship and possible job interviews.
- Students observe the presentation in order to make connections that guide them toward asking inquiry-based questions and creating responses grounded in critical thinking.
- Students gain an opportunity to practice basic narrative skills and share descriptive and active vocabulary.

How-To Tips for Show and Tell

- Provide an initial model for the students on how Show and Tell will be conducted, by doing it yourself. Introduce yourself and talk about whatever material or object you intend to share. Use the type of language and sentence structures you would want students to use. Request questions, and encourage the types of inquiry-based or personal questions you might want to hear, by displaying such interrogative sentences before you begin and mentioning them when you have finished talking about whatever you shared with them. Finally, state the importance of gratitude, and remind students to thank you, with words if that's what you want or with applause.

- We restrict our own thinking and fantastic possibilities in both ELA and social behaviors when we consider the concept of "Show and Tell" to be something only for preschool and kindergarten students. The "Show and Tell" can become a "Share and Tell" for students, if semantics are a problem. It can be a time when students read their poetry and short stories; when they offer a rap or a joke or a drawing or a photograph or, yes, a toy or game; and when they elaborate on their creative process, their reasoning for liking an item, and their reasoning for wanting to share.

- If a student seems to have nothing to share, the teacher can facilitate a share-and-tell moment by saying something like "Tell me (us) about something you saw outside today. Did you see a car you liked? Did you see . . .?" Or, "What did you watch on television (or book did you read or music did you choose or game did you play) last night?" That last question usually brings a response.

- Model respect by not interrupting (you may have to guide the sharing moment, but let the sentences or phrases be completed before you interject), effective inquiry by always asking the first two or three questions, and, always, additional respect by thanking the student for his or her answers.

- Playfully practice introductions each week (sometimes every day may help!): "Good morning! I'm your teacher, John Martin." Everyone applauds. "Now, I'd like to introduce you to . . . Henry Todd!" Everyone applauds. Henry takes his turn: "Good morning! I'm Henry Todd." Everyone applauds. "I'd like to introduce you to . . . Mary Grey!" Everyone applauds. Mary takes her turn, and so it goes.

- Be an attentive audience yourself. This is the time to make and model connections. Let go of paperwork, computer work, and phone calls.

- Develop a rotating schedule, giving each student an opportunity to share for no more than 5 or 10 minutes, with perhaps one to three students doing their sharing each time (you know your students and your schedule best; use whatever time you can). Consider offering this opportunity on the same day or days each week or month.

- Never force a child to sit or stand alone. If a child has difficulty in any way with participating in this experience, encourage a partnership with another student, or teacher (including yourself, but ask if you are wanted), or parent, or family member—anyone who can help build confidence and fill in what's necessary for the moment while still giving the student his or her chance to be the giver of information and the recipient of questions, responses, and applause. Always, applause for the student!

- Immediately after "Show and Tell" is a great time to incorporate some writing into your day. Students can write a thank-you note to the one who shared or describe what was presented and the presentation itself in a "Show and Tell" journal (with illustrations, if they would like). Display a model of what you would like students to share in their writing.

- Be alert for those teachable moments! If a student has presented something that you can follow with planned activities, take notes on your connections to the presentation and items presented and use them. Always make connecting student stories a part of your plans.

- Encourage students to recognize that everything they bring into class for "Show and Tell," and everything they do during their day, is a part of their own story.

2. **Tell, Then Read:** Whenever possible, share an anecdotal version or a summary of a story before you offer the printed material. When the printed material is a story you can tell, tell it (or invite a storyteller to share it for you) before students read it. This gives students two versions of the story and a chance to think about both.

3. **Reflect:** Add to possibilities for modeling reflection by thinking and talking aloud—"I'm thinking . . ." Let children hear your thoughts as a model of reflection, problem solving, and anticipation of forthcoming events:

"I'm thinking that if I hadn't left my umbrella at home, I wouldn't have gotten so wet this morning."

"I'm thinking that we might be able to work on this later today."

"I'm thinking that taking so much noise into the hallway might get us all into trouble."

"I'm thinking that there is probably an easier way to get this homework done. Any ideas?"

4. **Share (Daily):**

By structuring and role-playing emotional expression, recognition, and response (empathy): Spend a few minutes every morning taking an imaginary group selfie of how everyone is starting their day, or (if permitted) take a real selfie at the beginning and the end of the week focused on the same goal ("We started our week like this . . . . We ended our week like this . . ."). Use these photos as food for critical thinking, creative imagining, and story-sharing later in your grading period: "Remember when we all looked like this? I wonder what we were feeling? I wonder what was happening? I wonder what we might have been saying to ourselves?" See #2, "Add to your reflective possibilities . . ."

Try singing! (Example: Lyn Ford's "We Know Emotions Song" [to the tune of "If You're Happy and You Know It"])

We know happy, yes, we know it, show me now,
We know happy, yes, we know it, show me now.
Before happy time is through, share with me, I'll share with you,
We know happy, yes, we know it, show me now . . . happy!
We know sad . . .
We know angry . . .
We know excited . . .
We know silly . . .

By reviewing the planned sequence of the day in narrative format: Create an easily visible daily (or weekly) chart. Share its events using simple narrative or enumerative plotting: "The first thing we'll do (include time of day or 'in the morning . . .') is sing our morning song. The second thing we'll do is review our words for the day . . . the last thing we'll do . . ." or "First . . . next . . . then . . . finally. . . ," depending upon the vocabulary you wish to introduce or reinforce. Wrap up this review with "Here's the beginning of the story of our day"; point to it and then point and say, "Here's the middle of the story of our day"; and, finally, "Here's the end of the story of our day." Then, with the entire group's help: "*The end!*" And applaud!

Keep to that basic plot (plan) daily, but be flexible, thus modeling alternative action when necessary, and how that choice changes the story from beginning to middle to end (basic elements of any story). Guide students through a discussion of this story revision's outcome. Compare this process to the initial plan, emphasizing the fact that "things don't always go the way we planned, and, even when it annoys or frustrates us, we can be okay with that." Add such discussions to your day whenever you can, with the added vocabulary of "frustrating, frustrated, upset, tired, annoying, etc." Afterward, you can fill in a comparative chart (with routine times of events, if possible), reviewing the sequence of the day and comparing the facts of what happened and, perhaps, the fiction of what you thought would happen: "Here's what happened . . ."; "Here's what we thought we'd do. What changed? What stayed the same as what we'd planned?"

5. **Share More!** *Invite your school community into your classroom: attentive listening to the diversity of communication styles and diverse, nuanced voices is a skill that is honed by experience.*

   Encourage: Look over the school list of employees, the school administration, the PTA/PTO list, your parent list, and so on, and facilitate research about jobs that people have in the school. Students can then create a classroom guest speakers/storytellers list; write or record or illustrate invitations to visit and speak; and structure a schedule of dates and times for visits. This approaches many other curricular specifics and makes planning and preparation for each event a participatory student activity.

   Ask: The principal; teachers who are not from your own team/grade level/school; library/media specialists; special-areas instructors; office staff; guidance counselors; healthcare staff; maintenance workers; cafeteria workers; high school students (not just athletes!); security officers; school district administrators; government officials whose work directly connects to your classroom; parents; and other relatives to come in and spend "free" time talking with your students about who they are, what they do, and how they do it and their favorite childhood activities and stories and songs. These classroom guests might also answer prepared questions (another narrative exercise!); tell or read a story; sing a song; or share a favorite rhyme or poem as often as possible, acquainting students with the school district and the speakers with your students and their learning environment.

   Discuss, develop, and "record" students': one-sentence thoughts about visits; essays and illustrations on various jobs; list verses, a group verse, and other poetic formats on their feelings about each visit; or classroom news articles.

   Model gratitude: Thank-you notes after the visit, including group photographs (with the speaker whenever possible; these photos can become a classroom album)/recordings/illustrations, enrich the classroom story.

Resources

Hamilton, M., & Weiss, M. (2005). *Children tell stories: Teaching and using storytelling in the classroom.* Katonah, NY: Richard C Owen Pub.

Haven, K. (2000). *Super simple storytelling: A can-do guide for every classroom, every day.* Santa Barbara, CA: Libraries Unlimited.

Norfolk, S., Stenson, J., & Williams, D. (Eds.). (2009). *Literacy development in the storytelling classroom.* Santa Barbara, CA: Libraries Unlimited.

Index

Actual Size (Jenkins), 66
Aesop, 110–11
Aesop's Fables, 110
"Always Room for One More," 42
American Library Association's (ALA) Intellectual Freedom Manual, 62
American Sign Language (ASL), 99, 116
Anansi and the Moss-Covered Rock, 169
Andersen, Hans Christian, 86
"The Ant and the Chrysalis," 113
Arnold, Katya, 66
Attunement, 161
Aural (auditory-musical) learning styles, 25
Autism Spectrum Disorder (ASD), 50–55
  and Everybody Go activity, 51
  gathering students with, 50–51
  and social stories, 63
  and storytelling, 51–55
Autism Spectrum Disorder Reference Collection, 57

Between the Lions, 117
"The Big Bed," 44
"The Bird in Hand," 33–34
Boy on a High Dive, 76
"The Boy Who Flew Too Close to the Sun," 34–36
Brainstorming, 196

Call and response, 24–29
  adaptability of, 26
  culturally connected openings, 27–28
  described, 24–25

and learning styles, 25
  traditional folktale openings, 28–29
Carter, William Hodding, Jr., 182
Charlotte Mecklenburg Library, 56–61
Children with emotional/behavioral disabilities
  EBD and nonviolent problem solving, 47–49
  Special School District, 32–38
  storytelling strategies for, 31–68
Children with intellectual/developmental disabilities
  and Power Words strategies, 198
  storytelling strategies for, 69–114
Children with multiple disabilities
  scaffolding learning for, 138–40
  storytelling strategies for, 129–63
Children with physical disabilities
  interaction and adaptation for, 120–22
  storytelling strategies for, 115–19
  storytelling with deaf children, 116–19
Children with special needs
  sensory programming for, 56–61
  and Sensory Storytimes, 56, 58–59
Children with visual impairments
  challenges of storytelling, 123
  and illustrations, 124
  and sound effects, 124
  storytelling, 123–25
  using props in storytelling, 125
"The Chili Plant," 44, 45–46
Choral response, 24. *See also* Call and response

Chugga-Chugga Choo-Choo
    (Lewis), 65
"Cinderella:
    A Tactile Story," 137
Cognitive Neuroscience of Music, 86
Communication
    collaborative forms of, 158
    multilingual forms of, 158
    oral, 199–203
Comprehension, 4
Cook, Peter, 99–100
"Coyote and Skunk Woman," 97–98
Cut-and-Tell stories, 168

Dada, Idi Amin, 3
Deaf and hard of hearing students
    parents as storytellers, 118–19
    planning for storytelling, 116–17
    preparation for storytelling,
        116–17
    storytelling experience, 117
    storytelling with, 99–100, 116–19
    student storytellers, 117–18
Deliberate storytelling, 176–81
Denver Public Library, 62–67
Dodd, Emma, 65
*Dog's Colorful Day: A Messy Story
    about Colors and Counting*
    (Dodd), 65
Dracula, 190
Draw-and-Tell stories, 168
Dual sensory impairment
    (deafblindness), and
    storytelling, 126–27

Earrings (Viorst), 168
*Elephant Elephant: A Book of
    Opposites* (Pittau and
    Gervais), 168
Elephants Can Paint Too!
    (Arnold), 66
Emberley, Ed, 65
Embodied storytelling, 194
    and brainstorming, 196
    and building vocabulary, 195–96
    and Power Words list, 197–98
Emotional Behavioral Disorder
    (EBD)
    and children engagement, 47
    children with, 47–49
    and peaceful choices, 47–49
*Encyclopaedia of African
    Literature,* 3
Exceptional Experiences Team, 57

Expressive reading, 21
Expressive telling, 21

Fables. *See also* Folktales
    advantages of, 110
    described, 110
Falwell, Cathryn, 65
Feast for Ten (Falwell), 65
Folktales. *See also* Fables
    call and response, 28–29
    On-the-Fly stories, 83
    for social considerations,
        172–74
Frankenstein, 190

Gervais, Bernadette, 168
"The Gingerbread Man," 52–55
Go Away Big Green Monster
    (Emberley), 65
Graphic organizer, 78–79
Group storytelling, 97–99

Harrison, Annette, 76, 165
Hart, Betty, 4
"The Hound and the Hare," 111
*How Snowshoe Hare Rescued the
    Sun: A Tale from the Arctic,* 94

Inclusion, storytelling, 155,
        156–57
    vs. access, 156
    attachment, 161
    attunement, 161
    and communication, 158
    intensive interaction, 161
    and interaction, 157
    and Special Educational Needs,
        159–60
    strategies for, 167–71
    suggestions for, 158
    and Tactile Tales, 159, 162
    techniques for, 157
Inclusive classrooms
    deliberate storytelling, 176–81
    folktales for social considerations
        in, 172–74
    kindergarten learning, 182–87
    and narrative formatting,
        199–203
    and oral communication, 199–203
    strategies for, 165–203
Individuals with Disabilities
    Education Act (IDEA), xx
Intensive interaction, 161

Interactive storytelling, 141–48
  choosing and preparing stories,
    141–42
  preparing environment, 142–43
  warm-up story, 143–48

Jenkins, Steve, 66
Jennie's Hat (Keats), 78

Keats, Ezra Jack, 65–66, 78
Keller, Helen, 115

Lewis, Kevin, 65
"The Lion and the Mouse," 112
Literate populations, 3
Logical (mathematical) learning
    styles, 25

MacDonald, Margaret Read, 20
"The Magic Tree," 143–48
"The March Wind," 120–22
Martin, Larisa, 59–60
Meyer, A., 120
Mnemonics, 178
"The Monster on Grandma's Bed,"
    149–52
Multisensory storytelling, 20
  with children with complex
    additional needs, 131–37
  props, 132–33
  story scripts, 133–37
  story selection, 131–32
  and students with cognitive
    disabilities, 149–54
Music
  and brain stimulation, 86
  as motivational incentive, 87
  and senses, 87
  and students with verbal
    challenges, 86–91

Narrative formatting, 199–203
National Easter Seal Society, 18
Navajo Coyote Tales, 98
Nonverbal students. *See also*
    Students with verbal
    challenges
  countering disability stereotypes
    in stories, 72–73
  encouraging, in storytelling,
    70–71
  and Mad Libs game, 71
  reinforcing skills, 71–72

and storytelling, 70–75
teaching empathy, 73–74
North Carolina Autism Society
    of Mecklenburg County
    Chapter, 57

On-the-Fly stories, 80–85
  choosing familiar folktales, 83
  group retelling of the folktale, 83
  managing adaptations, 84
  new story prompts, 83–84
  story elements review, 83
Open Circle Theatre (OCT), 194
Oral communication, 199–203
Oral comprehension, 4
  and storytelling, 5
Orature, 2–3

Patel, Amrita, 60–61
Physical (kinesthetic) learning
    styles, 25
Pictures/images
  choosing, 78
  graphic organizer, 78–79
  infering, 76–79
Pittau, Francesco, 168
Power Words list, 197–98

"The Really, Really Big Enormous
    Carrot," 99
Rockwell, Norman, 76
Rose, D. H., 120
Rosen, Michael, 66

Scaffolding, 89
"The Seed Pod," 135–36
Self-esteem, and storytelling, 92–96
*Sensory Stories for Children and
    Teens with Special Educational
    Needs* (Grace), 139
Sensory Storytimes, 56
  additional activities for, 61
  at Denver Public Library, 62–67
  rules of, 61
  and special needs population,
    58–61
*7 Keys to Reading Comprehension:
    How to Help Your Kids Read It
    and Get It!* (Zimmerman and
    Hutchins), 4
Sheppard, Tim, 2
Show and Tell communication,
    199–203

Smart Start of Mecklenburg County, 57
The Snowy Day (Keats), 65–66
Social (interpersonal) learning styles, 25
Social stories, 63
Solitary (intrapersonal) learning styles, 25
Sound effects, 21
Special Educational Needs (SEN), and storytelling, 159–60
Special education (SPED) classroom and storytellers, 13–16
storytelling in, 7–12
Spooky stories, 188–94
descriptive anecdotes, 190–92
elements of, 192–93
fiction, 190
nonfiction, 190
Stories. *See specific types*
Story Tapestries (ST), 194
Storytellers
and children with emotional/behavioral disabilities, 31–68
parents as, 118–19
performance tips, 13
student, 117–18
tips for the SPED classroom, 13–16
The Storyteller's Start-Up Book: Finding, Learning, Performing and Using Folktales (MacDonald), 20
Storytelling. *See also specific types*
and children with ASD, 51–55
and children with emotional/behavioral disabilities, 31–68
and children with intellectual/developmental disabilities, 69–114
and children with multiple disabilities, 129–63
and children with physical disabilities, 115–19
children with visual impairments, 123–25
with deaf and hard of hearing students, 99–100, 116–19
described, 2–3
human brain and, ix
importance of, 4–5
instant response via, ix
learners and, ix–xx
and learning styles, 25

and literacy learning, 92–96
and self-esteem, 92–96
in SPED classroom, 7–12
tips and techniques, 20–23
Strange Case of Dr. Jekyll and Mr. Hyde, 190
Students with cognitive disabilities
creating own sensory stories, 152–53
and multisensory storytelling, 149–54
sensory stories for diverse audiences, 153–54
Students with disabilities
avoid labeling of, 18
etiquette of interaction with, 17–19
Students with verbal challenges. *See also* Nonverbal students
and music, 86–91
and story song, 87–90

Tactile Tales, 159, 162
"The Tailor in the Tower," 133–34
"Taily Po," 189
Teachers
multisensory storytelling, 20
storytelling techniques for, 20–23
storytelling tips for, 20–23
Thiong, Ngugi Wa, 2
Thirty Million Word Gap, 4
"The Three Bears," 172
"The Three Little Pigs," 126–27
Trumpet Practice, 76
"The Turnip," 183–84
Twarogowski, Tricia, 57

Universal Design for Learning (UDL), xx, 120

Verbal (linguistic) learning styles, 25
Viorst, Judith, 168
Visualization
and storytelling, 4
and vocabulary, 178
Visual (spatial) learning styles, 25
Vocabulary
building, for storytelling, 22
and mnemonics, 178
story, telling, 181

storytelling for framing, 176–81
and visualization, 178

Ward, Cathy, 76
We're Going on a Bear Hunt
      (Rosen), 66
White, Viviette, 58–59

"The Wide Mouthed Frog," 103–9
Wolfson, Carrie, 64, 66

Young, Karen, 129–30

Zirimu, Pio, 3

About the Editors and Contributors

About the Editors

Sherry Norfolk is an acclaimed storyteller, author, and teaching artist, performing and leading residencies and professional development workshops nationally and in Southeast Asia. As a performing artist, she is a dynamic storyteller, telling well-crafted and age-appropriate folktales from around the world. As a teaching artist, she uses storytelling as a strategy for teaching pre-K–12th-grade curriculum.

Working extensively in self-contained special needs classrooms as well as inclusive classrooms, she has led training sessions for VSA-Kennedy Center for the Performing Arts on the use of storytelling with diverse learners as well as professional development workshops for the CETA Professional Learning Series at the Kennedy Center.

Coauthor of four books on using storytelling in the classroom, *The Storytelling Classroom: Applications across the Curriculum* (Libraries Unlimited, 2006), *Literacy Development in the Storytelling Classroom* (Libraries Unlimited, 2009), *Social Studies in the Storytelling Classroom* (Parkhurst Bros., 2012), and *Science with Storytelling: Strategies for the K-5 Classroom* (McFarland, 2016), Sherry is a recognized leader in integrating learning through storytelling.

Lynette (Lyn) Ford, fourth-generation storyteller, author, and teaching artist has provided stories for libraries and schools; keynote and closing presentations; workshops at universities; education and literacy conferences; and featured programs at some of the most prestigious storytelling conferences and festivals in the United States and Ireland. Lyn is also a Thurber House mentor to young writers, an Ohio teaching artist in the Ohio State-Based Collaborative Initiative of the Kennedy Center for the Performing Arts, a certified laughter yoga teacher, and a great-grandma. Lyn is the author of two award-winning collections of orature from her family's heritage of tales: *Affrilachian Tales: Folktales from the African-American Appalachian Tradition* and *Beyond the Briar Patch: Affrilachian Folktales, Food and Folklore*. Lyn's latest two books are *Hot Wind Boiling Rain: Scary Stories for Strong Hearts*, and *Boo-Tickle Tales: Not-So-Scary Stories for Ages 4–9*, coauthored with friend and fellow storyteller and teaching artist, Sherry Norfolk.

Lyn's work is in many story anthologies and resources for educators, including the award-winning *The Storytelling Classroom: Applications across the Curriculum* and *Literacy in the Storytelling Classroom* (both from Libraries Unlimited). Lyn has been awarded the National Storytelling Network's Oracle Award for Leadership and Service and Circle of Excellence Awards and induction into the National Association of Black Storytellers' Circle of Elders.

About the Contributors

Judith Black retells history from new perspectives, tickles familial dysfunction, offers ironic explorations of aging, and most recently has turned her skills toward climate disruption. As a Wheelock College graduate and former teacher, she is able to draw storytelling through the educational landscape, showing its profound uses in cognitive, emotional, and social learning. Her work for adults has been featured 12 times at the National Storytelling Festival and on stages from the Montreal Comedy Festival to the Art Museum of Cape Town, South Africa. She is the winner of the Oracle Award, storytelling's most coveted laurel, and was recently given the Brother Blue and Ruth Hill Award. www.storiesalive.com.

Dr. Mollie E. Bolton completed her undergraduate work in psychology and graduate work in special education at Northeast Missouri State University. She completed her educational specialist degree in curriculum and instruction and her educational doctoral degree from Missouri Baptist University.

Dr. Bolton has worked in education since 1992. During that time, she has held a variety of positions, including cross-categorical special education teacher, functional academics special education teacher, reading specialist, and literacy coach. Currently she is the coordinator for curriculum and instruction at Special School District of St. Louis County and adjunct professor for Fontbonne University and Maryville University in the education department.

Mollie has presented at various state-level conferences and is currently a board member of the St. Louis Suburban International Reading Association as well as a state board member. Mollie is serving on various boards in the area, including schools, PTA, and volunteer organizations.

Gwen Bonilla has worked with people with intellectual disabilities as a social worker and a storyteller in the Denver area for the past 12 years. She created the StoryCrafters program in 2006 to bring multisensory storytelling to children in elementary schools. In 2009, she expanded her multisensory storytelling work and launched the Touching Stories program for children and adults with developmental disabilities. Gwen's passions for storytelling and for working with people with disabilities have informed every aspect of the Touching Stories program. To learn more about the Touching Stories program, please visit www.touchingstories.org, or e-mail gwen@touchingstories.org.

Betty Braun has been interpreting for the deaf for over 20 years. For the past seven years, Betty has been an educational interpreter. In her current position, she has worked tirelessly to provide accommodations to enable those students who are deaf and hard of hearing and/or deaf-blind learn to their fullest potential. She is always seeking ways to further her knowledge, whether it be taking courses and workshops or reading current literature that will help her further her skills as an educational interpreter and better meet the needs of her students.

Growing up in a family with 14 children, Betty credits her terrific parents, Bill and Pat Reagan, for encouraging her love of literature. Having been blessed with 11 younger brothers and sisters, Betty had ample opportunities to develop her storytelling skills. To this day, she still enjoys telling her version of "The Three Little Pigs."

Jeri Burns, MSW, PhD, is a storyteller, author, and radio essayist living in the Hudson Valley of New York State. Jeri, along with her husband, Barry Marshall, makes up the internationally renowned, award-winning musical storytelling duo, The Storycrafters, who perform and teach in schools, libraries, and festivals and conduct healing storytelling sessions with psychiatric patients. In addition to writing stories, articles, and chapters for various publications, her first book will be published in 2018. Jeri writes and records radio commentaries for *51%: The Women's Perspective*, a public radio show and podcast. She is adjunct faculty at SUNY New Paltz in the Department of Communication and a communication coach for the New York State Defenders' Association. Her greatest project is her family—she and Barry raised and homeschooled a wonderful son.

Patty Carleton earned an AA degree in child development in 1975, a BA in liberal studies (psychology, anthropology, history) in 1985 from California State University, Sacramento, and an MLS from University of North Carolina, Chapel Hill, in 1989. Patty has worked at St. Louis Public Library since 1989; in spring 2017, she retired from SLPL having served as director of youth services since 2004. Patty is an active member of the Association of Library Service for Children (ALSC), the Young Adult Library Association (YALSA), and the Coretta Scott King Committee of the Ethnic and Multicultural Informational Materials Roundtable (EMIERT). She served on the 2002 Newbery Committee, 2003–2004 CSK Jury, 2007 Sibert Award Committee, 2011–2012 Notable Children's Books, and 2016 Theodore Seuss Geisel Award Committee. She often presents at conferences, training sessions, and workshops.

Cherri Coleman is an arts integration consultant and teacher of dance, theater, storytelling, and heritage arts. Graduates of her student-led performing arts programs have gone on to Broadway, international tours, careers in stagecraft and graphic arts, video, music, and film. A native Tennessean, Cherri also keeps alive local traditions of storytelling, white oak and cane basketry, training the next generation of heritage art enthusiasts. Her current works include the Armillary Sphere Sundial Curriculum written for Tennessee's First Lady, Crissy Haslam, interpreting the Armillary Sphere Public Art installation at the Governor's Residence and "Math and the Art of Basketry," a hands-on exploration of geometry through visual art. Cherri has served on the Board of Directors of the National Storytelling Network, is on the Tennessee Arts Commission Artist Roster, and is a member of Artist Corps Tennessee.

Ailie Finlay is based in Edinburgh, Scotland, and has worked as a storyteller and puppeteer for the past 20 years. Ailie has run continuing professional development sessions for many organizations, including the National Museum of Scotland, Moray House (University of Edinburgh), Sense Scotland, and the Scottish Storytelling Centre. Since 2010, Ailie has specialized in multisensory storytelling work with people with additional needs, particularly those with complex needs. Ailie's work is underpinned by a belief that everyone can enjoy a good story, well told. For Ailie, it's very important that storytelling is as inclusive as possible and reaches out to everyone. www.flotsamandjetsam.co.uk

Annette Harrison is a storyteller, educator, and author. Annette Harrison's energetic, interactive, amazing storytelling has made her one of St Louis's most popular storytellers! For over 37 years, Annette Harrison has *wowed* her audiences at schools, libraries, museums, churches, synagogues, and Early Childhood and Young Authors conferences. Her book, *Easy to Tell Stories for Young Children*, is one of the best-selling storytelling books to date. She is passionate about teaching literacy, character education, diversity, environmental awareness, and American history through stories. The National Storytelling Network has awarded Annette Harrison the 2011 National ORACLE Award for Regional Storytelling Excellence. Netharbar@aol.com, www.annetteharrison.com.

Rachel Hartman is a children's librarian at the Denver Public Library, where she established the Sensory Storytime program and currently leads a baby storytime. As one of her duties, Rachel recently cochaired the 2017 CLEL Bell Picture Book Award selection committee. Before becoming a librarian, Rachel taught in infant and preschool inclusion classrooms, where she enjoyed working with children with a variety of special needs. Originally from Maryland, Rachel received a BA in studio art from Bard College in New York and a master's degree in library and information science from the University of Denver. She enjoys snowboarding and taking her daughter to storytime at their local library. Please e-mail Rachel at rhartman@denverlibrary.org with any questions about her Sensory Storytime.

Kendall Haven is an internationally recognized subject matter expert on the cognitive and neuroscience of story and now a distinguished visiting scholar at Stanford University. Haven has helped create the research field of the Neuro Story Science. A career performing storyteller, Haven has, for over 30 years, led the research effort for the National Storytelling Network and International Storytelling Center into effective story structure and into the process of story-based influence and persuasion.

Haven's two seminal works (*Story Proof* and *Story Smart*) have revolutionized our understanding of the neural and science aspects of effective story structure and story application. He serves as a story consultant to departments in various U.S. governmental science agencies (Navy, EPA, NASA, NOAA, and NPS) and to the Singapore Armed Forces as well as with numerous corporations, nonprofits, and educational organizations.

Katie Knutson is a professional storyteller, teaching artist, and writer usually based in Minneapolis but currently living in Chile. This "enchanting and magical" performer and "articulate, fun and inviting" workshop leader has delivered arts-integrated residencies, performances, and classes to well over 36,000 children. Katie spends her days blending storytelling and drama with math, science, ELA, Spanish, music composition, and visual arts to bring required curriculum and standards to life in an active and engaging way, all while embedding professional development for classroom teachers. In addition to leading storytelling and arts integration workshops for adults, Katie writes and curates the New Voices column in *Storytelling Magazine*, mentors new storytellers and teaching artists, and has taught with many Minnesota theater companies, including the nationally recognized Children's Theatre

Company. She has received grants from the Minnesota State Arts Board to be the full-time, yearlong storyteller-in-residence at two different schools. More at www.ripplingstories.com.

Dr. Amanda M. Lawrence has a BA, MA, and PhD in English with specializations in multiethnic American literatures, oral traditions, and pedagogy. After teaching on the college level for 21 years, she turned her focus to elementary education. She currently teaches fourth grade and works as an advocate for students with special needs, editor, and grant writer. She is the mother of two young boys, one of whom has multiple disabilities due to his premature birth. Her longtime interest in storytelling led her to cofound and codirect the Georgia Mountain Storytelling Festival, an annual event that brings the power and joy of storytelling to underserved populations in the area. She can be reached by e-mail at amlawrence@windstream.net or GAmountainstorytellingfestival@gmail.com.

Christine Moe is a teacher of the visually impaired, working with students with visual impairments in regular and special education classrooms as well as with their teachers and families. Her aim is to provide excellent instruction for her students while also ensuring that the supports they need are in place throughout the school day and at home. She has worked as an orientation and mobility instructor, vision consultant, Braille magazine editor, classroom teacher, and itinerant vision teacher since 1984. Her current job consists of teaching Braille, low vision, and computer technology skills to students, but she also spends time collaborating with teachers in K-12 schools, preschools, and early intervention programs to create vibrant and tactile learning environments for all the children in the classroom. In her spare time, she makes tactile books for her students who are emerging Braille readers.

Emily Nanney is the children's services coordinator for Charlotte Mecklenburg Library, and her responsibilities include designing and managing library services for youth ages birth to 11, coordinating system-wide children's programming and initiatives as well as special events for children and the adults who work with them and representing the library in the community. Emily also collaborates with staff that serve children throughout the system and leads staff in designing and developing innovative services for children while serving as part of the Lifelong Learning Team. Emily has worked in libraries since 1997 and held positions in Children's Services as library assistant, librarian, supervisor, and manager. Emily is a 2015 Public Library Association Leadership Academy fellow and chair for the 2016 Association of Library Service to Children National Institute.

Darlene Neumann is a library media specialist at the Science and Arts Academy, a gifted school for students in junior kindergarten through eighth grade where she uses storytelling in the library and in the curriculum. She tells stories professionally at schools, churches, and festivals. She and her husband, Larry Neumann, also tell stories in tandem as Two Voices Storytelling. She has led workshops for major conferences and has taught storytelling from preschoolers to college level as an adjunct professor. http://www.twovoicesstorytelling.com/index.html.

Suzanne Richard has a BA in theater from the University of North Carolina at Chapel Hill and is currently an actress in Washington, DC, performing at Ford's Theatre, The Folger Theatre, and Studio Secondstage. She is the cofounder and artistic director of Open Circle Theatre, a professional theatre showcasing the work of artists with and without disabilities, including *Jesus Christ Superstar*, which earned her a Helen Hayes nomination as outstanding director of a resident musical. She served on the Maryland Governor's Advisory Committee on Congenital and Heritable Disorders and the Governor's Advisory Committee for Careers in the Arts for People with Disabilities; received the County Executive's Award for Excellence in the Arts and Humanities Community Award; worked as the accessibility specialist for the National Endowment for the Arts and Outreach Coordinator for the U.S. International Council on Disabilities; and authored the chapter "Dealing with Being Different" for the book *Growing Up with OI.*

Arianna Ross and Story Tapestries create international, dynamic programs that weave the power of dance, music, theater, and spoken word. Her shows have been for audiences ranging between 50 and 10,000 people. Ross is known for her ability to perform for all ages with equal success, with solo as well as ensemble performances that are entertaining to large- and small-sized audiences. She does full theatrical events as well as outreach, custom designing her programs to fit the venue. For 20 years, Arianna has performed across the United States and Asia in festivals, concert halls, colleges, libraries, and schools and for organizations such as the National Theatre, East TN University, Hillwood Museum, and Washington Performing Arts. Her education work has been presented at locations such as the CETA Professional Learning Series at the Kennedy Center 2014, Johnson City Arts and Education Conference 2014, and National Storytelling Conference 2013. administrator@storytapestries.com; www .storytapestries.com.

Asha Sampath is a storyteller and the founder-director of Tale Spin. She gives storytelling performances covering a wide range of themes to suit all occasions and age groups. She also leads and arranges storytelling workshops (potentially featuring multiple trainers) on various aspects of storytelling. She lives in Bengaluru, Karnataka, India.

Geneva Foster-Shearburn, MA, CSC, MICS-M, works as an educational interpreter, freelance interpreter, video relay interpreter, teacher, and consultant with 40 years of professional experience. With a master's degree in teaching and a bachelor's degree in deaf education, she created and coordinated the Deaf Communication Studies-Interpreter Training Program at St. Louis Community College at Florissant Valley, cofounded the Florissant Valley Theatre of the Deaf, and created the Interpreter Training Program curriculum at Southwestern Illinois Community College. She has been the recipient of numerous awards and commendations but feels that her greatest awards are her marriage of 43 years with Pickering James, the blessing of their two sons, Cullen and Logan, and her deaf parent's gift of American Sign Language and deaf culture.

Erika Van Order, MEd, works as an itinerant teacher of the deaf and literacy leader, consulting with teachers and facilitating instructional intervention planning for students who are deaf and hard of hearing. She has been working with Special School District of St. Louis County for the past 15 years. Previously, she worked at the Central Institute for the Deaf as a lower school teacher for three years and taught overseas for four years on the island of Guam in the public school system as an elementary teacher of the deaf. She applied for and was granted federal funds to establish and coordinate a summer school program for the students in the Guam Deaf/Hard of Hearing Program for three years. Her passion is to help kids learn, especially those with the most difficult challenges to overcome.

Donna Washington graduated from Northwestern University with a BS in speech in 1989. She has traveled across the United States and has been internationally performing as a storyteller, speaker, and artist educator. She is the author of five picturebooks. HarperCollins published *A Pride of African Tales* and *The Story of Kwanzaa*. Katherine Tegen Books published *Li'l Rabbit's Kwanzaa*. Hyperion Books for Children published *A Big Spooky House*. *Boo Stew* is currently under contract at Peachtree Publishers. She blogs at *Language, Literacy and Storytelling* and has authored numerous articles about using storytelling in both performance and the classroom, including contributions to the National Storytelling World Winning manual, *Social Studies in the Storytelling Classroom*, and *Literacy Development in the Storytelling Classroom*. Donna's nine spoken-word CDs have garnered over 24 awards, including Golden and Silver Parent's Choice Awards, Storytelling World and Honor Awards, Children's Music Web Awards, and National Parenting Publication Awards.

Sheila Wee is a Singaporean professional storyteller and storytelling trainer. Because of her work to pioneer the storytelling revival in Singapore, she has been described as a godmother of Singapore storytelling. Sheila's storytelling work is deep and wide ranging. She performs for adults, teens, and children and is comfortable telling to small groups or to audiences of over a thousand. She trains students in storytelling skills and teachers of all kinds, from special needs teachers to university faculty, to use storytelling in their teaching. She also works with tourist guides, museum docents, military commanders, and corporate leaders, teaching them how to apply storytelling in their work. Sheila also works internationally and has performed and conducted workshops throughout Asia and beyond.

Ken Wolfe, by day, has spent 25 years teaching St. Louisan middle and high school scholars mastery in the ways of English. By night, he tells narrative lies and tall tales to anyone who will listen and pay him. He's a champion of the middle school underdog, winner of the Missouri State Liars Contest, a regular in the hip St. Louis storytelling scene, a unicycling coach, and a nascent author of darkly droll adolescent spy fiction.

Cassandra Wye, for over 25 years, has traveled the world telling stories from Barbados to Borneo, from temples to train stations, from the heart of the rainforest to the roof of the world. She is an internationally acclaimed performer, trainer, and director. She has worked as a literature consultant for British Council across Asia, as curriculum advisor for Ministry of Education in Hong Kong, and as a researcher of Sky-lore across the United States and Canada. Fizzing with exuberance and energy, her love of stories and storytelling knows no boundaries. She is a passionate and eloquent exponent of the belief that storytelling should be for everyone and has produced groundbreaking inclusive storytelling projects across the United Kingdom and Asia. www.storiesinmotion.co.uk.

Karen Young believes her storytelling appeals to the "young at heart and ancient in spirit." Her vivid character portrayals from history and folklore, as well as stories told in the voices from many lands and times, entertain and educate all audiences, anywhere people are willing to sit a spell and hear a story well told. A professional storyteller since 1992, Karen has been featured at storytelling events throughout the Midwest and is a storytelling and writing teaching artist with Springboard of St. Louis. She recently participated in two Very Special Arts grants from The Kennedy Center to teach students in the St. Louis Special School District (SSD) "The Art of Story" with storytellers Sherry Norfolk and Annette Harrison. Karen discovered that the SSD does so much more than simply educate students. The daily miracles she witnessed working with these students redefined her perception of the word "special." Contact Karen at youngstory@sbcglobal.net or her website www. kyoungstory.com.